MY LIFE IN LASERS

Gareth Emery

MY LIFE IN LASERS

ISBN: 978-0-578-73499-6

CONTENTS

dedicated to:

My Mum, and first ever mentor: Linda Angela Teresa Emery, 1954 – 2006.

Thank you for the unconditional love, and showing me what true hard work and discipline looked like.

all the thanks in the world to:

Kat, Sansa, Elise, for making me feel like the most fortunate person in the world every single day.

Kassy, my manager, for endless feedback, encouragement, and belief.

Gez, for great advice, fantastic edits, and dark humor.

Dad, for teaching me to think critically, and immersing me in books from a young age.

The 800 people who pledged over $50,000 on Kickstarter to bring this project to life. I'm continuously humbled to have such amazing supporters: each and every one of their names is listed at the back of this book.

And finally, thanks to you, for buying this book, unless I gave it to you for free, in which case you should be thanking me rather than scanning this section searching for your name.

PROLOGUE
THIS IS NOT AN AUTOBIOGRAPHY

I've always liked to tell a good story. Whether it's down at the pub with my mates, at dinner with my wife, or joking with other artists on the ride into a festival, I've always loved to share the good, the bad, the funny, and the downright fucking awful.

I'm sure I'm not exceptional in this, and like most of us, I have a few stories that have firmly cemented themselves as my greatest hits. And each time one of these 'hits' is retold to an audience, the DJ in me closely monitors the audience's reaction. Which parts of the story had the pub table glazing over or checking their phones? Which parts had them dying with laughter, or shaking their heads with incredulity?

Over the years, these stories have been refined and improved many times: not only to be more entertaining and comedic, but more insightful. What did I learn? What would I have done differently?

There are ten stories in this book: the same stories that form the backbone of my new album, with the color, emotion and wisdom of each tale being distilled down to a set of song lyrics. But it doesn't matter if you've heard the album or not.

Because now, for the first time, these stories are ready for print.

Before we dive in, some quick notes.

Firstly, I should point out that although vaguely chronological, this book is not an autobiography, or an attempt to provide an exhaustive account of my life. There will be gaps.

I've little interest in recalling particular moments, unless they happen to be part of a wider narrative. Plus, I don't really remember how I felt the day I played my first note on the piano, or first stepped onto a rugby field, and whilst I'm sure a competent ghost-writer could fill in those gaps for me, it wouldn't be real. It wouldn't be me. And it wouldn't be that entertaining.

But, fortunately, visiting over 80 countries over the last decade, performing thousands of shows at dance music's finest clubs and festivals has provided me with plenty that is entertaining.

Secondly, everything in this book is real. The stories, the characters, the places.

But of course, this book is my recollection of these events. Other opinions are available, and let's be honest, when there's booze and egos involved, the chances of everyone agreeing on the same storyline is quite slim.

That said, I've told stories from my perspective only, and have tried to stay away from second guessing the intentions of others, or speculating as to what went on in their heads. Where possible, I referred back to emails, text messages, or consulted people who were with me at the time to check if my recollection of events was correct. Where mistakes remain, the fault is mine alone.

Against legal advice, most people's names haven't been changed. When I've documented the misbehavior of others, I hope there's enough of my own bad behavior to provide balance. On the few occasions when I felt I couldn't tell a story fairly – it was too fresh, too raw, or I was still too angry - I removed it from the book. Those stories will need a few more years.

All in all, I stand behind everything I've written, even if I don't stand behind everything that I've done.

Thank you from the bottom of my heart for supporting this book. I hope it provides you with some value.

Or, at the very least, I hope that you don't think it's shit.

Gareth Emery
September 2020

ST. MARY'S
THE EARLY DAYS

Provence, France. July 2002.

It's 2am and I really should be in bed, but I'm still on the laptop, moving the last few puzzle pieces of this tune around. It's nearly done. The villa's big enough to provide a comfortable base for a family holiday, but not big enough that I can clatter around in the night without waking people up, so I'm being as quiet as possible, my mum, dad, and sister all passed out after too much French bread and wine. I stayed off the booze. I'm not much into drinking with meals. Not yet, anyway. That'll come later...

I've got a good feeling about this track, that it might be:

the one.

The one to get me out of my fucking job and into music full-time. I'm 22, but in my mind, I'm already there.

I'd left Warwick University a year ago. I'd had a fantastic three years, but in terms of starting a career, it was a waste of time, coming out with a useless Politics degree. Still, going to a UK top five university would keep my parents happy, and now I could figure out what I really wanted to do. Much to my mother's disappointment, I hadn't taken a job with one of the big investment banks or accounting firms. Those were the real prime jobs, the ones you were supposed to want. Deutsche Bank, Morgan Stanley, Credit Suisse. Names that meant little to me then, and even less now. In my final year, they all visited Warwick in a process known as the 'milk round' – the tapping up of the UK's top graduate talent.

I skipped most of their presentations, no doubt causing grave disappointment to my mother, but I knew even then that a lifetime of corporate slavery wasn't for me. If I was going to become a highly paid wage-slave, it was going to be on my own terms. There's a preconception that people who go to great universities end up doing the best, and whilst a degree *does* mean you'll make more on average, the majority of people coming out of Oxford, Cambridge, Warwick, and Imperial end up working for 'The Man'. Many of the people who are truly successful in my eyes - the entrepreneurs and artists, making things and building the next world for us - are often much less 'qualified.'

It's fair to say my background wasn't one that encouraged entrepreneurial behavior, and whilst artistic traits were encouraged, they were strictly within the realms of academic study.

It's different now. My own kids, growing up in Los Angeles, are surrounded by the complete opposite: people who've made their own way in life. Whatever it is they eventually want to do, I'd hope to be able to introduce them to mentors who've been there and done it. You want to start a tech company? Great, go shadow a friend of mine who's built up a company and sold it for half a billion dollars. You want to work in the music industry? Let's get you a coffee with Mark Gillespie, who discovered Calvin Harris on Myspace and has built an empire since then. You want to make art? Let's get you work experience at the studio of one of the hundreds of talented artists signed to my wife's gallery.

I'm very fortunate that my life contains huge amounts of talented, hard-working people ranging from musicians, artists, managers, authors, entrepreneurs – people who've fucked the system, carved their own way in life, and made it work.

Growing up in Locks Heath, Southampton, life was not like that. From a young age, my mother had planned out the ideal path for me, and it did not involve fucking the system. Finish school, get good GCSEs. Go to college, get good A-Levels. Go to University, get a good degree. Get a good job, work until you're 65 years old, spend a few decades in retirement, then die.

Inspirational shit.

In Mum's eyes, the prime careers were law, investment banking, accountancy, or best of all, medicine. My grandmother was a nurse, so actual doctors received superhero levels of worship in our family – and by the god-complex that many British medical professionals had, I imagine our family weren't the only ones who treated them with such reverence. My dad, humorously or perhaps jealously, disagreed, and preferred to refer to them as 'body mechanics'.

Fortunately, I already had a different path in my head – the first 'inspirational' content I'd ever encounter coming from an unlikely source. At the age of 12, I'd been introduced to the Los Angeles gangsta rap group NWA. My background was solidly middle class, but we lived in the orbit of a few council estates, and one of my friends, Ryan, came from that side of the tracks. It was at Ryan's house, hanging out with his drug-dealing older brother, that I first heard the music of Ice Cube, Eazy E, MC Ren, and Dr Dre, and I was fucking obsessed. His brother copied a few tapes for me to take home. I kept them under my bed, knowing there was no way my mother would allow this sort of music in the house, but fortunately my dad was a little more liberal, a few years later buying me the 2nd NWA album 'EFIL4ZAGGIN'.

I won't lie: part of what I liked was the swearing, the expletive-riddled music a huge departure from anything you could hear on the radio. This felt like truly black-market stuff. But there was also a rebellious attitude on there, a 'fuck the system' mentality. Locks Heath, Southampton was a long way from Compton, California so I couldn't relate first-hand to the issues people there faced – there wasn't even a single black kid at my school - but I was also stuck in a system, and I wanted to get the fuck out if it.

'Makin' more in a week than a doctor makes in a year.'

A throwaway lyric by Dr Dre, but one that embedded deep, without me even realizing it. All that time it takes to become a doctor, and Dr Dre, a record producer, is making more? Fuck being a doctor. I want to be a record producer.

Whilst music practice was encouraged in my household, it wasn't of the sort that would particularly help in actually carving out a career in music. I should say though, I don't want to come across as an ungrateful little fucker, or overly critical of my parents, because that's not the case. I had an amazing upbringing, and who can complain that their parents wanted the best for them? Plus, I like to rebel against the norm. If my parents had wanted me to be a rock star, I'd probably be an accountant right now, so things have worked out perfectly well. But, life's about evolution, and if I wasn't trying to improve on the upbringing my parents gave me, I wouldn't be trying very hard.

This excellent poem by Philip Larkin sums up parenting. I was taught it by my dad, who smugly recited it to me by heart.

This Be The Verse

They fuck you up, your mum and dad.
They may not mean to, but they do.
They fill you with the faults they had
And add some extra, just for you.

But they were fucked up in their turn
By fools in old-style hats and coats,
Who half the time were soppy-stern
And half at one another's throats.

Man hands on misery to man.
It deepens like a coastal shelf.
Get out as early as you can,
And don't have any kids yourself.

Alright, forget the last paragraph, having kids has been the greatest joy of my life, and I'm not saying that because I'm expected to - I fucking mean it. The point is: my parents were a product of their time, and they were doing the best they could. I'm also a product of my time, and I'm sure I'm also going to fuck up in many ways which my kids will no doubt tell me about when they're older.

As it turned out, we actually did have some of the right sort of artistic influences in a distant branch of my family, I'd just never been exposed to them. Aged 9, my dad headed to London to attend the memorial service of Sir Laurence Olivier, one of the UK's most famous actors of the 20th century.

"Why are you going to that?" I asked.

"Oh, he's your mother's third cousin, but she doesn't really want to go".

Are you fucking joking? A famous person? In our family? And he was proper famous. He'd been made a Lord! He'd been in over fifty movies. And nobody had ever told me about him until now? Admittedly, my mother had never actually met him, her interaction limited to one letter in her youth, but I'd take any tenuous link at that point. Laurence Olivier's fourth cousin. Yes mate. Going places.

But he was dead, and both my parents were teachers – my mother at a secondary school, and my father at a six-form college. For most of my childhood, our annual income was about £60,000. We never wanted for anything, and never felt poor in any way, primarily because everyone else we knew was of a similar wealth level. In fact, it wasn't until I got to university that I realized there were people much, much richer than us. That was quite a shock. The first day I met my friend Jim – still one of my closest friends to this day – he was driving a brand new, £10,000 Volkswagen Polo.

"Nice car," I complimented him. "Your mum or your dad's?"

"Mine," he replied, "18th birthday present". There wasn't a hint of pretension or boastfulness in his voice. That was just the way things were for him.

Me? I wasn't remotely aware of a world where people received £10,000 cars for their birthdays. I didn't even realize that people with that sort of cash even existed. I'd never paid it any thought.

Every young person I knew who owned their own car was driving a £300 death-trap, paid for by endless weekends working in a shop for £3 an hour. The few lucky ones with half-decent Fords or Renaults were driving their parents' car. I'm grateful though, in hindsight, for my lack of knowledge about how rich other people were. There was no social media, and the internet was in its infancy, and whether this was prior to obnoxiously materialistic shows like MTV Cribs and My Super Sweet Sixteen or not, I don't know, because we didn't have MTV. Four channels was our lot.

These days though, it's all in your fucking face. It doesn't matter how poor you are, because as long as you've got Instagram, you're going to be seeing some 16 year old cunt get a Lamborghini for his birthday. That's bound to make you dissatisfied with your lot, although in reality the poor fucker's likely going to be in therapy his whole life, if he doesn't die in a fiery crash first.

But yeah. My parents were a product of their time, and my mother's circles valued a very different sort of achievement to the ones I would ultimately end up valuing. You are the average of the six people you spend the most time with, and the six people my parents spent the most time with were teachers. Fuck, the sixty people they spent the most time with were teachers. It was literally all we knew. Teachers liked to boast about the achievements their kids were racking up. And that's only natural. When your one job is teaching kids, the accomplishments of your own kids are really fucking important.

What sort of teacher are you if you can't even railroad your own children into some success? Academic achievements were everything. Conversations between fellow teachers were fully of humblebragging, and went something like this:

"So tired, was up very early for Emily's Grade 7 Piano exam. She passed with distinction, of course…"

"John only managed two As and one B, but it looks like he's still going to Imperial!"

"David's still in his third year at University, but he's already been accepted for a job at Goldman Sachs!"

Now, whilst I understand why most teachers expect their kids to take standard jobs with 'the man', I still wish we'd learn to teach music differently.

For the most part, the education system is designed to turn out cogs for the machine. Diligent, hard-working cogs who slave away for 40 years before retiring. And for most people, that's totally fine. But the way we teach music to kids? Nonsense.

Listen up. If you've got kids, this is important. Do you want your kids to become classical musicians? No? Then don't force them to learn classical music pieces.

To this day, I still don't understand why music 'training' involves forcing children to mindlessly recite music composed hundreds of years ago. Not only are we breaking no new ground, we are complicit in taking our brightest young minds and telling them that the height of accomplishment is perfectly copying someone else's art.

Ridiculous example, I know, but that's exactly how we *do* teach music to children. Conversely, art training for kids is focused on doing your own thing, expressing your creativity, and it is a far superior approach.

Of course, learning pieces *can* be helpful in developing dexterity and skill – I've learned a lot from other artists' work. Learning 'Blackbird' by The Beatles taught me to finger-pick on guitar. Trying to copy Jools Holland's blues piano made me a half-decent blues pianist myself. But there are many, many ways to become good at an instrument other from learning another Mozart piece.

If you really want your children to take the classical music route, I'd highly recommend having them spend *at least* as long on creating their own compositions as they do diligently reciting the works of others. But me? Unless my kids really want to, and I mean really want to, they won't be taking classic piano exams, or playing in competitions / festivals – both of which I did, and found fairly stressful at such a young age.

You'd be surprised how adept children are at composition, if given the freedom to do so. Following this route *won't* get you parental bragging rights, but it might allow your child to actually succeed in a music career.

When I started writing my own music seriously, at 14 or 15, a certain degree of 'unlearning' my classical training was required, because writing your own music involves fucking off what's come before, and finding your own path: the polar opposite to diligent repetition. Frequently, the media praise contemporary artists who've achieved exceptional things *despite not having any formal training.* More likely, it's ***because*** they didn't have formal training that they made it!

I have a similar attitude towards any formal training for electronic music, or any other facet of the modern music industry. You do not need to go to college to learn about this shit. If anything, many people seem to use it as a reason to put off actually starting. *Well, right now I'm in college learning how to produce electronic music, and when I leave in two years, I'll start doing it.*

Fuck that. Leave college, save your money and start.

Now.

Everything you need to learn can be found on YouTube, podcasts, books or similar. Whether you want to become a master synth programmer, or music manager, or WHATEVER – trust me, it's out there. We live in a world where almost all the information you need is online for free, if you can be arsed to look for it. Plus, the world of music changes fast. Whatever they're teaching in college is almost definitely out-of-date already.

There are a few exceptions to this rule, though. If you can find a music school fully integrated with the scene you're looking to join, those can be useful. There's one such school in Los Angeles called Icon Collective, where I'll occasionally do Q&A sessions with the students. Their track record speaks for itself: many of their alumni are seriously successful artists, but this is because the school's in Los Angeles, in the heart of the electronic music industry. And whilst the teachers may not be working at the coalface, they have plenty of guest speakers, like me, who are.

But on the whole, almost nobody who's doing music as a full-time job took any sort of formal training. They just started doing it.

As a kid, the challenges of having a career in music were not discussed. It simply wasn't something that was even considered within the realms of possibility. Instead, the path my sister and I were sent down was the one best designed to engineer bragging rights to other parents.

"Gareth's gone to Warwick to read politics" – excellent.

"Gareth's playing on the computer in his bedroom trying to make music with it" – not good.

Sorry, Mum.

These days, I try and figure out my own motivations as best as possible. Why am I doing something? Is it for social proof? To impress other people? To post on Instagram? Taking a little time-out to ask *why am I doing this* is extremely helpful. It's also useful to plan large chunks of time which I won't post online, or indeed mention to anyone else. It's called **acting without social proof** and it's really fucking powerful. So, I might decide one afternoon to head down to the beach, ride bikes and watch the sunset, but my personal rule is: I'm not allowed to post about it online, or tell anyone that I've done it. Not only does it keep me more present in the experience, it stops me doing shit for the sole purpose of posting it online, which is remarkably easy to do.

Whilst my university degree was mostly useless, college did give me my first taste of entrepreneurship, which would form the template for my later life. In fact, by the age of 19, I'd already racked up two failed businesses, and was about to start my first successful one.

It's hard to explain these days how fucking exciting the internet was when you'd previously lived without it. Today, the internet is constantly evolving, so we don't tend to notice changes. However, up to the age of 16 I'd never been on the internet, then all of a sudden, I had it. This was fucking epic. I'd always loved computers, and this was a natural extension. All of a sudden, I was doing all of the things people take for granted these days, but it was exciting. Fresh. New.

I was finding chat rooms full of people who loved the Manic Street Preachers. Until now, I'd been the only person in my class to like this particular band, but now I could find hundreds of like-minded individuals. I could download MIDI files for popular songs, load them into rudimentary sequencing programs and reverse engineer them, figure out how they were put together. That's one that served me well in the future. I could Yahoo chat with American girls, and whilst it'd be nearly another decade until I'd meet any actual American girls in real-life, they were still a fuck load more exciting than the girls I knew.

But most excitingly, I could make money. My first couple of years on the internet had mainly been spent on social activities. But on arriving at Warwick University I realized very quickly that a lot of people there were a lot richer than me, and that would not do. It didn't matter when I had no cash back in Locks Heath, because nobody else had any either, but at Warwick other people in my friendship group were balling, and the fact that I wasn't was a fucking problem. I was already maxed out on student and parental loans, so I was going to need to figure this out. Fortunately, the internet was about to massively level the playing field.

At the age of 18, I had already started two businesses, neither of which lasted more than a few months.

The first, Strikeline Web Design got 'struck off' after I spammed a bunch of newsgroups looking to hire web designers. The internet was a highly regulated place back in those days. A small group of nerds had proudly built it up with a particular set of behavioral customs, and if you broke them, they'd come down hard on you. With our website domain revoked, our fledgling company was £500 in the red before finding a single customer or making a single sale, so understandably my business partner was out. I moved on fast. My next company 'Lottery Wizard' was rather more scammy, and not one I'm proud of. I set up a site where I masqueraded as 'The Lottery Wizard': a self-proclaimed master at predicting lottery numbers, with a money back guarantee. For the sum of £10, the Wizard (me) would give you your own, personalized set of lottery numbers based on your star sign, location, etc. If you used the numbers every week for a year, and failed to win your money back, I'd refund the £10.

Of course, I'd done the math, and it told me that most people would win at least £10 simply by playing for a year. I made one sale in the life of the company, although to my credit, he never returned for his refund, so clearly a satisfied customer. One sale sounds unimpressive now, but to me at the time it felt like potential. I'd managed to create £10 from nothing – a sum that I'd have to work in a bar for three hours to earn, so I was on the scoreboard, and the only place to go was up.

Success happened on the third try. Mobile phones were just starting to become a big deal. They didn't connect to the internet yet, but everyone had them, and they were fast becoming a fashion item. One day, I wandered into the bedroom of my roommate John, and saw a sweet Nike logo on his phone, which had replaced the usual 'Vodafone UK' text.

"Jesus, how the fuck did you do that?" I was in awe.

"Nokia Logo Manager. Here, let me show you".

John had not only figured out how to upload custom graphics to his phone, but also how to add new ringtones. It seems so wonderfully quaint now, but back then a custom ring-tone was a status symbol. Whilst everyone else's phones rung with the generic 'Nokia Tune', if you had 'Mission Impossible', you were the man, and we were about to make some serious cash off this fact.

Unlike me, John came from an entrepreneurial background. His dad was a publisher of some sort, he'd been to a solid private school, and had likely known entrepreneurs and their offspring, so to him the idea of selling shit to people was quite natural. I was shocked to find he'd already set up a website – mobiletones.net – selling these ringtones and logos online for £3 each, and the orders were beginning to come in. With little concern for originality, I roped in another friend, and we shamelessly copied John's idea and opened up our own shop, tones4fones.com. If this plagiarism bothered John, he didn't let it show – and I'm happy to report we're still friends to this day. Plus, it was 1999 on the internet. There was <u>plenty</u> of money to go around.

All of a sudden we had a viable business, and the orders started stacking up. I ran the website, and my partner, Joe, created the logos. Being an artsy sort, he made logos from all the top brands: Nike, No Fear, Chanel, and in brazen defiance of copyright law, we sold them. It was, in many ways, the perfect business. Once we'd set up the website, we could deliver the items for the cost of a text message and charge £3 for them. Over the next few years, the business became more and more sophisticated, and a good amount of my time was spent running it, rather than working on my degree. Soon, we were turning over £500 a day. Joe's dad, helpfully, worked as an accountant, so he was able to set up a company and arrange to pay us wages, pay our taxes, and make sure we weren't breaking any serious laws. My parents, whilst happy that their son was successful at something (although they would have preferred it be my college degree) wondered what I was getting into, making all this money on the internet.

"Are you sure it's legal?" my mum asked on more than one occasion.

"*Of course, Mum.*" I sighed back. Well, what could I really say? *Yes, Mum, it's mostly legal – except we've got the wrong license for music royalties and we're selling logos that likely infringe the copyright of some of the biggest companies in the world, but other than that, all good. Another cup of tea?*

Soon enough, we figured out the legal stuff, and tones4fones was both legal *and* profitable. My money problems were behind me, for now, and I was officially an entrepreneur before the age of 20. Good fucking times.

Two years later, I was leaving college and I had a new set of goals: dance music. My music tastes had completely changed over the past few years. In school, I'd seen electronic music as the devil, being purely into bands. Oasis, Blur, Manic Street Preachers, that sort of shit. But, just prior to college, I'd headed to Ibiza for a vacation, and it changed everything.

I had no interest in Ibiza, but it happened that one of my friends – Butcher – was into dance music, so when we chatted about where to spend our first holiday without our parents, he pushed hard for Ibiza, and the rest of us, not really caring either way, went along with it. We stayed in the horrendous Pieces Park hotel, an utter dump, even to an 18 year old lad's eyes. In the evenings, football chants from various UK teams would ring out across the balconies. Fights would happen on a daily basis. The girls, often louder, brasher, and tougher than the guys, came from an array of grim-sounding places I was only aware of because they had football teams. Scunthrope. Northampton. Doncaster.

But despite our spartan accommodation, Ibiza showed me a different side to dance music. Whilst I'd previously just seen it as music for drinking and meeting girls, in Ibiza, for the first time, I saw people dancing for the sake of dancing. Because they liked the music. And that was a big change.

I played in bands from the age of 14 to 21, and on occasion, had made some progress. My first band, joined at 14, was called The Counterfeiters, primarily playing cover versions of Clapton, Dire Straits and Black Sabbath. But, like all bands, we soon evolved. Realizing covers weren't going to get us far, Rob, the leader of the band, decided we needed our own songs, and brought in a girl we were at school with called Janet, who apparently was working on some songs of her own.

I'd been at school with Janet for years and had never paid her much attention, but the day she walked into our practice room and showed us what she'd been writing, I remember being blown away by the sheer quality of her songs. She had a great voice, but most importantly she had an abundance of songs she'd written herself, and they didn't sound like anyone else's. She wasn't an especially accomplished musician, but that was likely her secret weapon: unlike us, she hadn't spent the last decade learning the rules of other people's songs, and therefore had the freedom of a complete blank canvas when creating her own. Her songs had chord patterns I'd never heard before. They took strange directions. The lyrics were personal; funny; poignant, and I still remember the excitement every time Janet turned up with new songs. She'd hand us sheets: lined A4 paper, blue pen, schoolgirl handwriting, and we'd be excited to see what brilliant new songs she'd written this time.

Rob and I realized that Janet was fucking good, and it was clear that our route to success involved rebuilding the whole band around her. We changed the name to Munch, kicked out anyone who didn't like this new direction, pivoted our entire sound around her songs, and started getting some gigs. I was on the keys – I hadn't learned guitar yet – Rob was on drums, and we had a few different bassists come and go. We were the best band in our school by miles. Janet wrote the songs, and Rob and I were both solid musicians with a taste of blues, so were able to find some weird hybrid between UK guitar music and delta blues. It was fucking cool.

At 16, as we left school and headed to sixth-form college, we got better and better. By this point, we were starting to get gigs in the local music pubs – including the legendary Joiner's Arms in Southampton, where the likes of Nirvana and Oasis had played. We even had some sort of fan base who'd turn up and watch us. It didn't matter that we were 16 - licensing laws were lax back then. We practiced multiple times a week, and I believe - had we not all fallen out spectacularly the following year, as bands tend to do - we could have made it.

So arriving at university, I'd had a small taste of success in a band with Munch, and also had some small grounding in electronic music from my Ibiza trip. For those next three years I bounced between the two. On the band side I quickly formed a group with a few mates, called The Dynamos - these are the earliest demos of mine that I still have - and during the next few years, I started writing songs, and by that, I mean writing the music.

I never wrote the lyrics. I didn't know where to start and I had zero life experiences to base them on, but fortunately the lead singer's brother, Mick, was a legitimate poet, who banged out hundreds of beautifully crafted poems each year. I'd simply take his poems, set them to music, and those were our songs. Every time Jim, our lead singer, would go home for the weekend, he'd return with a thick folder full of new poems from Mick and boom, I'd be off.

I probably wrote close to 100 songs in that period – I was prolific.

But whilst the Dynamos were fun, I was also starting to experiment with electronic music. Early in my first year, I attended a night at the university nightclub called 'Quench', where I heard music unlike I'd ever heard before. Whatever had been missing from dance music for me in the past was here. This was the most exciting music I'd ever heard. I'd go out and spend hours at the front of the stage doing nothing more than being totally and utterly lost in the moment.

Problem was, I had no fucking idea what this style of music was called.

Sitting around in the kitchen one night, I tried to see if anyone else knew.

"What sort of music even was that?" I asked. "That's not like any house music I've heard before."

"Nah," my mate Will confirmed. "Quench isn't really house. It's quite… trancey".

Trance. There you go.

The first time I'd hear the word that would come to define much of the rest of my professional life.

Shortly afterwards, Ministry Of Sound released an album entitled 'Trance Nation'. All of a sudden, this incredible music officially had a name. *Trance.* That was my thing. Furthermore, I could start to find the names of the songs I'd been hearing. There was no Shazam back then, with the DJs at Quench playing off unmarked white label vinyls, so finding out the name of a song was almost impossible. But now, Trance Nation laid bare some of these songs. System F – Out Of The Blue. Lost Witness – Happiness Happening. Chicane – Offshore. ATB – 9pm. I didn't know it at the time, but many of the creators of this music would become colleagues, friends, and nemeses. The album was mixed by Ferry Corsten / System F, a young Dutch DJ leading the charge in this new style. I was going to see a lot of him over the years.

In that same year, Craig David exploded, and whilst his music was a million miles from trance, he was from fucking Southampton! He'd gone to the college where my dad taught! Finally, proof that someone from my home town could make it. Now, there's been fuck all successful people from Southampton since Craig David, but this was major. Before him, famous bands came from other places, Manchester in particular. But Craig was putting Southampton on the map. His first hit, Rewind, wasn't trance, but that didn't matter. It was a Southampton anthem.

Inspired, I naturally wanted to start making some trance music too, but that was hard. At this point, electronic music wasn't made on laptops: it was made in very expensive studios which cost tens of thousands of pounds. I didn't know where to start. But, I got myself a keyboard – a Yamaha DJX which came with some in-built beats and a very rudimentary sequencer – and started putting together some demos in my college dorm-room. Soon, I had three tracks I was pretty happy with, so I burned CDs, blasted them out to 20 of my favorite record labels, and waited for the big deal, my big moment, to come.

Nothing.

Not a single response.

The weeks went by. I couldn't even follow up because I didn't have email addresses for any of the labels. At that point, whilst most labels put their physical addresses on their vinyl sleeves, none of them published emails or phone numbers. This was an industry where business happened beneath the surface, and trying to get in you were faced with an iron wall of impenetrability.

Then, nearly a month later and entirely out of the blue, I received a phone call from a guy called Glenn Dobbs, at a label called UCMG – Undercover Music Group. He was a German techno DJ running a fairly prominent label group.

"Listen, Gareth" he told me. "I've heard the demo, and it's not right for us, but I can hear the potential. Give me your address. Let me send you some CDs to show the sort of stuff you should be making."

Glenn sent me a package full of mix CDs from the label, which introduced me to a world of new and underground sounds. I carried on producing, improving, and started uploading my tracks to a fledgling internet music site called IUMA.

'DJ Gaz is a solo artist living in Southampton, UK, writing and producing totally uplifting trance and house tunes' said my first biography. Engaging stuff. The time was coming where I'd need to market myself, and do it well.

After I graduated I started to spend almost all of my time on electronic music. The band was done, and all of our members headed back to our respective home towns. Electronic music would have to be my shot. I'd upgraded from the Yamaha DJX to a crappy IBM laptop and had acquired some rudimentary software, and I was improving, fast. Annoyingly, I'd also had to take a full-time job. After a great run, tones4fones wasn't paying what it used to. Ringtones weren't as hot any more, there was more competition in the market, and I'd been phoning it in for too long, running the business on auto-pilot whilst my real focus was on dance music. I took a job in Southampton at a local web-design firm called Webtastic – the CEO, impressed by my entrepreneurial history, didn't take long to offer me the position. The salary was £18,000 a year – less than half of what I'd be making in a proper graduate job - but my parents were relieved. At least it got me out of the house.

I spent this period essentially doing two jobs: working my day job from 9 to 5, and on music from 7pm-2am. Sacrificing sleep and friends in pursuit of a goal isn't something I'd now recommend or endorse – it's not sustainable long-term and if you burn the candle at both ends for extended periods, you'll eventually burn yourself out, requiring real time which undoes your good work. The fact is, the cornerstone of long-term success is daily cumulative wins – getting in a few hours every day, rather than hero-style 18 hour sessions. However, the all-nighter strategy *can* work for some short sprints, and I did many in this period.

I was also lucky to be living at home with my parents with no rent and few commitments, so I was able to pour all my efforts into work. The work at Webtastic wasn't particularly demanding, so whilst in the office from 9-5 I could answer my music emails, listen to BBC Radio 1 Essential Mixes, and continue my self-schooled apprenticeship in dance music. In the evenings, I'd work on music from 7pm to the early hours of the morning before dragging myself, bleary-eyed, back into work the next morning. This lifestyle wasn't sustainable, but fortunately, it wasn't to last long.

I realized quickly that whilst my production skills weren't yet up to scratch, I could hack the system by starting to make bootlegs instead of original tracks, where I could use samples from other, better made tracks. My first attempt was a bootleg of The Shrink's 'Nervous Breakdown' a Dutch hard house track. Deciding this was good enough to send out to DJs, I dropped nearly my entire monthly salary and invested £1,000 pressing up a few hundred vinyl copies – most clubs didn't have CD players at this point, so getting tracks to DJs was expensive. By this time I'd started to collect various DJs' addresses. Whilst record labels were still impossible to contact, I'd found many DJs were a lot more accessible with emails on their websites, and after reaching out I'd managed to score the mailing addresses of a handful of top DJs.

When the time came to press the record, I used a day's holiday and took the hour-long train journey up to London to hand in my master CDR. The staff at the pressing plant all seemed impossibly cool and barely spoke to me, uttering a few disdainful words as they took a hopeless CD from this chubby 22 year old. But sure enough, a few weeks later, a huge box of unmarked black vinyl records arrived at my house in Southampton, and they sounded great. These were 12-inch vinyls and not only did they sound beautiful, but they looked beautiful too: totally unmarked, jet-black, and with that vaguely narcotic smell that new vinyls tended to have. Just holding my music in my hands on a vinyl record made me feel like I was halfway there already. Assisted by my family, we set about printing labels and sticking them onto the records. After that, I headed to the post office to mail them out to any DJs whose addresses I'd managed to blag.

This time, the response was quick. A week or so later, a West Country accent left a message on my answerphone.

"Alright there Gareth. Chap called Brisky here from Chemical Records over in Bristol. I'm friends with Eddie Halliwell, and he gave me a play of your record. Could you give me a call to have a chat?"

Fuuuuuuck! Eddie Halliwell hadn't responded to the promo (nobody had) but he was clearly into it. At this point, Eddie was the hottest young DJ in the UK. Even though he was about the same age as me, his career was a lot further on, headlining shows all over the country, and with his own show on BBC Radio 1. Eddie was doing what I wanted to do. If I could get support from him, I was on my way. I called Brisky, who confirmed Eddie Halliwell loved my record. We then cut a deal to press up another few thousand records, which he was confident he could sell in his shop. A few weeks later, Eddie Halliwell played the track on BBC Radio 1 in a live Essential Mix.

It's hard to overstate the influence of BBC Radio 1 in the UK. The US is a big country, so in order to have success, you need to get played on a lot of different stations. In the UK, you only need one: BBC Radio 1. It was everything. It's where Pete Tong and numerous other huge names started – and to me, it was the only radio station that mattered. Now that I'd been played on Radio 1, I'd practically made it. A few days later I received a phone call from a guy called Eddie Gordon, from Neo Records – a label I'd reached out many times before with no response.

He'd heard the track on Radio 1 and wanted to release it. I half expected to get a bollocking for the illegal samples, but Eddie had released the original Shrink record, and wanted to connect me with the track's Dutch writers so it could get an official release. The Shrink record went on to be played by a raft of other hard-house DJs, but that wasn't quite where I wanted to be. Trance was my thing, and I needed to score some points there. Fortunately, things were about to start moving very, very fast.

Whilst I'd worked on The Shrink, I'd also been writing some original music under the name GTR, and my first release - a double A-side with two tracks called 'Flood Control' and 'Psiclone' was getting pressed to vinyl too.

I knew that I had to capitalize on the hype of The Shrink, but again, I had no money, and so I had to find a way to press the records up. A bloke I knew, seeing that I was trending in the right direction, offered to fund pressing the vinyls, so we started a label called Influential Records to get it done. Neither track was especially successful, but it led the way to something much bigger. By this time I had the address of Paul van Dyk, one of the biggest DJs in the world, and as I was sending him 'Flood Control / Psiclone', I decided to throw in a CD of something new I was working on. This new track didn't even have a name, and I doubted Paul even played CDs, so the whole exercise was pretty pointless, but something in my head told me to include it.

Although the new track had no name, I'd played it to a few friends, and just a couple of weeks later I received a message on MSN Messenger that would change my life.

"PAUL VAN DYK IS PLAYING YOUR NEW FUCKING TRACK LIVE ON THE RADIO FROM NATURE ONE IN GERMANY".

This. Was. *Insane*. Paul van Dyk was playing *my fucking track*?!

Before long I received an email from someone called Alexis Hooper at Five AM Records, offering a deal.

Five AM was a *proper* label. None of this self-funded crap. They'd released plenty of legit artists, and I even had a few of their records. Alexis had heard the track in the Paul van Dyk set, as had a few other A&Rs, but he was the fastest to track me down, and offered me £500 to sign the track to them.

I bit his hand off, and signed the fucking deal.

The track, now called 'Mistral', felt like it was going to do big things for me. My friends loved it. Paul van Dyk loved it. Even my mum loved it. Its name, a suggestion by one of my parents, was a nod to the winds of the Provence region of France, where we'd spent numerous wonderful family holidays, and where I'd finished the track.

By now, I was starting to get some hype. I was 22 years old, which at the time was extremely young by music producer standards, and 'Mistral' arrived at the perfect time.

The track exploded.

With Five AM now doing the promo instead of me, 'Mistral' would be arriving from a trusted source, meaning that DJs would give the record a proper chance. At this point in time, labels sent records out with feedback sheets: a piece of paper that asked a few questions. *Rate this record from 1-10. Are you supporting this record? Any other comments?* DJs would fill in the little survey, fax it back, and let the label know what they thought.

The 'Mistral' feedback sheets flowed in.

Armin wrote back saying he loved it. Ferry Corsten, too. Paul van Dyk was already on board, so that was the A-list of trance sorted. Then, last of all, the name that I'd been hoping to hear from most of all.

Tiesto.

In terms of hype, there was nobody even close to Tiesto at this point. He might not have had the history of Oakenfold or Carl Cox, but in terms of buzz, there was nobody bigger. Not only did he write back that he loved the record, but he also sent over a licensing request for an upcoming album.

This was massive. His 'Nyana' album was released a few months later, and he chose 'Mistral' to close out the first CD. I had a bona-fide anthem.

Things happened fast after that. These days, in order to receive press or publicity I need to actually do something worthwhile – but back then, I was riding the wave of hype. I was hot as fuck, and when you're hot, everything is easy. Muzik Magazine made 'Mistral' their single of the month. Mixmag came down to interview me in Southampton and wrote a full-page article entitled 'Boring DJs be very afraid: Gareth Emery is about to kick your arse'. I'd literally released three records and had no business being in Mixmag, but like I say… hype.

Soon I was paid a £10,000 advance for a publishing deal: more money than I'd ever seen, but I didn't plan to keep any of it. I was on my way, and reinvestment was the name of the game. So instead, I headed to a shop called Digital Village and dropped almost all of it on pro studio gear. Finally, I had a proper computer, proper speakers and real software. With the cash I had left I paid a local handyman to build a studio desk in my bedroom. I wasn't likely to be moving out of home anytime soon, so I might as well at least make my bedroom/ studio a decent place to work.

I found an agent, booked my first ever international gig in Jonkoping, Sweden, and soon after that a tour of Australia, which required me to quit my job. I managed to book shows at all of the UK's top clubs. Places where I was still going as a clubber! This wave of hype wouldn't last forever – and I'd struggle to follow up my initial success of 'Mistral' - but at the time I was riding high. My job was gone, and for the first time in my life, I was a full-time DJ / record producer.

I was 23 years old, and I was on my fucking way.

"ST MARYS"
written by Gareth Emery & Anthony Galatis

heading to st marys, i cross the avenue
the last time i came here, i'd just turned twenty-two
i should be a hero in this town
but that's alright, i'm keeping my head down
it all started here, walking on a road like this
singing at the joiners, bowing down to matt le tiss
move like a suburban hurricane
red and white blood running through my veins

tell the city that i love her, and i miss her way
but only fools hold on to their glory days
when memories fade, and friends move on
i'll never forget where i come from

all i've got are memories, that's good enough for me
walking past the old dell, remember '93
rewind on the radio again
t-shirts with 6-3 all over them
post relegation, following the northern lights
foreign destinations, california in my sights
a thousand airports and i feel the same
red and white still running through my veins

tell the city that i love her, and i miss her way
but only fools hold on to their glory days
when memories fade, and friends move on
i'll never forget where i come from

walking through the suburbs and the world i left behind
looking for your headstone, '06 still on my mind
don't think that i've felt this way before
decades past still knocking at my door
it's way past sunset, i'm feeling kind of strange
old gang out drinking, some things they never change
9pm, and it's time to board my train
another year till i'm round here again

tell the city that i love her, and i miss her way
but only fools hold on to their glory days
when memories fade, and friends move on
i'll never forget where i come from

I SAW YOUR FACE
THE MANCHESTER YEARS

Manchester, 2019.

The steaming red curry arrives in front of me, and I wonder if it's as good as I remember. Manchester is where my obsession with Thai food began, and being back here, eating this same food, is having... a strange effect on me.

I try the curry. It's good, just sweet enough, deliciously thick, the pungent mix of spices coinciding with a curious mix of thoughts: part melancholy for days gone by, and part gratitude for how far I've come since then.

I suppose that I shouldn't be surprised. Tampopo is one of my favorite restaurants in Manchester, and when I lived in the city, I had lunch here a couple of times a week. I was first introduced to the place by my wife Kat, who'd gone there for a work function to meet the owner. The guy had allegedly spent years trekking around South East Asia, sampling the street food, getting the recipes down, then creating the restaurant based off his experience. It might be total bullshit, but the food's legit. Robust prawn crackers with sweet chilli sauce, pork gyoza (delicious little parcels served with a light soy sauce), followed by a Thai curry of some description with jasmine rice. Dessert's usually a pass, but the Vietnamese coffee is well worth it, served in its own mini-cafetiere type device, with a thick sludge of condensed milk sitting on the bottom. Sweet, strong, excellent.

Back in the day, I'd come here most often with Adam Flexer, who was my business partner of sorts, and as the smell of the curry fills my nostrils, my mind drifts back to The Manchester Years.

The past is a strange place for me to be, mentally, in that I have almost no interest in it. For as long as I can remember, I've been almost entirely future focused – my mind overflowing with plans for later today, tomorrow, next week, month, and year.

What's my next album going to look like?

What am I going to do with the kids at the weekend?

What do I need to learn next? Spanish? Flip turns in the swimming pool? How to do 20 pull-ups?

What books will I read?

Where are my gigs?

When are my flights?

When's my ride to the airport?

You get it.

My obsession with the future is so complete, that for large chunks of my life I've neglected the present moment and those around me, my mind constantly off in a distant future. If I didn't know better, I'd blame it on cell phones, but I've been like this as long as I can remember. *Somewhat bright, but spends far too much time staring out of the window,* was the gist of my school reports. And why the fuck not? The dreams in my head were far more interesting than the shit I was learning.

Being future-focused is an excellent way to accomplish a lot. Plan things, do things, on to the next. I still love to learn new things now. Making music's my job, so I have to constantly learn new things there - refine my skillset, and get better - but I've always got some other shit on the go too. Typically a learning phase will last 6-12 months. A few years ago, my obsession was cameras. I bought a DSLR, learned about lenses, aperture, shutter speed, ISO… essentially, how to use the thing in pro-mode, and for half a year I took my camera everywhere.

Currently, my learning obsession is focused on Spanish. I love this joke:

"What do you call someone who speaks three languages?

'Trilingual.

'What do you call someone who speaks two languages?

'Bilingual.

'What do you call someone who speaks one language?

'English".

So over the past year, I've been working on Spanish. It's almost entirely useless, as I don't live in a Spanish speaking country, most native Spanish speakers I know speak good English, and in a few years our phones will likely translate perfectly for us, but I'm totally fine with that. I'm just learning it because I enjoy learning. People often ask me where I find the time, and honestly, it's mainly at the expense of the things I don't do that almost everyone else does. I hardly ever watch TV, and spend as little time as possible on social media (due to my job, a certain amount is mandatory). I'd just rather spend my evenings learning than being entertained. That's absolutely no judgment on people who like to spend their evenings binge-watching six Netflix episodes back to back. I've done that too. But for the most part, I'm happier actively learning something new than passively consuming media.

I've decided that getting 80% good at a new skill is the sweet spot. That's where most of the fun is. With a lot of skills, you can reach an 80% level pretty quickly, and have fun doing it. When it comes to taking photos, I'd say I'm 80% as good as a professional, and I learned that in six months.

But don't think I'm over-rating myself.

I'm not a good photographer.

Because being a good photographer requires being *better than 80%, and getting past 80% is very fucking difficult.*

Let me explain. Whilst you might be able to get your photography skills to an 80% level in six months, going from 80% to 90% will take you another decade and thousands of hours of practice.

Getting above 90% will be a pursuit that lasts the rest of your life, and even then, few people will ever crack the 95% mark.

My favorite example is sprint training. According to a sports coach I know, your average man, with about a year of training, can apparently run the 100m sprint in about 12 seconds. There's your 80%. Practice for a year and you could probably do it. But improve that by just two seconds and do it in 10 seconds, and you're qualifying for the Olympics. Improve *that* by just another 5% and get to 9.50, and you'd hold the world-record.

Like I say. It gets hard after 80%.

Of course, in music, I'm gunning for 100%. I want to be the best in the world and I'll continue to invest thousands of hours trying to become 0.1% better. Because at a professional level, a little improvement means a lot. But in everything else, 80% is just fine.

My issue of course, in spending so much time in the future, is that I have a tendency to neglect the present, and more than one relationship has fallen by the wayside to a string of mumbled answers by me, failing to hear vital information from a girlfriend, because in my mind I was walking onto the stage at Coachella:

Did you even hear what I said?

Uh, I think so.

What was it then?

Fuck.

Fortunately about five years ago I discovered meditation, which is an incredible technique for keeping you in the present moment. I'm not going to drone on about the benefits of it, except I'd recommend anyone try it a few times. Not only has it generally made me happier and less difficult with people around me, it's allowed me to experience my shows a lot more fully.

When I'd first play major festivals, I'd often entirely fail to absorb the experience. Before the show, I'd be frantically going through tunes on my laptop, planning my set. Then the set would start, and I'd be plunged into the world of real-time problem solving, as DJing at a high level often is.

Is now the right time to get on the mic?

Do I play this song in its entirety, or edit out the second breakdown?

Is this a trance crowd, or a little more commercial?

What records can I play so I can better figure out what they're into?

How long do I have left?

Are they ready for the confetti on cue?

What am I going to finish my set with?

Where's the next DJ?

And so on.

And before I'd know it, the hour would be over, and I'd be walking off stage, cheers of 10,000 people behind me, but I'd barely noticed, my mind already thinking about what was next:

Where's the golf cart?

Do we have interviews to do?

I'd like a vodka red-bull please.

Where's the afterparty?

It's not an exaggeration to say that until I learned how to meditate, I never fully experienced any show that I played. I did a good job, usually, but I saw my role as a professional, like the athlete on the sports field, going out there to win rather than to enjoy it.

But meditation changed all that. These days, whilst there's still a large chunk of 'problem solving', I'm much better at stepping back into the moment and just experiencing it. Looking out over the sea of people, and just thinking: wow. I'm fucking lucky. Absorbing it all. And it's fucking beautiful.

So, as you can imagine, the past isn't a particularly natural place for me to spend time, mentally. It's not because it's unhappy. I've had a great fucking life, and fortunately the good memories outnumber the bad ones drastically. It's just not how I'm wired. But being here, in Manchester, in this fucking place, drags me right back.

I'd never have thought that I'd end up living up North. Fuck, I'd never have thought I'd live anywhere other than Southampton, but that's life.

I'd initially left home in 2006 to move in with Kat: my girlfriend at the time, and I'm proud to say that she is now my wife.

In my earlier drafts of this book I didn't write a lot about our relationship: primarily because enough of our lives are public already, and that wasn't entirely her choice. Unlike me, Kat has never chased fame or public limelight: probably because she's naturally confident and self-assured, with few of the neuroses or grudges that typically make people want to get on stage in front of thousands of people.

I chose this life, and I accept both the good and the bad of living in public. I might get called a talentless failure by a random stranger on the internet before I've even got out of bed, but hey, at least I can get a good table at a busy restaurant!

But whilst I can deal with both the pros and cons of public life, I'm always conscious about dragging those around me into it. I'll often edit down or delete social media posts if I think I'm oversharing about my home life. Naturally, I like to be outspoken, but I have to think about how what I say and do in public impacts those around me. That said, it wouldn't feel right if I didn't write a few words about the most important person in my life for the last 15 years, so here goes.

Kat and I had initially met through mutual friends in 2006, at the UK superclub Godskitchen, Unfortunately, I wasn't actually playing that night, so I didn't have any of the kudos of being on the line-up. However, I already knew who she was: although social media wasn't really a thing at this point, the UK's clubbing community had a healthy online network on various message boards, and I might have stalked her profile a few times. Kat was clearly out of my league, but sitting in my bedroom-studio at my parents' house, a boy could dream.

Over the past few years, I'd met numerous people in real life after observing them online, and many disappointed. The Godskitchen Message Board had a school-playground like environment, but often the loudest and seemingly most interesting characters were rendered wordless mutes when you encountered them in real life, whereas others who could barely type a coherent sentence could light up a room in the flesh. Some of the most popular characters from the message boards could be rather unpleasant in real life: strutting around the club like mini-celebrities, rendering themselves entirely unapproachable to anyone who didn't have the status of 20,000 posts. Looking back, it was an interesting time. These days, it's so natural to connect with people online before meeting them in person that we forget things weren't always this way. Even as late as 2006, meeting up with 'internet friends' was still considered a little unusual, and there were some nutcases out there. You never quite knew how it would go.

Kat, thankfully, was refreshingly normal – her real-life personality seemed identical to her online persona, and she looked even better than her pictures. The same certainly couldn't have been said for me: each of my online profile pictures had been carefully chosen from hundreds of precisely angled webcam shots to minimize facial flab.

The biggest blessing on the night that we met was that I was only passing through the club on my way to do a show elsewhere. This meant that I was driving, so I was sober, and we were only able to chat for a minute or two. Any longer and I would inevitably have fucked things up by getting black-out drunk, or thrown out of the club, and I might never have seen her again. However, my sobriety and pressing appointment elsewhere meant we could only chat for a minute or two before I was on my way, and it went well.

Soon we were direct messaging on MySpace. This was the early days of the network, and for a while, I'd been the only British person I knew that used it, but Kat was clearly ahead of the game. I'd been introduced to it myself on a trip to Los Angeles the previous year, which meant that I already had the good look of a couple of thousand American friends, making it a place where I could play to my strengths.

After a few months of chatting online we went on a few actual dates (to nightclubs, of course), and soon enough we agreed to start dating properly. I vividly remember the moment her Myspace profile changed from 'Single' to 'In A Relationship', three words I'd been visualizing appearing for months. I was so happy that I punched the fucking air.

Even though we lived 180 miles apart and hadn't been dating long, I imagined us being married right away: something that I'd never felt before, for anybody. Jogging around my neighborhood of Locks Heath, my mind would drift to the future, and I'd picture her in a wedding dress, and how the day would look. *This was fucking mental.*

Although I didn't realize it at the time, this was a form of *visualization* - where you imagine something you want to happen in your future life - and it's bizarrely effective. I won't drone on about the powers of visualization and how powerful it's been for me, as there's an awful lot written about it already, but I will say this: <u>it works</u>.

Visualization has been given props by everyone from Oprah to Richard Branson, plus numerous sports stars. England rugby player Jonny Wilkson – arguably the best English goal kicker of all time – undertook an intense visualization routine prior to kicking on the pitch, taking a moment to forget the stadium around him and vividly imagine the ball sailing through the posts after a perfect connection with his boot. In the earlier parts of his career, Wilkinson's rather odd pre-kick routine used to draw a few laughs and even a little scorn, but that ended when England won their first ever Rugby World Cup in 2003 – with 15 of their 20 points in the final scored from Wilkinson's boot. So how does it work? On the surface, it seems laughable that simply imagining something could increase its chances of happening, but when you think about it, there's plenty of confirmatory information. We all know that glass-half-empty character: the natural victim who's always catastrophizing about bad things happening to them. I know a few of them, and they all also seem fairly unlucky, with many of their forecasted doomsday events actually coming true. Visualization is just the same, in reverse.

Of course, some of the best-selling books on visualization are flat-out nonsense. There are no magic powers at play here.

Instead, the best explanation that I've heard is related to the way your brain filters information.

We don't realize it, but our brains are constantly filtering out unwanted information and focusing on the important stuff. For instance, if I'm in a noisy pub, I won't hear a single thing amidst the conversation of the room, unless something on my radar jumps out:

"Blah, blah, blah, blah, blah, blah, blah ***Gareth Emery***, blah, blah, blah…"

Shit! Did I just hear my name?

We've all got filters unconsciously set to pick up on things that are important to us. Our own name is an obvious example, but I'm sure you've experienced it in other areas. Perhaps you were considering buying a new Ford Focus, then all of a sudden you started seeing the fucking things everywhere. Filters.

Visualization employs this same mechanism.

Let's say you want to get into great shape. Obviously, merely imagining yourself running a marathon won't change a thing. But, it might help you to notice a poster for a local 5k run that's coming up. Then, you might complete the run, meet a few other like-minded people, and start training for a marathon together. Before you know it, your fitness and life are radically changing.

The same goes for making money, creating art, and… yep… getting married. Because just six years after we started dating, Kat and I were getting married in Manchester.

At the time of writing, Kat and I have been together for 14 years now, and things have worked out pretty fucking well. We've two amazing children in Sansa and Elise, and have a great life in Los Angeles. Although it was my career that initially brought us here, Kat's own business – an art gallery which she co-founded – has become incredibly successful. In short, if you'd shown me back in 2006 where we'd end up, I would have been very fucking happy, and whilst my personality is geared to look for things to improve upon, rather than appreciating the present, I often try and get my head back to those early days to see how far we've come.

Has it all been plain sailing? Of course not. But we're a team, and every time we've faced adversity we've ultimately come out of it stronger. In any long-term relationship you're going to have challenges. Kids. Work/life balance. Money. Travel. People who will try and drive you apart. But as long as we've remained a team, we've faced these challenges together and come out of them stronger than before.

Back when we first met in 2006, marriage was still a long way off, but after a few months of dating we did move into our first home together, starting a journey that would land us in Manchester a few years later.

Initially, we got a pad together in Derby after just three months of dating. We both have a tendency to rush into things we're enthusiastic about, but it worked out well, and I'd highly recommend it. The fact is, living with someone will *vastly* accelerate how well you know them. I'd say a couple of months of living with someone is the equivalent of a few years of dating, so move the fuck in. You'll find out if they're right quickly enough, and if not, move on. Life's fucking short: why drag it out?

In Derby, we'd found a small ex-council house at 56 Ward Street. The rent was £500 a month, but our occupations of 'student & dj' hadn't impressed the landlord, who rejected our application without further consideration. However, I was able to convince them to let us rent the property on the basis of paying the entire six-months rent of £3,000 up-front, so I found the money from somewhere, and we were in business.

Now, 56 Ward Street didn't have much by way of amenities, but it did have a 'combination boiler' that created hot water on demand, which to me was pure luxury compared to my childhood home, where there never seemed to be enough hot water, and when it was gone, it was gone. No more waking up at 1pm and finding only cold water left for the shower: I could be as lazy a fucker as I wanted, and enjoy warm showers round the clock. Other than that, it had a convenience store across the street, where we could buy tins of baked beans from the unsmiling owners of Lynton Stores. It's still there according to Google – certainly not for their customer service.

After a year in Derby, Kat was done with college, and it was time for her to get a job. From my side, I was flexible – I'd move anywhere. As long as I could get to an airport in a couple of hours, and our home had a room I could requisition for a studio, I was gravy. That said, I hadn't considered the realities of living in the countryside.

I am *not* a country person.

Sorry.

I wish I was, and on some days, I still vaguely entertain thoughts of a life where I walk the dog through muddy fields, feed a horse, then stroll back into to my country house miles from anywhere to make a pot of tea on the Aga, or whatever the fuck else country people do.

And I love the country for an afternoon. A weekend at most. But ultimately, I like cities, and I always want to live in them. The buzz. The buildings at night. The people. The food. The potential, the possibilities. Just fucking cities mate, they're where it's at. So yeah. I like cities, and I can live in the suburbs for a bit if I don't have to stay too long (it's where I'm from, after all), but the countryside can fuck off.

Kat was working the food industry, which required relocating to East Anglia: one of the shittiest bits of the UK I've ever experienced. No doubt I'm being harsh to East Anglia; there are surely worse parts of the UK, but I haven't lived in them. Kat was working in Wisbech which is a charmless market town, but we were living up the road in Elm, a genuinely picturesque country village, in an old converted pub. Elm was a village of a few hundred people, and it was genuinely beautiful, with a lovely old church, a post office staffed by some of the most miserable people I've ever met, two pubs and at least five Indian restaurants. But it wasn't for me. It was cold, wet, the locals were unfriendly, and every time I jumped in my car to drive down to Heathrow airport, I was fucking glad to be out of there.

The drive to Heathrow was always a bit of fun though: partly to be getting out of the countryside, and partly because the road was a big, bouncing death trap: a good few hours of snaking country roads through dark, nameless villages. The roads always seemed to have rivers right next to them. "*Think, don't sink!*" the signs grimly warn you. I took my chances and thrashed the car anyway.

Sinking in the car was a real prospect, though. That entire part of the country sits below sea level, so one particular road called 'The Wash' would flood every few weeks. Often, I'd arrive at a 'Road Closed' barrier and wait it out – it was easy enough to skirt around the barrier and take your chances, but I never fancied my car getting stuck in the river, so I'd usually wait until someone in a better equipped vehicle came the other way. Once a Range Rover or similar arrived, you'd wind down the window and ask "How bad is it?" and you'd get a response which varied between "It's fine, go ahead", or "Not a fucking chance in that car". You'd then proceed to drive down into 'The Wash', where the water would swell right up to your bonnet, you'd hold your bollocks and your nerve, and hopefully you'd power out the other side. I often took my chances on this road because I was typically running late, and often making a flight (and a gig) depended on me making it through The Wash.

These are the only good stories I have from my time in Cambridgeshire. The vast majority of the time it was miserable, boring country life, so when Kat was offered a job in Manchester, I was all in. I didn't care that it was too far north, that I didn't know anyone, or that my family was a six hour drive away. I'd work it out. I needed to be out of the fucking countryside.

We were moving to Manchester.

A few years on, and having discovered Tampopo, I'm digging into a red curry that has cooled down to the point that it's just about edible without burning my fucking face off. I love the food, but why do they always serve it so damn hot? Across the table, Adam Flexer is frantically blasting messages backwards and forwards. Tonight we're throwing a party in Manchester, and the buzz is off the fucking charts. I'm playing a three-hour set, as is our guest Sander van Doorn, and upstairs we've got Wippenburg and Josh Gabriel. We've sold well over 1,100 tickets – the night's technically sold out, but there's no doubt Sankeys will sell a few hundred more on the door, dodgy fuckers that they are. It's going to be a crush in there.

I'm not sure how I transitioned from DJ to promoter, but it's working out well for me. My career's on the up, and finally I might be cracking the UK, which has been the hardest piece of the jigsaw so far. Over the past five years, I've managed to turn my career around. Five years ago, at the start of 2006, it nearly all ended. Three months without a single professional gig, ready to apply for jobs, and I managed to fucking fix it. Over the previous five years, the buzz on me and my music had been gradually building across the world with bigger crowds in every country, but the UK was always the one where it refused to happen. Whilst fucking annoying, it's natural. We're not huge fans of success, us Brits. We like our artists in the early stage of their careers, when they're small, intimate, just like us – but any sign that they're getting too big for their boots, and we'll shoot them the fuck down. However, by starting this series of nights in Manchester, I think I might have finally cracked the code.

My career as a promoter started in 2007, and taught me a very valuable lesson: the only thing that club bookers understand is *strength*. If you are getting the shitty end of the stick - a bad deal or whatever - you need to have the strength to walk away. Keep your pride intact. Go do your own thing, demonstrate your value. They'll be back.

In London, I'd been playing at the legendary Turnmills club for a few years at their flagship night The Gallery, when I fell out massively with Mr Thong, the promoter. I don't recall the exact circumstances, but we were backstage after a set. It was me, Thong and Paul Oakenfold, and the booze was flowing. Before long, fueled by booze and fat lines of coke, Thong started giving me hassle for some row he'd had with my agent.

"You know Gaz, what Neil's asking for you is a fucking joke, mate. I'm already paying £750 a gig and he wants a grand, plus 2nd bill? Let me tell you mate, I don't give a fuck where you came in the DJ Mag list."

I don't enjoy confrontation, and if I'd been sober I'd probably dodge the conversation, blame it all on the agent or whatever, but I was drunk, so I made the dubious decision of engaging.

Oakenfold, seeing the way this was going, slipped off, leaving us to it.

"You're entitled to your view, but I honestly don't agree. Look at your 2nd bill last night. Guarantee I sell more tickets than they do."

"Shut up mate. We booked you when you were a fucking nobody for £300, now I'm paying £750 and that's already too much. There's just no fucking loyalty. This club's done so much for you."

"I appreciate that, Thong", I shrug.

"Well why are you asking for more money then?" He's really pissed now. He goes on.

"How about this? Next time I'm halving your fee. It's going back to £300. What you gonna fucking do?"

"Dunno mate. Sounds like you want me to go elsewhere."

"Good luck with that. There's no other venue in London close to ours and you know it. Go and play for those fucking muppets under Vauxhall Bridge if you want, and see where your career goes then."

I'd had enough.

"Mate, fuck off. If you don't want to book me don't fucking book me. I don't give a fuck."

I clearly did give a fuck.

"Alright then, I won't.' He shoots back. 'Seriously mate, your ego's out of control. You sell 20 tickets for us, that's it. 20 fucking people, that's all you bring in"

I leave the club and text Neil. *Had a kick off with Thong. Not going to be playing here for a bit I imagine.* Neil can probably smooth it over on Monday when everyone's sobered up, but I've got an idea.

For my next London play, I decide to go elsewhere, but Thong was right; there's literally fuck all other clubs worth playing for in London, so I decide to throw my own show instead. We find a tiny venue, just a couple of hundred people, and throw a night called "Gareth Emery's Podcast Party". I get everyone from our record label to play, promote the shit out of it, and sell about 250 tickets to a combination of family, friends, and super fans – not bad, for a start.

The night of the show, Thong's boss, J Darwin Huffer calls me up. He owns the venue itself, and is a major player. Tonight, he's sarcastic, arsey, and hopes we've shat the bed.

"Heard about your little show tonight. What are you on? Fifty tickets? Hope you're not blowing the savings on it".

"Actually J, more like two hundred and fifty. Basically sold out"

"Oooh, two hundred and fifty tickets. Remember, you could have been here. We'll do over a thousand tonight. Think I give a fuck about two hundred and fifty poxy tickets?'

"You should do. It's two hundred and fifty people that aren't coming to your club."

Got him.

Fact is, despite J's posturing, I'm in a good position now.

Club promoters tend to base the value of an artist on two things: hype, and tickets. Hype is a valuable commodity but it only applies to new artists. But, as I'm digging into this story, let me explain How Hype Works.

An up-and-coming artist does something of note: makes a big record, or get the world's attention in some way. Suddenly, they're proclaimed as the 'next big thing', and promoters scramble to book them. The media follows suit, and before you know it, said artist is literally everywhere, not because of achievements, but because the industry's been whipped up into a state of frenzy. Promoters book the artist with a sense of FOMO, not wanting to miss out on the next global star. When you've got hype, you're untouchable.

A small amount of artists translate hype into a real career, but most don't. Have you ever seen an artist who seemed to appear on every single lineup for a year or so, or an actor that – suddenly – was in every TV show you watched? That's the power of hype. Have you also noticed how those people often disappear as quickly as they appeared? Hype again, or the lack of it. It's a fickle beast.

Now, I've been around a while, so hype's not on my side, so my only other option is tickets. If you can demonstrate that you can sell tickets, that's the holy grail. And I, for the first time in my life, have demonstrated that I can sell tickets.

This is good for me. Not only has Thong's assertion that I could only sell 20 tickets been shown to be utter bollocks, but both J and I know that two hundred and fifty people times £20 equals £5,000 in ticket sales, and these are extra-special tickets, because they are what we call in the trade '*hard tickets*'.

The primary difference between hard and soft tickets is the following. When you play a club, it's known a *soft ticket play*: because the club likely has an in-built crowd who go there every week. So even if you sell out a nightclub, selling, say, five hundred *soft tickets* isn't all that helpful to demonstrate your value, because most of them might have been going anyway. On the other hand, when you do a show in a theatre, or some other space that has no in-built crowd, it means that every single person who's coming, is coming to see you. Those are *hard tickets.* Doing hard ticket shows are not for the faint of heart: you can lose a lot of money very quickly, and if nobody comes, your lack of actual fans is exposed quickly, brutally, and publicly. However, if you get it right, selling hard tickets is one of the most effective ways to demonstrate your value.

Different acts have different strategies on this. Some acts do zero hard ticket shows, instead preferring to stay in the safe, protected lanes of clubs and festivals (the ultimate soft ticket play). I believe there are a number of DJs who essentially have almost zero actual fans who'd go out of their way to see them perform, but have managed their careers extremely smartly, kept to soft-ticket plays so their true fanbase was never exposed, and have built to headline status. Fair play to them. For me, I've never had a lot of industry hype, meaning I typically need to prove myself to a promoter before they take a chance on me. And that meant doing hard tickets.

Selling 250 hard tickets in London was a game changer. I'd now demonstrated that I could sell £5,000 worth of tickets, and whilst my fee in London isn't going to jump from £750 to £5,000 overnight, I can be sure that when Turnmills make their next offer, I'm going to get the fee and billing I want. The London show didn't make money - in fact, it probably cost a grand or so- but that'll get made back many times over in the future.

It was a *great* investment.

As I planned our move to Manchester in 2008, promotion was on my mind, but first, I needed an employee. Hungry and ready to fire my career to the next level, I wanted to start to build a team. I already had Andrew, who worked remotely on my radio show, but I wanted an office, and somebody in there every day.

Adam Flexer was that person. I'm not sure how I knew him, but he was in his early 20s, fresh from abandoning his university degree, and had helped us out on our London show. I got chatting to him on Facebook, and not only did he want a job in the music industry, he planned to move to Manchester as he had a bunch of friends there. Perfect.

"I'm not in Manchester yet, still living in Wisbech, but we'll be there in a month or so," I told him. "Get yourself on a train, come up here next week, and we can chat about this".

Adam took about fifteen trains to get himself to the middle of nowhere. We chatted, got on well, and agreed that he'd start working for me at the sum of £500 per month.

Reconvening in Manchester a month later, we got down to business.

"I've found a pretty decent office", he told me. "It's £600 a month but it's in the old mill above Sankeys, and the bloke before has been using it as a studio, so he's already got some sound-treatment in there. It might be perfect."

I checked it out, and it was indeed, fucking perfect. Beehive Mill was an old textile mill in Manchester's Ancoat's district. To say the area was 'up and coming' would have been kind. Desolate and murderous would have been more accurate, but it had a buzz about it, and the building was full of creative-type businesses that made for good neighbors. There was a nightclub, a flyer distribution company, the bloke next door had a DJ school called Make Me A DJ (which became highly successful) and our room was already divided into a studio and office. It was great. And so my mind turned to promoting events.

At this point in time, trance music in Manchester was non-existent. The city had plenty of house and techno music and some amazing legacy dating back to the notorious Hacienda nightclub, but zero trance. The prevailing wisdom was that Manchester just didn't have enough trance fans to sustain a scene, but as far as I could see, nobody had ever tested that assumption in recent years. Often, bits of established 'wisdom' get repeated so often they become widely accepted as fact, despite the fact that they might no longer be true… or were never true in the first place. The good thing is, if you're able to spot where everyone else is missing a trick, there's a lot of opportunity there.

Trance in Manchester was about to be one of those things.

Another piece of established promoter wisdom was that throwing events in January doesn't work. The logic is that people have spent all their money over Christmas, and in January they're poor, on a diet to shift the Christmas weight, and basically have no interest in going out. That might have been true at one point, but most UK promoters followed this to an insane degree, refusing to throw a single event in January, which always struck me as utter bollocks. Once you get to the third week of January, Christmas was three weeks ago and people are ready for some action.

So for our first event, we decided to stress test that assumption. Personally, I quite like the idea of January dates – there's fuck all competition because of every other promoter essentially shutting down for a month, so good venues are easier to get, and artists tend to be a bit cheaper too.

Sankeys, at this point, had an air of untouchability. A dark basement known for drugs and hypnotic underground music, it was one of the hottest clubs in the country, packed every weekend. From hiring our office we knew the owners, and whilst friendly enough, they had little interest in giving their club to a 'commercially toxic style' like trance music. Sankeys was cool. Trance was not.

However, they'd just opened a small 2nd room, attached to Sankeys, which could also be operated as a stand-alone venue called Spektrum, and it was beautiful. Spektrum was brand new, had a luxurious VIP feel, some innovative ceiling lights based on legendary Berlin club Watergate - and the fact that it was attached to Sankeys – a place where no trance fan would ever have set foot – immediately made it cool as fuck.

For a small fee, Sankeys were reluctantly willing to let us hire their baby venue for the night, and so we launched 'The Gareth Emery Manchester Podcast Party' at Spektrum. The capacity was only 300 people, and the room was tiny. Looking around, I figured even with 100 people in there it'd look half decent, so even if it turned out that there indeed were no trance fans in Manchester, it wouldn't look too bad in there. Kat had a decent network of friends, so I figured she'd get thirty or forty people down there, so at worst we should do 100 – not a total failure. Capping your downside and considering the worst-case scenario is important when promoting an event.

However, even though we'd capped the downside, we threw everything at the event. We stacked the fucking line up, pulling in every favor, and counting on the fact that it was January to get decent fees, booking Cosmic Gate, Lange, Andy Moor, Activa, and Jerome Isma-Ae. For a 300 person room, this was an absolutely bananas line-up, but I wanted to hit it with everything so if we failed, we'd at least have given it our all. None of the acts had ever played in Manchester before, so the sell was pretty easy.

"Look, it's Manchester", I told each of them. "There's no fucking trance scene here, it's January where you've got no gigs anyway, so give us a good deal, come over, have some fun, and let's see if anyone's into this music here. It won't interfere with anything else you're doing".

Our designer Mike made a stunning flyer, modelled on one of my favorite films, *Lock Stock & Two Smoking Barrels,* giving it a gritty, UK feel, and with that the tickets went on sale, *and they fucking flew.*

Over half of them sold on the first day. The excitement was incredible – promoting is extremely hard work, but when things go well, the buzz is unreal. I was checking our ticket account a few times an hour. Within a week, we were down to 50 tickets left. We announced at that point the event was nearly sold out, and then, it was!

We'd fucking done it. *Sold out.* In the eyes of the UK promoters, this was the moment where I started to transition from Gareth Emery: trance nobody, to Gareth Emery: who sells out fucking shows. Looking at our ticket data, people had come from all over – we'd had people from The Netherlands, Germany, all over the UK, but the most encouraging thing?

75% of ticket buyers came from Manchester or the surrounding areas.

The event lived up to the hype. Manchester was on the trance map, and so was I.

The Monday after the show, Dave Vincent the owner of Sankeys headed down to our office. He was a notoriously difficult character. A short Jewish promoter in his mid-forties who'd seen it all, and done it all, and who also owned the building we were in. He hadn't spoken more than a few words to me in the months we'd been in the building, but all of a sudden he wanted to chat.

"Do you know how fucking rare a sell out is?' He told me. 'You need to go bigger. It's the full club for the next one. We're giving you Sankeys. Book a headliner. You've got to strike while you're hot".

I was nervous as *fuck*. Sankeys was a 1,200 capacity venue, and going from 250 tickets to 1,200 felt like too big of a step.

"Dave, we sold 250 tickets, but you're talking five times as many. It's a huge risk"

"It really isn't." he insisted. "Look, you've already shown you can sell 250 tickets way in advance. Even if your presale ends up being just 450 tickets, we'll get two hundred walk ups, and then you've got 650 people in the club, and it looks fucking great with 650 in there. Trust me."

Predicting how a club would look with a certain number of people is, I would learn, a skill every single club owner has. Dave knew his legal capacity, and how many people he could actually cram in before someone called the police. He knew how many people looked like a sellout, even if the night wasn't sold out. He knew how many people looked like a busy, thriving night, even if the club was way below capacity. And he knew how many people would make the club look empty: the number that would lead clubbers to happily enjoy the fact they had so much room to dance, and DJs to decide they'd never be coming back. All club owners know these numbers.

"OK," I gave in. "Let's see who's available. Not saying we'll do it, but let's at least see."

Big DJs are extremely difficult to book – not only do they cost a fortune, but getting the dates is tough, as is figuring out billing, flights, and almost everything else, if they even want to do the show in the first place. But we did some shopping around, and it turned out Ferry Corsten was available for the date. Corsten was a trance legend and the sort of name we would need to try and fill the entire Sankeys venue. He was a little past his peak, but had maintained his career well and had plenty of fans. Better still, he was in the middle of changing European agents, meaning his American agent Paul Morris would handle the booking. I was glad we didn't have to deal with a European agent who'd know a lot about Sankeys, and would probably dig into the economics of our night and ask us what the fuck we were thinking trying to sell 1,200 trance tickets in Manchester. None of that was relevant to Morris, who was thousands of miles away, and who told us that Ferry was ours if we could afford his £6,000 fee.

This made me extremely fucking nervous. With other costs, I'd be risking nearly £8,000 on the show, and I didn't have that cash, meaning if we shat the bed and the show was a fail, I wouldn't be able to pay Ferry's fee. I was making good progress in the industry, and getting known as the guy who stiffed Ferry-fucking-Corsten for six grand wasn't a reputation I particularly wanted.

I told Dave the idea was a no go. It was too risky.

Being a professional promoter, unlike me, Dave came at this from a different angle. First, he had a lot more money than me. Second, he was much more tolerant of risk, and third, he could see what I couldn't: that our night was fucking hot, and with Ferry there it was going to explode. He offered to co-promote the night with us: he'd cover all upfront costs, meaning Ferry Corsten would definitely get paid, and if the night profited we'd split the proceeds 50/50. I was still really fucking nervous because if we lost money I'd need to pay Dave back, but he wouldn't take no for an answer.

"Stop fucking shitting yourself, Gaz! Trust me, the night is going to fucking sell out. Do you know how long I've been doing this? It's a great fucking date, there's loads of buzz, and people are desperate for the next night."

"Ah mate," I went on. "It's just the costs are..."

"Listen," he told me. "We're into this now. You've got a quote from his agent, if you back out he'll never deal with you again. Plus, if you pull out now, I will be extremely fucking offended that you have so little faith in my ability as a promoter that you don't think I can project ticket sales. And, if you bottle it, *maybe I'll just do it my fucking self anyway*!"

I was in a pickle. Do the night, or burn my bridges with Dave and Sankeys. And worst of all, if Dave who hated trance decided to go it alone and made it a success, I'd be forever kicking myself. The fucker had me by the balls.

With no other options left, I decided to roll the dice.

If we thought the buzz on our first show was good, nothing prepared us for what would come next. Garuda @ Sankeys, featuring Ferry Corsten & Gareth Emery, was announced. Rather than stack the lineup with loads of supporting acts, we decided that both me and Ferry would do three hours sets. Today, every man and his dog does extended sets, but at the time, they were very rare and people lapped it up. Trance! At Sankeys! In Manchester! With Gareth Emery and Ferry Corsten! Three hour sets!

The three-hour sets were also particularly helpful for building my own name. I was starting to get known as a solid producer, but I really wasn't ranked as much of a DJ yet. I felt like my skills were getting good: I'd been professionally DJing for six years at this point, so I was comfortable enough behind the decks and felt my track selection was pretty fucking solid, but people just didn't know me. I knew Ferry Corsten would bring a lot of his fans who'd have no idea who I was. Playing for three hours before him would hopefully give me the chance to convert a lot of those to my fans as well.

The Ferry Corsten show sold out. I think we sold our online allocation of 1,000 tickets in advance, then another 200 on the door, and everyone made money. Walking to the venue, I looked down the street to see 500 people lining up, and couldn't believe it was for our night. The air was cold, but the buzz was palpable. We were at the start of something new. Something great. I'd never experienced anything like it before, but this was just the beginning.

Over the next few years, we did four shows a year, bringing in Above & Beyond, Sander van Doorn, Markus Schulz and many others alongside me. We also threw our busiest party yet, celebrating the 100th episode of my podcast, which saw Sankeys cram in nearly 1,500 people, and an all night, seven hour set by me, which sold out withn days.

Aided by these nights, my UK career finally got moving. Being behind one of the hottest nights in the country was finally delivering some hype, and being able to play extended sets meant I could showcase my skillset as a DJ and demonstrate that I was actually pretty decent. Finally, I was making some money too. The Sankeys nights didn't pay much, but they were having an explosive effect on my fees in the rest of the world, and the festival bookings were beginning to come in. Around this time, Sankeys was voted by DJ Mag as the world's best club, further adding to the buzz. DJ Mag's polls are famously corrupt, and Sankeys probably contributed most of the votes themselves, but it didn't matter. We had the number one trance night in the country, at the best club in the world. We were untouchable.

Finally having some spare cash in the bank, I bought an apartment on Cotton Street, a two-minute walk to Sankeys. This was incredibly convenient: I could live, work, and throw parties all on the same street. I didn't need to drive anywhere. Knowing I was having a 'moment', I worked hard to capitalize on it.

Around the start of 2010, Kat and I had broken up after 3.5 years together, and although we'd get back together two years later, I took the time to throw myself into work like I never had before. I was incredibly productive, but I had little else happening in my life other than work, and my personality took a bit of a dip.

I'd be in the office or the studio Monday to Friday. Every weekend I was on tour, often in North America. I became one of British Airway's top few thousand flyers in the world, gaining their elusive Concorde Room card. I had zero hobbies and my only 'relaxation' consisted of huge amounts of alcohol, always after shows. Worse still, I lost contact with my old friends, and exclusively interacted with people who worked for me in some way.

Many artists turn into dickheads for a while when they first get big. They believe the hype, surround themselves with sycophants, disconnect from their true friends, and I followed that tried and tested path. In losing Kat, I'd lost one of the few people in my life who could be honest with me: who could tell me when I was being an arsehole. I still had my sister Roxanne, who did her best.

Creatively though, it was a remarkably productive time. I wrote and produced my debut artist album 'Northern Lights'. The lead single 'Sanctuary' exploded worldwide, having a particular impact on US radio, which was entirely new to me. Within the next year, my US bookings started going through the roof as the record worked its magic, laying the foundations for my mission to conquer America, which would come a few years later. We also threw our most ambitious event yet, the 'Northern Lights Concert', to nearly 2,000 people at the O2 Academy in Leeds, where I experimented with live instrumentation for the first time. During the night, Kat – now in a new relationship - came out to support me . As I stepped off stage, the roars of 2,000 people fresh in my ear, she gave me a hug, congratulated me on the show, then headed out, as she was going on holiday with her new boyfriend.

I'd stayed off the booze as I was flying early the next day, and as I drove back to Manchester - alone - I couldn't shake a nagging feeling of loneliness. I guess I was missing Kat. My career was at its absolute peak, but for the first time ever, I started to wonder what it would all cost, personally.

But Northern Lights was a life-defining album for me. When I look at the cover of that album, all I can see is the hunger and drive I felt at the time. I was going places, and knew I had hype, and I was going to throw every fucking thing at my career.

As pivotal as those years were for my career, it wasn't all smooth sailing, and sometimes, I felt like most of our time was spent fighting fires. The Garuda Manchester operation felt a little like a beautiful plane, sailing through the sky, every graceful arc admired by the watching crowd, whereas on the inside, we were frantically running around making repairs with duck-tape and doing everything we could to stop the fucking thing from crashing. To the industry we were untouchable, but on the inside we were rapidly imploding, as was our relationship with Sankeys.

Sankeys were difficult fuckers to work with. Nightclubs tend to be run by faceless, soulless corporations, or total fucking wide boys, and Sankeys was of the latter type. Everybody who worked there took drugs. Dave, the owner, was so well-known for his ketamine intake, that he had an alter-ego of 'Ketaman' who he'd occasionally dress up as, super-hero outfit and everything. They could be a nasty bunch too. Not to me, but Adam constantly got shit from them. He was in the process of having a bunch of procedures done on his teeth to repair some childhood issues, which led to them giving him the unfortunate nickname 'Browntooth.'

The poor guy constantly had to do battle with Greg Vickers, Dave's #2 who did most of the day-to-day running of the club. Vickers was a genuinely good guy, but he had to do Dave's bidding, so he was always kicking off with us. He's also the closest I've come to a fight in recent years. One day we were having an explosive argument over the phone, and he was screaming at me. Eventually, he yelled. "Gaz, you're driving me fucking mad mate! If you were in your office, I'd walk down there right now and smack the shit out of you!".

"I am in the fucking office mate!' I responded. 'Come on down!"

"FINE! I FUCKING WILL!" he screamed, and slammed down the phone.

Adam looked up from his computer quizzically.

"Everything OK?"

"Um, I think I've just agreed to a fight with Vickers"

Seconds later, the door flew open. It was Vickers, sweating, and bright red.

"Gaz, can you step outside please?"

I stepped outside.

For an indeterminate amount of time, we stared each other down. I wondered if he was actually going to him me. Should I hit him first? I wasn't even that bothered about it. The whole thing was a fucking joke. I broke the tension and laughed.

"Mate this is fucking ridiculous. What are we even fighting about?"

He laughed too. The moment had passed.

"Fucking drinks tokens. Dave's killing me. He's a nightmare".

We made up, and got on a lot better after that. Funny how nearly coming to blows with someone can improve your relationship.

But every show seemed to produce some sort of battle, requiring us to find a new solution. The door staff, a bunch of angry roid-rage meatheads, would deny our personal friends entry even when they were on the guestlist, meaning that we had to send one of our own crew down for the first couple of hours to make sure our guests got in. We'd send an email to all our guests saying get to the club by midnight. If you turn up before midnight, our girl will be there, and she'll get you in. If you turn up after midnight, good luck and godspeed.

Then there were constant battles over drinks. As Manchester was our home town, we knew a ton of people who attended every show. This was great, and I loved the fact we were throwing events that everyone in a 100 mile radius was desperate to attend, except for the fact that all our friends and DJs wanted to drink... on us. Garuda @ Sankeys was not a night anyone attended sober. Unless you had a legitimate medical reason, or were a recovering alcoholic, you were getting fucked up. *Don't book a gig the next day, you'll miss the flight. Book yourself a spa day. You'll fucking need it.*

The issue was that Sankeys charged us for all drinks, and their prices were extortionate. It didn't matter that it was our guests: nobody at Sankeys drank for free, and any alcohol spend was diligently deducted from our statements after the show. Bringing in our own booze was absolutely not allowed, and we'd already had a serious kick off when I tried to bring in a bottle of vodka in my DJ bag.

Two incidents told us we had to get things under control.

The first was when Andy Moor and his entourage managed to drink his entire drinks rider of multiple bottles of vodka, champagne and beers in under 30 minutes. I still recall Adam, incredulous at the sheer thirst of Andy's friends, calling me from the club with his voice shaking. *They've literally drunk everything! What do I do?*

The second was our first £1000 drinks bill. It was time to get our house in order.

Our approach for this was two-pronged. We'd split our guests into two lists: Tokens & Green Room. Guests on the tokens list were people we wanted to hook up a little bit, but not too much. They'd each be handed five or six drinks tokens which could be exchanged at the bar for a drink. Enjoy, use them up, then don't fucking come back for more. That's your lot, enjoy. That would at least limit the damage the Andy Moors of the world could do. No doubt they'd be coming back for more tokens, but it would still be better than having an unlimited stockpile for them.

Then, for a small selection of close friends and artists, we figured out an ingenious solution. We worked out that although our office was two floors up from the club, by taking a convoluted route through the back corridors of the old mill, through various abandoned areas and security coded doors, we could make our way from the belly of the club to our office. So, we threw some sofas in the office and turned it into a green room. We could fill the fridge with booze during the day when the Sankeys police weren't around, and siphon off our most important guests to the office where we could listen to music in the studio, drink, and basically do whatever the fuck we wanted prior to show time. It was great fun and meant we'd avoided getting gouged by Sankeys, although they would have gone fucking berserk if they'd found out. One night, I wandered up to find Simon Patterson passed out on the sofa an hour before he was due to play. I woke him up.

"I'm not fucking playing!" he slurred in his Irish drawl, good natured as ever, even when threatening to cancel a gig. "Adam won't pay me, so I'm not playing".

"I've told you three times," laughed back Adam, looking up from his laptop, "I'll pay you *after* you've played. If you can play...".

Patterson looked a right state, but professional that he was, he sobered up enough to play a set which many on the internet reported to be the best of the night.

We also had major issues with Sankeys filling the venue far beyond its reasonable capacity. As the promoter, we had zero control over the door, and there was very little we could do if they decided to sell 200 extra tickets on the door. When we started to get complaints about how busy the nights were, the responses were typical promoter backchat:

"It's a good problem to have. Do you know how many promoters wish their nights were too busy? Every fucking one..."

"Those extra 200 tickets at the door for £30 each put £6,000 on the bottom line, and you're fucking complaining?"

But the venue was brutally hot and insanely busy. Sweat would literally be dripping off the ceiling. To get to the DJ booth, I'd need two security staff to help shove through a solid mass of bodies. It was absolutely nuts. Soon the internet starting talking, and reviews of the night made me convinced we needed to act.

At some point soon, somebody is going to die at a Garuda night, and Gareth Emery and his whole crew will have blood on their hands. The conditions in the club are inhumane and it's down to nothing more than greed.

I'm sure the writers of those words weren't a massive fan of me anyway, but most other posters, whilst noting the tone was a little over-dramatic, agreed our nights had become far too busy. Besides, I wanted our nights to be fucking amazing in every way. Not uncomfortably full. Eventually we came to an agreement with Sankeys that we'd restrict the main room to a comfortable 900 people, so while we never did the same numbers again, the nights were a lot more fun for everyone who attended.

But as the years went by, inevitably, things became a little less special. Dave decided he wanted to bring Armin van Buuren, the world's #1 DJ at that point, to the club. But after chatting to his agent, there was one catch.

"Armin's up for it, but he won't play as part of your night. Says it's just got to be an Armin show".

This wasn't surprising – most big names in the trance scene got there by very carefully ensuring they did as little as possible to elevate the status of their competition, but I was still pissed off. I'd brought trance to Sankeys, to Manchester, and now they were going to do an Armin show without me, and who was our next headliner? Markus Fucking Schulz. Hardly comparable. But, there wasn't much I could do, so I reluctantly gave it my blessing, as long as Adam could also play on the night, a show which I knew would be a real treat for him. I was working him to the bone, and still paying him too little, so this would keep me on his good side.

A few days later, Dave sent me the flyer. ARMIN VAN BUUREN / BROWNTOOTH. I called him:

"You're a dick, mate".

"We fucked up Gaz. We made it as a joke in the office and it accidentally got sent to the printers. They've made 10,000 of them".

"Are you fucking joking?"

"No, this is real."

"This cannot be fucking real. You're about to ruin Adam's life".

It turned out he was joking. Living in the US now, I've got to be careful about this work-based banter. People take things seriously, and any humor that Americans lamely call 'mean-spirited' in nature can you get into serious shit. Some of the antics that went on at Sankeys would have lead to multi-million dollar lawsuits for emotional damage. For us, it was just another day in the office.

The Armin show set a precedent though. For Above & Beyond's next show at Sankeys, they also decided they didn't want to play under the Garuda brand. And again, I understood it. Back when they played for us, I was a virtual nobody, no competition in any way. Now I was starting to get somewhere, getting booked on the same festivals as them, and there was no fucking way they were going to help me out. It didn't matter too much, because I'd built enough of a fanbase to more or less sell out Sankeys on my own now, but it was clear that the Manchester effect, which had supercharged my career for the last couple of years, was coming to an end.

As well as our increasingly fraught relationship with Sankeys, my own team was rapidly falling apart. The stress of running my operation for years had been hard on Adam, and he'd fallen into a serious drug and alcohol problem – a huge occupational risk in the music industry, where this sort of behavior is acceptable and normalized. He'd always had a taste for the white powder, gaining the jokey nickname 'Pablo Flexibar', but as his reliability fell off a cliff, and he began to miss work, it didn't feel such a joke any more. Each weekend, his partying would roll over into the week, and he wouldn't turn up until Wednesday, ignoring emails and phone calls for the first two days of the week. This had to change.

Whilst I tried to get him back on track, I wasn't exactly setting the best example. I might have had my shit a little more together, but I liked to drink to excess, especially after shows, and culture flows from the top. Perhaps with a few more years of experience I might have been able to guide him through it, but this was my first time dealing with a struggling employee, and I had a lot to learn. Sitting drinking expensive tea in Teacup in Manchester's Northern Quarter, I tried to get to the bottom of it.

"What is it mate? I know you're not really enjoying it anymore, but how can we fix it? We've come so far together. It's shit the way things are right now".

Adam shrugged, looking down, likely on yet another comedown.

"I don't know. I'm not happy. Maybe I want to do other stuff. The nights are great, the record label's great, but I just don't know. Maybe I want be an agent. Maybe I want to focus on my own DJing…".

"I'm down to help with all those things, but I seriously need you to start turning up for work again. Every time you disappear, people who are trying to get hold of you are kicking off with me. It's a terrible look for the company".

He shrugged.

Years later, Adam would tell me he had an air of invincibility at that point – that he felt his job and position in the industry was so secure, he could behave however he wanted – and he'd still be fine. And many others, in his position, might have felt the same way. He'd gone from nothing to running one of the top nights in the country in years. In the eyes of many juniors in the industry, he was a major player. So what if I sacked him? Someone else would snap him up.

Unfortunately, reality was about to come crashing down. His absences from work became more frequent, the excuses more far-fetched. Eventually, after a full week of no contact, I had to let him go.

Prior to a show in Dubai, sitting at the pool bar, I fired off a long email telling him it was over. Towards the end, I wrote:

> I am not ruling out you coming back to work with me again at some point in the future if you wanted to. But right now, on a personal level, I just can't work with you. I feel you need some serious time off to sort your own head out, address your own personal issues, and spend some time working elsewhere.
>
> In six months, a year, once you've done something else for a bit, if you still want to come back, let's talk. The door will always be open and I'd genuinely like to work with you again. But for your own good, you need to be doing something else right now. I genuinely believe long term this is going to be more beneficial for your overall career and character building, regardless of how hard it seems at the present.

I gave him three months full pay, and that was it.

It weighed heavily on my mind. I'd done everything I could for him, and gave him a crazy amount of chances, but I'd never let somebody go before. These days, it's easier. Working relationships come and go. Some people last forever, others move on to bigger things, others stop performing, and at the end of the day, whilst I'll do my best to pull someone through a rough patch, you can't save everyone. But letting Adam go was huge. He was the first person I'd ever hired. We'd built our dreams together and reached places we never thought possible. And now he was gone.

After Adam left the city, Manchester was never quite the same. I hired his replacement, a hard-working, serious DJ called Craig Connelly. He'd come up to me in Sankeys one night and asked if he could watch me work in the studio, and I thought, fuck it – why not? It'd be good for me to mentor someone, and at least if he's there in the studio with me, I'll be somewhat productive. My studio sessions at the time had become extremely unproductive, quickly descending into social media or pornography binges, and at the very least there would be none of that with Craig sitting in the corner.

So we'd done a few sessions and built up a rapport. At that time, he was working in the Apple Store and was desperate to get out of there into the music business, so I figured it was worth a shot.

Over coffee at Starbucks, I chatted about his aspirations for his own career.

"Basically mate, I want your job," he told me. "I want to be a famous DJ, producer, the works. I know my music isn't good enough yet, but it's all I've ever wanted."

"Look, come and work with me," I told him. "Run the label, work on the nights, and you can learn from me. As long as you run my label well, I'll teach you everything I know, both in and out of the studio, and when you're ready to go it alone I'll carry on supporting you."

It's rare that things pan out exactly how you planned them, but Craig's career did. He ran Garuda for the next five years, helping my next two albums reach iTunes Dance #1 in over 15 countries each, before taking the leap into his own career, where he's been ever since. He's still a grumpy little fucker, but he's done remarkably well and I'm proud of him.

But Adam leaving represented the end of an era. Things had become more serious. Businesslike. Craig was an exceptional team member, a serious, hard-working, drug-free professional who always turned up for work, and did an incredible amount for my career, but that meant the entire vibe changed. There were no more benders on Tuesday nights. We cut down on the nights at Sankeys – there was too much competition, and it wasn't quite as special any more. I decided to vary things up by doing a few headline shows at their arch-rivals, The Warehouse Project, including an epic Boxing Day five hour set. With nearly 2,000 people in there, it would end up being my biggest Manchester show ever, but as incredible as the night was, as I stepped off-stage it felt more like an ending than a beginning.

At the start of 2012, after two years apart, Kat and I got back together. My career had dramatically changed during that time, but I was convinced that she was the person I was destined to spend the rest of my life with.

Despite this, Manchester no longer felt like home. It was full of ghosts. Sankeys, no longer the best club in the world, was approaching bankruptcy. Dave Vincent, overwhelmed with the stress of running the club, had been committed to a mental institution (his alter ego of 'Ketaman' might have had something to do with that, too). Adam was gone. Old friends were leaving. On the work front, I also was concerned about how much of my time promoting the nights was taking up. One day, whilst collecting some flyers, the bloke who owned the flyer distribution company offered me some useful advice:

"The problem is Gaz, you don't want to turn into a promoter anyway. You're an artist. If you spend all your time on your night, you're making decent money, but you're building up other artists, and you turn into a promoter just like any other. Is that what you want?"

It wasn't.

For various reasons, Manchester just didn't feel like it did before. It had served its purpose well, but the excitement was gone. I was in search of a new challenge; one which would soon present itself 5,000 miles away.

Trance in Manchester had its moment from 2010-2011, but dance music in America was only beginning to boom. The first time I realized this was flying to Los Angeles to play the EDC festival in 2010. Having never played an American festival before, I had little idea what to expect, and was utterly shocked to arrive to find 100,000 ravers at the Los Angeles Memorial Coliseum. I'd never seen anything like it. As I looked out over the crowd, it became very clear to me: America was where it was at, where I needed to be.

A few months later, I was in Russia to play the Global Gathering festival. Leaving my hotel, I headed down to reception to find a stressed looking promoter waiting for me.

"You need to go, now," she told me. "Steve's been waiting in the car 20 minutes and he's not happy"

Steve who? I thought, not entirely happy at having to share a ride. Fuck Steve.

Walking out, I jumped into the back of the car to find Steve Angello from the Swedish House Mafia. We'd never met before, but Swedish House Mafia were on the cusp of becoming the biggest dance act in the world. They'd just released 'One', a record that would launch the EDM revolution and re-define dance music for the next five years, and Steve was the creative genius behind a lot of their incredible branding. Fortunately, he was lovely, and due to the appalling condition of the Russian roads and our driver's navigation skills, we had two hours in the car where we chatted about every topic imaginable. I felt lucky to be getting this sort of insight from someone I admired greatly. Clearly, Steve understood the magic of thinking big. He'd left Sweden for Los Angeles and was taking the US by storm. What the fuck was I doing, holding onto the past in Manchester? I'd already scored a hit with Sanctuary on US radio and I was in demand there. I already had the perfect springboard to launch my career.

Los Angeles was where I needed to be.

Fortunately, Kat was up for the move. She'd been in her job for the last five years as a corporate buyer at a large UK supermarket. The money was great, and it came with real power, holding a budget of tens of millions of pounds, but Kat was up for a change. Over curry at Wagamama we discussed the various options for getting her a visa.

"So, we can add you on to my Visa. I'd have an O1 visa, and you'd have an O2 visa, which means you're support personnel for me".

"But can I work under that visa?"

"No..."

"That won't work. I'm not moving to Los Angeles to sit by the pool all day".

"Well, there is one more option…" I suggested.

"I could upgrade my visa to a green card, then you'd be able to get a green card too, if…"

"If?"

"If we got married".

"Hmmmm. Are you asking me to marry you?"

"Well… it seems the most logical option, right?"

I have many strong points, but clearly romance ain't one of them.

"Sure.' My wife to be agreed. 'Let's do it".

Kat and I got married in December 2012 at the beautiful Manchester Town Hall, then threw an epic party afterwards. A few weeks later, we boarded a plane for America. The Manchester chapter was over. The Garuda Manchester flame only burned for a few short years, but changed the trajectory of many people's lives and careers, hopefully for the best.

Manchester, 2019.

A decade after those times, as I finish my food at Tampopo, I look up and see Adam walking out of the restroom. I get up to greet him, then realize:

It's not him. Just a look-alike.

I thought I saw your face.

As I wait for my coffee, memories of the Manchester Years wash over me. Man, it's hard to be back here.

Way too many ghosts from the past.

A few weeks later, I go for dinner with Adam in London, and I'm happy to see he looks well. We're at London's trendy Hakkasan restaurant. I knock back a few beers, Adam joins me, and for a moment, I worry that I'm maybe not setting the best example, again. Then again, he's out of the music industry now, working as a chef, and I can't help but feel it's good for him. I tell him about how fucking strange it was being back in Manchester, and he agrees. He's hardly been back there since he left, but every time has felt exactly the same.

"It is what it is, but it's not what it was." he laughs.

"Fucking hell mate," I reply, "I think that's the most profound thing I've ever heard you say."

We leave the restaurant after two beers. No more drinks, no afterparty. I wander back to my hotel for an early night, and he heads for the bus. It's good to see him, despite how much we'd both changed.

We weren't the only ones.

"I SAW YOUR FACE"

written by Gareth Emery and Anthony Galatis

nothing in this place looks the same
from days gone by
but it's like i've never been away
that same old sky.
expecting you to walk in like you do
and laugh with me
all the dreams we built together here
just history
i was sure i saw your face
but we're somewhere else
both gone without a trace
darkness taking over the street
it's only three
way too many ghosts from the past
they follow me
and it will never be the same again
that much is true
just keep on moving forward and forget
the life we knew
i was sure i saw your face
but we're somewhere else
both gone without a trace

WAY TO YOU

IDENTITY BATTLES, CALIFORNIA LIFE, AND FAR-FLUNG PLACES

After Manchester, moving to California happened, and it was easy.

"Don't you miss England?" I'd be asked on visits back home.

"Of course," I'd reply, dutifully listing off all the things I missed, like chocolate biscuits, orange squash, and black pudding, but in reality, I could happily live without all of it. Frankly, there's not a single day I've felt homesick in my seven years living in Los Angeles. I'll get a little frustrated when the Six Nations Rugby is on, because seeing a game involves a 10 hour flight instead of a two hour car journey, but that's the extent of it.

Moving was easier, because I've struggled with identity my whole life. Even as a child my national identity was an issue. I was being raised in Southern England, but neither of my parents embraced Englishness in any way. My father, who'd grown up in a Welsh mining village of less than 10,000 people called Treorchy, has always firmly identified as Welsh. If anything, his sense of identity has heightened in his 40 years living in England.

In order for the next few pages to make sense to my international readers, I'll need to dive into a quick UK101: a brief explanation of the United Kingdom and the four countries that comprise it. Brits, you'll know all this already, so feel free to skip. Americans, you may benefit from reading it twice.

To most people in the United States, 'England, 'The United Kingdom' and 'Great Britain' are thoroughly interchangeable. One and the same. Sure, they might find it strange that the country has three names, but then again, the majority of Americans don't tend to be overly curious about worldly affairs. Those that are, however, tend to be incredibly curious and more than make up for the rest of the country, so don't take it badly.

But, yeah. UK 101. The United Kingdom is the 'master' country name, if you will, compromising all four countries of England, Wales, Scotland and Northern Ireland. But whilst we refer to these four countries as, err, countries, in reality they're more like states or provinces. There are no borders, they all accept the same money, and everyone travels under the same passport, regardless of which country they live in.

Then, you've got Great Britain, which refers to England, Wales and Scotland but <u>not</u> Northern Ireland. Northern Ireland sits on a separate landmass, the island of Ireland, where it borders the Republic of Ireland, which actually *is* a separate country. Great Britain exclusively refers to the three countries on the main British island.

Our passports, attempting to make sense of this mess, are titled:

UNITED KINGDOM OF GREAT BRITAIN AND NORTHERN IRELAND.

Long-ass country name, I know.

Part of what confuses the rest of the world is that the individual countries pre-date the term the United Kingdom. The United Kingdom was established in 1707, but England has existed since 927, nearly 800 years previously, with Scotland, Wales and Ireland also enjoying long, colorful and bloody histories. Is there any surprise the United Kingdom hasn't quite caught on in the same way?

So, we're four countries, operating as one. Now, in the United States, identity seems to be fairly evenly split between the country of the USA and local state/city identities. People will be fiercely proud to be Texan, but also fiercely proud to be American. On the contrary, in the UK, being English / Welsh / Scottish or Northern Irish is far more important than being British.

My dad, despite having made his home in England, had a healthy disdain for the English and everything about them. This tends to be true for many Welsh, Scots, and Northern Irish. They literally fucking hate The English. Now, this doesn't apply on a daily basis: after all, we've all got to work together, but the moment there's a sports fixture, it's tribal warfare. As a child, my dad drilled this simple rule into me: if you're Welsh, and the England football or rugby team are playing, you always want them to lose, regardless of who they're playing against.

Even against Germany, who we fought two world wars against.

The Scots and Northern Irish are similar, actively wanting England to face defeat any time they're on the world stage. But what about England? Do English fans tend to want their neighboring teams to lose? Not generally in my experience, no. Most of them just don't give a shit - maybe because they win more often. Sure, I've heard the odd England fan muse something like this:

"Well, I suppose I can't really support Wales, as you lot always seem to want us to lose, but I shan't be watching anyway, so…"

This likely all boils down to the inferiority complex that the Welsh (and I sort of include myself in that), Scots and Northern Irish face. England's the dominant country. It's got the capital city, the population, the wealth, and the world stage branding. They're the conquering colonial power, and we're a couple of oft-forgotten tagalong countries with inferior sports teams. When people do remember that we exist, which isn't often, we're an afterthought lumped in alongside England, so it's understandable we'd be bitter.

Plus, without sounding too much like my dad, English rugby fans *are* smug. I'm sorry, but they are. Attending a rugby match at Twickenham – the home of the team – is one of my favorite experiences, but if you've ever wanted to see the English class system in action, that's the place. From the champagne picnics in the back of Range Rovers in the car parks, to fans recognizing each other from boarding school or chatting about the last Henley Royal Regatta, it's a microcosm of the English class system, and one of the few times where you'll get a glimpse of the people who *really* run the country. When I was younger, it was enough to make me want to start a class war. Now that I'm well-off myself, my desire for a class war has faded as I'd likely be on the wrong side, but still: I'd never fit in with that lot.

I'll never be one of them.

Growing up, I'd managed to pick up a fairly strong Welsh accent from my dad, despite the fact that I'd never lived in Wales, which immediately messed with my sense of identity. Despite being a small country, the UK has hundreds of regional accents, and, if you're well attuned to the local dialects, you can discriminate between accents of just a few miles apart. This meant that I was frequently asked:

"How long have you lived in England?"

"Uh, all my life..."

Was I English or Welsh? On one level, I'd only ever lived in England, attended an English school and all my friends were English. Yet, I somehow had a Welsh accent, and had been drilled by my dad that the English sports teams were to be my primary object of hate. Whenever England played in a major soccer tournament and our school was abuzz with excitement, I'd be the odd one out: sitting around sulkily hoping the team would lose.

My mother, despite seeming as English as they came, wasn't exactly overflowing with English pride either. Whilst she was proud to be British, and felt remarkable warmth for the achievements of our country, the 1980s were a particular time in history where the concept of Englishness itself had become associated with many of the wrong things. The English flag, the St George's Cross, had been adopted by the far right, which meant celebrating Englishness felt only a short step away from football hooligans, the British National Party, casual racism and anti-immigrant sentiments. So instead, my mother instilled a sense of pride in me for our international roots. Her father, my grandfather, was a first-generation immigrant to the UK – a Yugoslav / Italian WW2 veteran who spoke seven languages – and this was the source of far more pride than our Englishness.

This lack of Englishness meant that growing up, my Welshness was my dominant identity. But when I attended rugby matches in Wales, I didn't exactly feel like I belonged there either. My accent wasn't thick enough. The National Anthem was all in Welsh so I couldn't sing a single word (I still can't). So what the fuck was I? Even my Dad didn't seem to know.

"You kids are basically English, anyway", he gruffly told me and my sister one day. Well, thanks, Dad! If that's how you felt, you could have made sure I supported England and spoke with the right accent from the start, and this would all have been a whole lot easier.

Of course, these days, I'm quite happy for all the confusion. Not quite knowing who I was as a kid has meant my identity has also been fairly malleable as an adult, and that's been a good thing. It's meant that I've been able to subtly change the person who I am over the years – to pivot when my personality was no longer serving me or the world well. And flexibility in this area is important. At 22, I could decide that I was a famous DJ, even though I hadn't become one yet. At 30 I could decide that I was no longer a person who drank alcohol every night, taking long sober breaks and only drinking on rare occasions. At 32, I could decide that I was now a healthy person, eschewing burgers and fries for sushi and salads. None of these were difficult. They would have been harder if I'd had a clear identity, and that identity involved being at the pub five nights a week, as it still does for many of the people I grew up with.

Besides, as I reached my teenage years, I was soon to find the first identity that truly resonated with me.

Despite national confusion locally, I was very clear where I was from. Southampton, mate. I'd been born at Southampton General Hospital, in the middle of the city. My address had always had Southampton on the bottom of it. It wasn't up for debate: that was where I was from. And when I reached the age where I could attend football matches on my own, I was set. It didn't matter that I had a slight Welsh accent: when I walked into The Dell with 14,999 other fans wearing my red and white colors, the Southampton accent proudly swelled up, and that was who I was. Along with a couple of mates from school, I had a season ticket at Southampton Football Club from my early teens until I left for university. Whilst we were never a particularly good team, frequently languishing towards the bottom of the league, we had some great players: most notably Matthew Le Tissier – in my biased view, the greatest player the England national team never gave a proper chance to. His nickname was 'Le God', and to us, he was.

My Southampton identity received further affirmation when I took a weekend job selling furniture at a store called MFI – a long-defunct British Ikea equivalent. At 16, finding a part-time job had proved challenging. There was no minimum wage back then, and people got paid fuck all. I had taken a job behind the counter at a local shop – Alldays – for a meagre £2.08 an hour. The job itself was alright. The customers, often drunk students from the local Maritime Academy provided good banter, plus, at the end of the shift, I was able to take home any uneaten doughnuts and pastries left in the cabinet, which I always did. In fact, I'd take home so many that I'd need an industrial sized trash bag to carry them in. I'd pretend that they were for my family, but in reality, I'm not sure anyone else ever ate any.

After a few months though, I knew it couldn't last. The money was shit and I was getting fat from scoffing five chocolate doughnuts after every shift. Plus, I had to hang around for 30 minutes after my shift ended to 'cash up' the till, and was expected to show up 30 minutes before it started – both unpaid. Whether shop workers are still subject to these types of exploitative practices today I don't know, but even then, I knew that working an extra hour for free was bollocks. I needed to move on. My girlfriend-of-sorts, Emily, had bagged a sweet job, working at B&Q – the British equivalent of the Home Depot – where she received a £3 basic wage, but double time on Sundays, and triple time on holidays! She was making £6-9 per hour and I was making £2. This would not fucking do at all.

Unfortunately, there were no more cushy jobs available at B&Q, so I wasn't able to nick Emily's idea and work there – I'd have to find my own path.

Fortunately, I was about to find something much, much better.

I'd seen somewhere that MFI were looking for staff. Without any idea of the pay or job, I applied. It had to be better than working in the shop. I was called in for an interview the next day. Before the interview started, I was given a tour of the premises by the sales manager, Olly Gilbert, who would become a bit of a legend to me.

"It's a sales job, you know that, right? Not the warehouse or anything. You'll need to wear a suit."

"Yeah, that's fine" I replied. I had no idea what sales involved, but I spotted various people in suits sitting around tapping on computers. Looked fucking easy.

"So, the basic's low. £3 an hour. Double time on Sundays and holidays..."

Low? That was already better than what I was currently getting. Olly continued.

"But, we make up for it through commission. You'll get commission on everything you sell. The rates vary based on products. Sofas are the highest at 10%. Bedrooms can be up to 5%..."

As he went on, my attention drifted to the sofas in front of us. £500! Sell one of those fuckers, and I'd make £50? This was insane. I just had to interview well. Eventually, we finished our mini-tour and stopped by the front door. Olly looked at me.

"What do you say then? You want the job?"

What the fuck? That's it?

"Definitely".

"Alright then. Start Saturday. Wear a suit."

Fuck yes.

My time at MFI was one of the happiest of my life. Even though I only worked weekends, I was fucking good at selling, and I hustled hard. I actually had a real advantage over most of the full-timers. As they'd been working all week, by the time the weekend rolled around, they were likely tired, hungover and not on top form. But, the weekends were at least three times busier than the weekdays. They were where the real money was. Those were the days you needed to be on your game.

So, every Saturday and Sunday I exploded into work. I'd stopped going out, or when I did I went light on the booze, because I had a limited window to make as many sales, and as much money, as possible. Fortunately, I was good at selling, soon figuring out what worked and what didn't. Too many of my fellow employees tried to put a positive spin on everything. *Oh, it's a wonderful cabinet, very classy.* Fuck off. I soon realized that being honest was what generated sales. I made sure I knew our range well, buying a few cheap pieces for my parents' house, and assembling them so I knew them inside and out. There was no bullshit from me.

'Yeah, look. I personally love these pieces, I've got three of them at home. It's chipboard, so while it looks good, it's obviously not going to last as long as the solid pine stuff over there, but at this price it's still a great deal'.

'I love this one. I actually bought it for my parents for Christmas. I will tell you, it'll take a while to put together, because it's got the deluxe runners made with the ball-bearings. Took me four hours… but once you've done it, you won't regret it. The drawers are smooth as silk.'

Honesty all the way.

Although my basic wage was less than £100 a week, I was able to get that up to £250 with commission, and on a good month I'd be earning £1000 working just two days a week. This was nuts. It was also a fantastic grounding on how to sell: skills I'd need in abundance later in life.

Working at MFI was one of the first times I really felt independent. To some people it would have been a brutal environment. No punches were pulled between the staff: if you messed up, you were getting told. But there was no discrimination between the staff, male or female, old or young, gay or straight.

Of course, some of the antics would never be allowed today. When I returned from my first term at university, a stone heavier, my nickname became 'Fat Boy' until I'd dropped the weight. When I messed up assembling a new piece of furniture for the sales floor, Olly asked me if I was 'on day release from the retard center'. Sam, a gay employee who I liked a lot, had a number of nicknames. All of them would be lawsuit-worthy in 2020, but he took it in his stride and gave as good as he got.

In short, as long as you were good at your job, you'd be fine. Was it right? Probably not, but it was a product of the time. What I do know though, is that while the language was boorish and offensive, that was where the discrimination stopped. It was essentially all front, surface level stuff. Whereas today, our language is sanitized and constantly changing in order to be politically correct, but often with a dark underbelly of real discrimination lurking beneath the surface. Personally, I'd rather it be out in the open.

But it was good times. I'd passed my driving test, so I could drive to work, work as hard as I wanted (which usually was pretty hard), banter with a great group of people, eat what I wanted, and make money. Here, it didn't matter if I was England or Wales. All we all cared about was the job.

And these days, of course, I've made peace with being 'English'. On first moving to Los Angeles, when asked 'Oh, you have an accent, are you English?', I'd tend to reply that it was complicated, or give them the honest 'Actually, I'm Welsh but I lived in England for 30 years'. But now, sure. I'm English. Whatever. I don't even mind anymore, and even supported the England Football Team for the first time in my life in the 2018 World Cup. It only took 38 years. Sorry Dad!

Living outside of your home country has the interesting side-effect of showing how similar you actually are to your fellow compatriots. Growing up in Southampton, with our arch-rivals Portsmouth just 20 miles away, I felt very different to people there because I was entirely focused on the divisions. Whereas travelling the world does a lot to unite you with people from your own country. Even though there are many of us here, I still like meeting fellow Brits in Los Angeles – we all started out on a small island in Europe, and we're now on the edge of the world trying to make it in a new, vast continent. We likely have a lot in common. And it's fair to say, when I was in Syria, having been detained at Damascus Airport for not having the correct visa, or in St Petersburg, Russia, in a similar scrape, I would have given anything to have someone from the UK show up next to me.

Even if they were from Portsmouth.

DAMASCUS, SYRIA, 2010.

First things first, we need to set the stage here. Syria in 2010 was about to slide into a hell I cannot even imagine, but it wasn't like what we think about the place now.

That being said, it's been less than 30 minutes since I got off the flight, and I'm already feeling that knot in my gut best described as - *ohmyfuckinggodwhydidIagreetocomehere.*

The Syrian immigration border guard doesn't speak a word of English, but body language is international, and he isn't happy, shaking his head at my barrage of questions. I'm trying to buy a visa-on-arrival, perfectly legitimate for a British passport holder, but there's one small problem. The only currencies accepted are Syrian Pounds, and US dollars, and I have neither. I do have a wallet full of credit cards, British pounds, and Euros, all of which I have attempted to wave in front of the border guard's face, and all of which have been flatly rejected.

"Come on. How about British Pounds? They're still Pounds..." I hopelessly offer, attempting to slide a few crisp £20 pound notes across the counter, in the hope that he'll pocket them and issue me the visa anyway. Is this bribery? Not sure, but it has worked for me in the past. In Ukraine's Kiev airport – historically a terribly disorganized and long-winded airport, you used to be able to stick a couple of twenty euro notes in your passport and head through the diplomatic channel. Maybe this'll work here.

But no. Border guard shakes his head, and gestures me to move over to the side. He's got other passengers to serve. *Fuck.*

I take a seat on a hard plastic chair and curse my agents for failing to tell me that I needed US dollars: acquiring some at London Heathrow would have taken less than a minute, but now, stuck in Syrian immigration limbo with no ATMs or credit card machines in sight, I'm fucked.

"Excuse me, but are you OK?"

A Middle Eastern gentleman in a sharp suit sits down next to me. He's seen my problem, and his English is impeccable.

"I've seen you have some problems entering our country, may I ask if I can help? Perhaps I can arrange entry for you and give you a ride to wherever you need to go after?"

I decline his request. He's probably just being kind: the Middle East is rather like that, with people far more willing to go out of their way for strangers than in the West, but this is fucking Syria after all, and I'm not taking any chances.

I check my phone for the 100th time since landing: no service. I've got a phone number for the promoter, but it's fucking useless unless I can get a signal. I turn it off and on again.

Eventually, after processing the rest of the passengers, Visa Guard closes up his booth and pulls down the blind. He's closed: no more visas today. It's 10pm, dark outside, and there are no more flights today.

I'm due on stage in two hours.

Visa Guard gestures for me to come with him, and leads me to a back office where a bunch of other border-guards sit around laughing, smoking, and chatting in Arabic. One by one, they listen to my story and shrug, laughing together about their lack of understanding. I'm pretty confident that I'm not in any real danger, but they clearly have no idea what to do with me. After being ignored for a few minutes, I stand up, and make to head for the exit.

"Alright, thanks a lot then, bye!".

"No! No leave!" I'm told, like I'm a naughty schoolboy.

Fuuuuuck.

I find the promoter's phone number, and show it to the border guards, who reluctantly agree to call it. At first, there's no answer, but I persuade them to call again, and again, and eventually they get through.

A seemingly endless conversation in Arabic takes place, before one of the guards leaves, returning five minutes later with a new person wearing civilian clothes. He's my promoter. He introduces himself and I immediately forget his name - sorry, but I was shitting myself at this point - but nonetheless I'm grateful as fuck to see him.

"Gareth! Here you are. Come, quick, you have to be on stage in an hour."

Here's the small advantage of airports in developing countries: a well-connected individual can find themselves 'backstage' smoking cigarettes with the immigration officers. Syrian Pounds are handed over and a visa produced for me. Then some very clipped, abrupt conversation – some sort of argument – and we're out of there.

"What was that about?" I ask promoter.

"Nothing really. We were arguing about how many names he could have on the guest-list tonight. We're close to sold out so I'm limited in capacity."

"The immigration officials… are coming to the show?".

What the actual fuck? This would not happen in London.

"Yes, of course. A small token of thanks for them not deporting you."

As we blast through the streets of Damascus, I try to see something of the city. It's dark as fuck outside and there's little to see, but I can tell this place is ancient and wrapped in history, and look forward to seeing it in the morning.

Promoter speaks up: "So, we've had a little change of plan. The government removed our license for the original venue, so today we moved the entire event outside…"

Last minute venue moves are never generally good, particularly tonight – it's barely above freezing, but soon we're close to the venue, and my set is minutes away, and I need to change: my track-pants, selected for a comfortable flight, are not quite suitable for stage wear. With no green room at the venue, our car pulls into a restaurant.

"There, you can change in the toilets," the promoter tells me.

Cigarette smoke hangs heavy on the ceiling of the restaurant, and Arabic music pipes through the speakers. I feel very out of place. I nod hello, and head to the bathroom for a Clarke Kent-speed change.

Soon, we're in the venue, and the show looks good: there must be 5,000 people here. With 15 minutes to go, I head to the VIP balcony, and am immediately struck by how fucking rich everyone seems to be. This isn't your normal VIP – there's plates of food being served, glass cabinets showcasing bottles of cognac – it's a serious affair, and even more impressive given they've built the whole thing on a day's notice. Another thing about developing countries is that whilst there may be millions of people in poverty, the ruling classes are insanely fucking rich, and that's the crowd that are on the VIP balcony with me. There are more designer clothes and expensive watches than you'd find in a Hollywood nightclub. My friend the promoter introduces me to a friend of his, Aline, and we chat for a few minutes. Then:

Showtime.

I'm not sure why, but I've always been drawn to dangerous places, particularly any disputed territory. It's a strange obsession. Perhaps after travelling to over 85 countries I'm numb to the upside of safe, boring, Western countries. Austria? New Zealand? Greece? Been there, done that. Give me excitement, culture-shock, and danger.

Of course, in 2020 and now with two young children, I don't travel as much as I used to, and safety is more of a concern, so the chances of me actually going to places off the beaten-track is rather less than it was. But still, I'll live those dreams vicariously through others: spending my nights reading reviews of road-trips through the Democratic Republic of the Congo, bribery in the unrecognized Soviet republic of Transnistria, or guided tours in North Korea.

That said, I've had my fair share. Over the past decade, I've played in the Olympic Stadium in Baku, Azerbaijan, during the closing ceremony of the inaugural European Olympics. I've played in deserts in Jordan, festivals in Guatemala where our own private security carried machine guns at all times, and I've tapped into my heritage to visit North Macedonia, formerly Yugoslavia – the ancestral home of my great-grandfather.

And I have only a few regrets. On a trip to Israel, I desperately wanted to enter Palestine to visit Bethlehem and the birthplace of Jesus Christ – despite not being especially religious, I felt a strange draw to make the pilgrimage, but my lovely Jewish hosts, who would not be allowed to travel with me, were nervous about the security of me travelling alone, so reluctantly I decided against it. I was having such a good time with my hosts, who'd showed me fascinating parts of Israel, from Jerusalem to Be'er Sheva, that I felt taking an independent, unauthorized trip into Palestine would be poor repayment for their hospitality. A few years ago, my dad travelling on a cruise ship docking in Israel *did* manage to enter Palestine and visit the Church Of The Nativity, so at least one member of the Emery family has managed it.

For the most part, regardless of where I travelled, I was met with good fortune, excellent food, and friendly locals. I could likely write a book on my travels alone, so I won't dwell on this part of my story, but I feel fortunate to have experienced few 'incidents' during the thousands of flights I have taken over the past 15 years. In China, traveling at the peak of the swine flu epidemic, officials in full HAZMAT suits entered our plane to test each passenger: our plane had three suspected cases and the unfortunate passengers, along with anyone sitting near them, were hauled off to a quarantine hospital. In 2006, I flew to the US days after a terrorist plot to use liquids to bring down planes was discovered. Traveling out of Heathrow with the domestic security alert at 'severe', all hand luggage was banned, and we boarded the plane with nothing more than passports and wallets.

Most situations I have found myself in were self-created. In Russia in 2010, after playing a festival in St. Petersburg I arrived at the airport to return home, and realized I'd left my passport back at my hotel. This wasn't entirely my fault: Russian hotels at that point insisted on keeping your passport for a few hours after check-in (presumably to run your details through some KGB-esque database or other), and they'd not returned it to me. The problem was that the hotel was an hour away, and I was due to fly home to meet a gathering of friends and family in Manchester for my 30th birthday.

Like many frequent travellers, I have two passports. It's a little-known rule that if you travel enough to frequently need visas, and visit 'incompatible countries' (where one country won't let you in if you have a passport stamp from another country they particularly dislike), you can request your government issue you a second passport in order to make your travel life easier. So, I decided to leave the country using my 2nd passport, and have the hotel courier my 1st one back later.

However, at St Petersburg Airport immigration, my plan encountered a problem. As the immigration officer leafed through my passport for the third time, shaking his head, I realized something was up.

"Entry stamp. Where is entry stamp?" he asked.

Oh fuck. I hadn't thought about that.

Leaving on my second passport meant I had no entry stamp.

Which meant… he would assume I was in the country illegally. Fuck!

This immigration officer barely spoke any English, but before long, a more senior officer with a couple of guards arrived.

"This way, please".

Ah, the immigration back-office. I was becoming quite used to these now. As we sat down, I explained myself carefully, and he listened, seeming to understand.

"I understand. So, you are a DJ? You play the music for Russian people?"

"Yes, last night. At a festival, look, here are some pictures…"

"I see, interesting. And you have the two passports, why?"

"Well, I travel a lot, being a DJ…"

"I understand".

A long silence.

"And you are also working for British government, no? You must tell me truth".

Fuuuuuck.

Eventually I persuaded him that I wasn't a spy, but there was no way I was being allowed on that plane.

"You are very stupid man. No entry stamp, no exit Russia. Go back hotel, get passport, come back. Other flight later. Better for you."

He throws the passport across the desk at me. I'm dismissed.

The next flight isn't for 12 hours, so I've missed my own birthday party. I return to the hotel, check back into my room, and collapse on the bed. My friends and family send me a photo of them all gathered in my favorite restaurant.

Man, this job. I fucking love it.

The Syrian set goes without a hitch – the crowd, witnessing only the 2nd or 3rd dance music show ever in the country, lap it up despite the freezing temperatures. It's now 2am but I'm buzzing and I need a drink. The party's beginning to wind down, but I head back to the VIP and the promoter and friends are heading to Aline's place in the city for a few drinks.

On one hand, I'm buzzing from the show. On the other, I don't know this country, plus I've got a flight home in a few hours, and going to a random afterparty in Damascus could lead to all sorts of unintended consequences. All things considered, it's pretty clear what the move is. I agree to go.

Before long, we're back at Aline's parents' place, a palatial accommodation situated in the old town of Damascus. Promoter's with us too, and he's my ride back to the airport, so at least my chances of making the flight are solid.

"What do you drink?" Aline asks me.

"You have any red wine?"

She shows me a rack of serious looking bottles.

"Most of the best stuff is at my parent's place in the country, but they keep a decent supply here in the city too…"

I pull out a few bottles and check the dates. 1982. 1999. 1962. Not a single bottle is under ten years old, and many are decades old. It looks like the sort of wine collection people spend a lifetime amassing. I pick the least-expensive looking bottle and crack it open, and after giving it ten minutes to warm up, it's stunning. Rich, full bodied, like nothing I've ever tasted before.

The three of us drink and chat for a few hours, before Promoter pulls out a joint and offers me some weed. *What the fuck?* The Middle East has notoriously strict drug laws, but by this point, I've drunk enough not to care, so I get involved. When's my flight again? I fucking love Syria!

Minutes turn into hours, and then I'm struck by a beautiful, haunting voice over the city, so I take up a spot on the balcony to listen. It's the first Muslim call to prayer of the day, the *Fajr* prayer, which happens 'between the very beginning of dawn and sunrise' in Muslim cities around the world, projected by loudspeakers across the whole city. I listen intently as the first light of dawn emerges amidst the darkness. The last time I heard this prayer was in Jerusalem, a similarly historic city on a similar morning, and I remember my surprise at hearing the prayer drift over from the Arab neighborhoods in the city's east. Whilst not especially religious, I do consider myself spiritual, and it's hard not to be moved by the beautiful voice of the *muezzin*. For a short time, task lists and career aspirations are forgotten and I allow myself to simply exist in the moment. Basking in my view of the awakening city, I watch the cracks of light appear amidst the ancient streets of the old town, and feel profoundly grateful for my life.

Then, it's time to head to the airport.

Arriving back at Damascus airport, it's now daylight, and as I walk through the airport, my life seems faintly ridiculous. I've been up all night, partying in Syria, and now I'm walking through Damascus airport, stoned. When my passport is stamped without issue, the sense of relief is palpable. I board the plane for London and pass out.

Ten weeks after my visit, a brutal civil war strikes Syria, which will eventually be responsible for five million refugees and half a million deaths. I never see either the promoter or Aline again, but every time I see the conflict on the news, I hope they're OK.

For me though, as always, I'm happy to be on my way.

"WAY TO YOU"

written by Gareth Emery & Anthony Galatis

i've seen the summers
the fallen winters
reaching for the moon
i've walked a thousand
miles just to be here
and not a day too soon

looking back at
the life that we had
the things that we've been through
remember this day
as i go my way
that leads me back to you

when the last note plays
the music fades
and i've done all i can do
won't be afraid
to walk alone
cos i'm on my way to you

soon a new face
will take up my place
the circle will renew
another chapter
forever after
i know i'll see you soon

when the last note plays
the music fades
and i've done all i can do
won't be afraid
to walk alone
cos i'm on my way to you

LITTLE CELEBRITY

BELIEVING YOUR OWN HYPE WILL KILL YOU

I think there's a point in every artist's career where they turn into a cunt. Usually, that's just after they first make it big.

It certainly happened to me. For years, I'd been getting bigger and bigger, and all of a sudden I was *making* it. Unfortunately, the sheer competitiveness meant I didn't have a scrap of gratitude for what I was achieving. It was about getting bigger at all costs. I say *bigger*, rather than better, because that's all that mattered. I was surrounded by the wrong people. Our goals were bigger billings, superior set times, more production, more money. Making music that inspired us didn't come into it. It took my career plateauing, and a lot of self reflection, to choose a different path. A path where I tried to make the most inspired music I possibly could, regardless of whether I thought it would be successful or not. A path where I realized that success has a price, and if the price of success was lying, cheating, manipulating, or making music that I fundamentally wasn't proud of, then it wasn't worth having.

I feel I'm in a good place now, but over the years I've seen many others fall into this trap - often people who worked for me. However grounded someone is at the start, fame and money changes everything. These two things are amplifiers. Whatever your natural traits are, they'll be amplified. If you're a bit cocky, fame and money will make you extremely cocky. If you're a bit anxious, fame and money will make you very anxious. Of course, they can amplify good traits in your personality too, but that usually takes a bit longer. I've known many Little Celebrities in my life, and the song could apply to them all, but I want to also color that with my own experiences. Some of the following stories relate to a period of my life I'm not particularly proud of. However, I learnt valuable lessons, which have served me well since then. Perhaps reading about my bad decisions will prevent you from making some of your own.

2012.
Manchester, UK.

Mood: Livid.

I am fucking furious. After battling for years to get my name higher on the bill, I've managed to get my name to 2nd place at the main trance stage at Godskitchen Global Gathering 2012, and yet it's all going wrong.

There are three key components to booking a show: fee, set-time, and billing. Fee is obvious and requires little explanation. Set-time is important and the source of much negotiation, particularly at a festival. You want an artist before you who can play an appropriate set: nobody too similar to you, in case all your good tracks get played before you arrive, and certainly nobody who's going to play far too hard and steal your thunder. Plus, it's important to know who's on the other stages – if you have a similar but larger act playing on a different stage, you're going to get murdered. Better to ensure the other stages feature artists who are totally different.

The third - and most controversial - piece of the puzzle is billing: the order in which the artists' names appear on the flyer. Billing is important. It means almost nothing to fans, but everything to artists – particularly those on the way up. The artist at the top takes *top bill*, the next along *second bill* and so on. The top billed acts usually get paid the most, get the best set-times, and the most production. The lower down the bill you are, the shitter your lot is. This has the curious effect of keeping the big acts big and the small acts small, as the deck is almost entirely stacked against them, which makes breaking into DJing's top tier extremely difficult.

When I first played the Global Gathering Festival in 2010, I was given a schooling in how this all worked. I was excited to play on the incredible Godskitchen Boombox stage, and planned out the perfect set which I felt should have been one of the best sets of the day. But on turning up, I found the sound system was insanely quiet, and I had almost zero production – no lights, shitty visuals, quiet sound, so regardless of how good my set might have been, it didn't move the crowd. Dance music is designed to be loud: if you can't hear the bass even in the front row, it's hard to impress, and it's also highly visual. Essentially I was playing whisper-quiet music in a dark tent.

A few hours later, Above & Beyond, the day's headliners arrived – and being headliners, they'd made sure they'd negotiated all of the prime production elements in their favor. I watched as the sound system reached maximum volume and their set was complemented by confetti, fireworks, and perfectly coordinated visuals, with the crowd roaring on cue. I'd not won the day as I'd hoped, but this was a good lesson: work hard in advance to make sure the deck's stacked in your favor, because you will get fucked otherwise.

The next year, in 2011, I wasn't making the same mistake. This time, I brought a proper production crew, including a VJ to control the visuals, an LD to run the lights, and a sound guy to make sure I wasn't getting fucked over with low volume again. I blew my entire fee on production, paying out of pocket for fireworks, confetti, streamers, CO2 jets, and spent an incredible amount of time preparing my set. This time, I got it right. The reviews online were incredibly positive, many even saying I'd outperformed Above & Beyond. Production matters.

So now it was 2012, and after my stellar performance the previous year, Godskitchen had offered me 2nd headline to Above & Beyond, above Ferry Corsten. This was huge.

Billing is a horrible thing to get involved in. Music is meant to be art, and none of us got into this game to try and convince promoters why we're bigger than other artists, many of whom are our friends. Unfortunately though, it's very important and in the industry it is war. Agents are brutally aggressive in negotiating billing – and the smallest slip will cost you dearly. There's always someone trying to trip you up and the smallest mistake can last for years. For instance, we'll often be asked to take second billing to someone in a particular territory.

"Now, I know you've never heard of DJ Blob, but he's huge in Brazil, he's all over the radio there. And as the gig's in Brazil, it makes sense for you to go below him. That OK?"

No. Not OK. Because from then on, every single time I'm sharing the stage with DJ Blob, his agent's forwarding over the Brazilian flyer; *Look, Gareth played below us here, so we're definitely bigger, and should be billed higher this time, too.*

So you don't give a fucking inch. Even going as far as turning down shows if the billing isn't right.

Of course, there are some acts that simply blow up and become undeniably huge very quickly, and when that happens, everyone tends to stop battling. This happened with the likes of Avicii, Hardwell, Garrix, etc., but generally, you fight for your billing, and so going above Ferry was a big deal. It was my initiation into the top tier of trance. The same names had been ruling the genre for the best part of a decade, with hardly any artists joining the top table. Getting above Corsten meant that I was finally in the club, and I felt like I deserved it.

It was just three short years since I had brought him to Manchester to play Garuda, but in my - admittedly biased - view, I should have been top, particularly as the show was in my native UK.

'Sanctuary' from 'Northern Lights' was still a big track, and earlier that year I'd had 'Concrete Angel', which acquired classic status almost instantly. When the lineup arrived we felt victorious. Even though 2nd bill was part of our offer, you never quite know until the flyer arrives.

ABOVE & BEYOND
GARETH EMERY
FERRY CORSTEN.

We'd fucking done it.

Or had we?

A week later, the online flyer and lineup suddenly changed.

ABOVE & BEYOND
FERRY CORSTEN
GARETH EMERY

What the fuck? I called Thien Dinh, my agent in the Netherlands. A few hours later, he gets back to me.

"It was just a mistake, check the website. You're 2nd again".

And indeed I am.

But a few days later, the website changes again, and Ferry's back 2nd. What the fuck is going on here? Thien reaches out to the festival again, and receives some utter bullshit back.

> Hi Thien,
> You must have an old version of the web page.
> Try emptying your internet cache and reloading it.
> Gareth's definitely 2nd name, as contracted.

This bullshit goes on for five or six weeks, with the names changing every couple of days, before Global Gathering come clean. Thien calls me.

"So, they've admitted they've fucked up. They accidentally contracted 2nd bill to both you and Ferry".

"Bullshit, that was no accident. They knew neither of us would settle for 3rd place, so they just told us what they knew we wanted to hear".

"That may be so," Thien admits, "but they can't give you second bill now. They've offered a compromise where they keep swapping your names every few days up until the festival, which Ferry is happy with."

Fuck this. I'm furious. Because this clearly isn't a mistake, and because of the utter bullshit we've had from the festival over the last month, who have told us every lie in the book rather than just admitting their mistake. By running the clock down, they've also made cancelling extremely difficult. A month ago, we likely could have cancelled quietly – now, the festival is weeks away, and if I cancel it's big news.

"Thien, can we cancel? Breach of contract?"

"Yeah, you can. But it's a terrible idea. I think..."

"Yeah, yeah yeah. I know. I'll get back to you".

For a few days, I mull it over. I've never had to cancel a large show like this before. I've never cancelled any show for anything contractual. And cancelling clearly comes with a lot of repercussions. That said, if I back down now, I'll get fucked like this every time. There will be no point agreeing anything with the festival, because they know that they can change whatever we've agreed, and I haven't got the bottle to do anything about it.

With hindsight, I really could have used some mentors at this point. Someone older, who'd been there, done the cancellation thing, and could explain to me how it would go down, so I understood what I was getting myself into. Unfortunately, I didn't have anyone who fitted the bill. I knew no people in the industry, except those who worked for me.

My ego had also taken a hit. I felt under attack, and victimized, and making a decision based off those factors is usually a bad move. Either way, I was angry and upset, and I wanted to fight. I called Thien.

"Tell them I'm fucking cancelling if they don't give me 2nd name like we agreed."

"Already have done. They won't do it".

"Then we're cancelling. Sorry Thien, but tell them we're out, please."

Thien wasn't happy, but he agreed to deliver the news. A few hours later, he called back.

"The festival understands you're cancelling, but they want to make up a story you can both get behind. An unavoidable family commitment perhaps? Or maybe you can just pretend a few days before that you're sick? They're ok with any of that."

"No, Thien. Fuck that. They've breached contract. I'm cancelling publicly and telling the world that they breached their contract".

I'd boxed myself into a corner but there was no going back. Thien hates this course of action. The festival hate this course of action. Many acts cancel festivals all the time over stuff like billing and set-times, but usually they'll find a mutually agreeable excuse for the cancellation and do it quietly, with some bullshit reason that doesn't draw attention to it. Not me. I'm going to do this publicly.

A day later, we pull the trigger.

> [mgmt] CANCELLATION GLOBAL GATHERING UK. We are sorry to announce that due to numerous contractual breaches by Global Gathering, Gareth will no longer be playing at this year's Global Gathering UK. Please understand that after three great festivals in 09/10/11 (including producing the festival's theme tune in 2010),

> this was the absolute last thing we wanted to do, and we made every attempt to rectify the situation, but in the end Godskitchen / Global Gathering gave us no choice. International Global Gatherings in Russia and Ukraine are unaffected. Sorry to all of you who had bought tickets hoping to see him play - hopefully some of you can catch him at UK festivals South West Four or Creamfields over the summer instead. GE MGMT

The internet goes berserk. Speculation about why I've cancelled is rife, and Global Gathering's Facebook page is a warzone. The festival are copping some serious flak, 99% of people are on my side, and I'm coming out of it well.

'You guys are a fucking joke' one commenter writes. 'Every year artists end up cancelling with no explanation. Never buying a ticket again'.

If this is the end of it, I've come out of it well...

But it's not.

Global are taking an unprecedented amount of shit, and they need to respond. So they do. And what do they do?

They tell the fucking truth.

Fuck.

I don't know it yet, but I'm about to learn a very valuable lesson. If you get into a public showdown, you need to be OK with all the details eventually being leaked to the public. If you're not alright with that, keep your gob shut. If you're meant to be paid £50,000 for a show, and the promoter decides he's only going to pay you £25,000 – then yes, I agree that the promoter's the bad guy here, but back in the real world, £25,000 is still a spectacular amount of money for playing records. The public ain't going to be on your side.

Global make a statement saying that they did indeed make a mistake relating to the billing of the arena, and that I had cancelled because my name was 3rd rather than 2nd.

This is, quite clearly, not a story that makes me look good, and the angry internet mob now turn their attention from Global Gathering to me. The comments on my Facebook page are brutal; How dare I try and put my name above a legend like Ferry Corsten? My ego's out of control, I'm a narcissist, etc., (probably true at this point). It's brutal. I'm getting killed.

"Gareth Emery drops out of Global Gathering UK because his name was advertised 3rd and not 2nd on the bill." Says one person. "Is this what DJing is becoming?"

Desperate to do some damage control, I post one further statement blaming 'management' for the cancellation (false) but pointing out that it only occurred after months of bullshit, and if the festival had simply owned up to their mistake at the start, we could have resolved it (true). The fans are split on whose side to take. What's very clear, is that there's no winner here.

It takes a while to cool down, and the whole incident left a shitty taste. A few months later, flying out to a gig, I run into Above & Beyond's manager James.

"Quite the kick-off with Global Gathering." He says, honestly. "We were rapt watching it all unfold in the office. It was like Reality TV. Looked like you were in serious trouble for a minute, but you did well with that second statement. Really pulled it out of the bag."

He doesn't even dig for the gossip on what actually happened. He knows what festivals are like, and he's no doubt had plenty of similar scrapes himself.

"Cheers mate" I reply. "I won't be cancelling any festivals any time soon though. Don't think anyone came out of that one well".

Hilariously, rather than being black-balled for life, Global Gathering doubled my offer the next year, and give me a much better set time in a prime arena. My bad behavior seems to have paid off handsomely, but I don't care. This isn't the way I want to do business, and I won't be doing this shit again.

I lost fans for life. Some people have never forgiven me for cancelling, even seven years later. I don't read too many comments these days, but occasionally someone will pipe up with 'Never been a fan since you cancelled Global Gathering'. It was one of the biggest mistakes I have made, but not from a business point of view. However, the Global Gathering cancellation taught me a few important lessons. Firstly, the public don't give a fuck about stuff like billing or money. And whilst, as an artist, you do what you can to stack the deck in your favor, cancelling is almost never worth it.

Secondly, my ego was out of control. I needed some more people around me who could give me better counsel at times like this.

I needed to build a team.

LOS ANGELES, 2018

It's the day of our headline play at Los Angeles's 15,000 strong Dreamstate festival, and we seem to have another Global Gathering situation in the making.

This time, I'm six years older, a little wiser, but I'm still fucked off. And who am I pissed off with? Ferry Fucking Corsten.

Again.

A few years previously, we'd launched our Laserface show – a stunning live production with record-breaking numbers of highly choreographed lasers - and it had been a ticket selling machine. We had 8,500 people in San Francisco, 5,000 in Vancouver, and we were riding high. Every show was selling out. Our next play was the highly ambitious Forum in Los Angeles, which would have been my biggest play yet, at 15,000 people.

Yet there's a hitch. Of course there fucking is.

Dreamstate festival are desperate for a headliner, and they want to persuade us to cancel our own show, and instead bring Laserface to the festival.

It's an interesting offer, but I'm not sure. We're on a good path with this show, and we don't really have any need to take it to festivals where other artists' egos might get involved. I listen to their offer, though. They must be really desperate as they throw the kitchen sink at us. Our agent calls to tell us more.

"They really fucking want you. They're willing to give you overall headline billing of the entire festival, a huge fee, and they'll pay for all the lasers. Plus, nobody else on the same day can have lasers in your arena, so the excitement of the laser show is reserved just for you. But, on the downside, you have to cancel your Forum show".

This is a tough decision. Their offer is very good, but I've had my heart set on the Forum for some time.

"Nobody else having lasers before us? Will the other artists be OK with that?"

"They won't like it, but Dreamstate are offering it, and they're willing to write it into our contract, so yeah, you'll be the only ones".

We decide to take their offer. The show's announced, and as promised, Laserface by Gareth Emery sits at the top of the bill.

The night before the show, we head down to the cavernous aircraft hangar of a venue to do a visual check for the show. Our old friend Ferry Corsten's playing before us, and his VJ is already there, running Ferry logos on the screen. Our VJ tries to gain access to check if our visuals work, but Ferry's guy isn't having it. He looks like he's been here for days, his skin pallid and hair greasy, and by his attitude, he needs some sleep.

"This is actually our rehearsal time,' he says. 'You can't have your visuals up now".

"We only need five minutes,' my VJ tells him. 'I thought you just said you were finished?"

"It doesn't matter if I'm finished or not. It's *my* time. I'm not moving".

To drive the point home, he sticks a Ferry Corsten logo on the screen, sits back and folds his arms.

For a moment, I imagine punching him in the face as hard as I possibly can, then my meditation training kicks in, and I instead calmly chat with our team about when we can find a slot. Then, I overhear Ferry's guy saying:

"So, about the lasers that we'll be having…"

Our team hears, and wanders over to join the conversation. One of them politely asks the question we're all thinking.

"Hey guys. Pretty sure we were promised exclusive use of the lasers as part of our deal, were you aware of that?"

"Yeah," sneers Ferry's guy. "But we threatened to cancel the performance unless we had lasers too, so we've got them. Good luck with your show. Not sure how much impact it's going to have now though after we've run every laser in the place an hour before you though..."

He turns away. My blood is boiling. Is this really happening again? With Ferry Corsten?

We head back to the hotel, crack open a bottle of wine, and discuss options.

First, we call up our agent who booked the show.

"Ah yes, quite the nightmare. The thing is, this doesn't actually constitute a material breach of contract, you see? If they didn't give you lasers, that's a material breach and we could likely sue them. But by giving your production to someone else, there's not really anything we can do about this".

Thanks for the fucking backup, guys.

I'm raging. We could have done our own show at the Forum without any of this bullshit, but instead, we took their money and now we're involved in a stupid stand-off with Ferry Corsten. Again.

We chat through options. My team is young, and they're angry; at the festival, at Corsten's team, and at our agents for not helping us. There is serious talk of cancellation. Maybe we could disable

Corsten's lasers? Sabotage the smoke machines during his set so even if he has lasers, they look like shit? We all head to bed without any real conclusions.

The next day, the agents call back. They've spoken to the festival.

"So, here's what the festival are saying" our agent tells me. "Ferry's threatening to cancel over this lasers thing, and they really don't want that. So instead, they'd like you guys to make an exception. Ferry's team have asked for just six lasers, which they want to use for three songs. Is that OK?"

"Fine," I tell them. I'm not getting into a cancellation stand-off again, and I'm also proud of our show. I know that when all's said and done, our set's going to be the most talked-about of the day, and Ferry having six lasers won't change that.

During the day, I hang out at the hotel, hit the gym, meditate and get ready for the night. I know this show has the potential to be a little stressful, so I want to make sure I arrive at the festival relaxed, energized, and ready to deal with whatever shit the world throws at me. Arriving on site, our team are stressed as fuck.

"We're getting totally fucked," our project manager tells me. "Ferry's team promised they'd use the lasers for just three songs, but they've run them for the entire first 30 minutes of his set without a stop. It's like they're trying to fuck us as much as possible".

"Don't worry about it," I tell her. "Our show's going to win the day. Let them do whatever they want".

I fire a group text message to our team.

> Team. I know today has been stressful as fuck. But in 30 minutes, we're on stage, and people are fucking STOKED to see the show. There are 15,000 people here and all the indications are that we're going to have the biggest crowd of the day by far. The buzz online is unreal. We've worked hard as fuck on this show for months and nothing before can change that. It's going

> to blow our minds. Don't get stressed about this stupid political shit – in two hours time we'll have forgotten it all. Just look out at the crowd, and remember why we're here: for them. We're only going get to do this once so remember to enjoy the moment. SO PROUD OF YOU ALL. GAME ON!

I finally take the stage. The show goes off without a hitch. We've got by far the largest crowd of the day, and nobody's talking about what came before. The show is a huge hit.

It's an important lesson to me: trying to play the production war can only take you so far. If someone else has better music, and a better show, they're going to come out on top.

A few months later, I run into Ferry at a festival in Poland.

"That stuff in Los Angeles was so stupid, mate" I tell him, and he agrees.

"I never even knew you guys were headlining," he tells me. "I thought I was headlining, then when the flyer came out, you were top, and I was getting fucked. So I felt I had to try and keep up with you guys in some way".

He's a decent guy, Corsten, and I'm sorry that we've been pitted against each other twice by the industry. On a personal level, we actually get on very well – I like him a lot more than most other people in the industry, and he's just trying to make his show look as good as possible, same as anyone else would. But I'm grateful for the lessons I learned during the Global Gathering cancellation. Yep, production, billing and all that shit is important – but you know what's more important? Making great records that can change people's lives. Embracing that as my mission in life has made me a lot less likely to get dragged into this sort of nonsense, and I'm glad to say it hasn't happened any time recently.

"LITTLE CELEBRITY"

written by Gareth Emery, Anthony Galatis, Geraint Jones

i got your message and you're moving on
we always knew this day would come so, here's your song
from san francisco, la, singapore
we should have been so grateful but you wanted more

what did i do to make you leave like this
three years down, we were still crushing it

believing your own hype will kill you
drown you in a lonely sea
many took that road before you
but now you'll walk it without me
i pushed you, pulled you, took you further
gave you opportunity
i only wanted the best for you
good luck, little celebrity

a sea of people, smiles on every face
remember why you started out in, the first place
did i give you far too much too soon?
fame's a drug and just like me you're not immune

what did i do to make you feel like this
three years down we were still crushing it

believing your own hype will kill you
drown you in a lonely sea
many took that road before you
but now you'll walk it without me
i pushed you, pulled you, took you further
gave you opportunity
i only wanted the best for you
good luck, little celebrity

YOU'LL BE OK

TERRIFYING TRAVEL AND THE LOVE OF LIFE

Helicopters.
Hawaii, January 2020.

I lie down on the beach on my own, feeling satisfied, but vaguely bemoaning the fact that we haven't got an umbrella. It's our first vacation in years – our first vacation ever without the kids – and I'm being cooked in the sun. Although I'm not a ginger and can't think of any in our family, the medium-rare look of my skin suggests otherwise. Any more than ten minutes in the sun in a place like Hawaii and my skin becomes immediately bespeckled with hundreds of freckles. Ten minutes later and I'm burning. Tanning simply isn't an option.

That said, it's been a good morning.

Kat dragged me out of bed at 8am, much to my dismay**.** *It's our first fucking holiday in years! It's only 8am! I want to sleep in!* But now, at midday, I'm glad of it. We'd taken advantage of the beautiful weather, headed to the Ala Moana beach, and spent an hour in the ocean on paddleboards – a good workout. Following that, I hit the water for a long swim, looking for turtles in the crystal clear water. And now it's food time.

Kat arrives back to our spot on the beach with some food

"So, the only gluten-free thing they had was chicken and rice, but it looks good. I hope I did OK..."

As usual, I'm on some sort of rather extreme eating plan, which, amazingly, Kat usually manages to keep up with. This vacation, it's gluten-free and caffeine-free.

"Terrible news from Los Angeles. Absolutely terrible news."

But, her voice doesn't sound stricken with tragedy, so I already know this doesn't affect anyone we know...but more likely a celebrity of some sort.

Even if I had a phone with me, I'd be unlikely to know whatever has happened, because these days I try to avoid all news. That sounds a little extreme, and it is, but by nature I'm a news junkie. Having majored in politics, I can easily spend hours a day on my phone immersed in the latest political sagas, but I realized a couple of years back this is not a good use of my time.

Part of the problem of reading the news, is that it feels like work. *I'm just being a good citizen, informed about the state of the world!* But, in reality, that's nonsense. Unless you actually work in the fields of politics or news, an hour or two a week is likely all you need to stay informed.

Of course, it would be easier and more logical if I could have simply *reduced* the time spent reading the news... down from two hours, to about fifteen minutes, and then, I'd be able to enjoy the news and it wouldn't be wasting large chunks of my day that could be spent on more productive things. The problem is, I'm not good at moderation: I'm an abstainer instead.

The wonderful writer Gretchen Rubin has written extensively about moderators vs abstainers, but I'll paraphrase her badly here. Like Gretchen, for a long time, I struggled to stick to diets – where the typical advice went something like this: *"Be moderate. Don't have ice cream every night, but if you try to deny yourself altogether, you'll fall off the wagon. Allow yourself to have the occasional treat, it will help you stick to your plan."*

That advice works great for one group of people – *moderators* – who do better when they avoid strict and absolute rules. But me? I'm an abstainer. No ice cream is far easier than some ice cream. No news is easier than some news. Because, *some news,* would lead to a thousand other questions popping up in my head each day. Is it time for my news fix yet? How long can I have today? Do I deserve this? Etc.

In short, I find it far easier to give up something entirely than to reduce it, and so, for news it's none, and that works rather well.

This doesn't mean I'm ignorant about the state of the world though. In recent months, I've read many books about history, and I generally find that events are better viewed when a little time has passed and the dust has settled, rather than in the heat of the moment.

Not only does not consuming news save me time, it also preserves my sanity, because consuming news dramatically fucks up your perception of risk. The news, after all, is something of a greatest hits of everything terrible going on in the world – and reading it often left me feeling pretty glum about the state of things; Terrorist bombings! Police shooting innocent people! Deadly pathogens! Environmental disaster!

Then I'd walk out of my house into Los Angeles, and watch people happily bumbling around in yoga pants, being generally cheerful to each other. This world didn't represent the one I'd been consuming via my phone. In fact, things seemed pretty good.

We live in the safest time in human history. Today, there are fewer wars, less crime, and even less risk of terrorism than ever before. That's not to say there aren't issues: of course there are. But looking at the last thousands of years of human history, things are pretty fucking good right now.

So why is the news so fucking depressing?

Because the business model of news organizations revolves primarily around selling advertising. The likes of CNN and Fox are private companies, with an aim to make profit, which means keeping us coming back as many times as possible. Good headlines don't tend to keep us coming back ('World safer than ever, just like yesterday') so the news reverts to fear and despondency based programming.

Not reading any news tends to put me in a better mental state. Plus, when something happens that affects me, or my community, I'm likely to hear about it anyway.

Kat continues.

"Kobe Bryant. He's dead..."

"Fuck. How?"

"Helicopter crash. His daughter was with him too, and a load of others."

I'm not a basketball fan, but I am hugely respectful of anybody who has worked themselves to the bone to achieve greatness in their field, so the news that Kobe had passed leaves me saddened. As a father, knowing that his daughter died with him leaves me gutted for his family.

Fucking helicopters.

For my entire life, I've avoided helicopters. They just seem to crash far too often, and whilst I'm sure they're still far safer than my car, I'll never take one.

I was just 16 when a close friend of my dad's – Raymond Deane – took a helicopter ride with the then-vice-Chairman of Chelsea Football Club, Matthew Harding. The fact that Chelsea's ground now has a Matthew Harding Stand gives a hint as to how this particular helicopter ride turned out. Flying back from a match in bad weather, the helicopter plunged into the Cheshire countryside, killing all on board. My dad went to the funeral.

I've only ever taken a helicopter once, during the EDC festival in 2013. Having already played the show, I received a phone call from my manager the following day.

"You want the good news or the bad news?"

"The good news."

"EDC want to interview you for the documentary they're making. They're only interviewing the biggest DJs so you're in good company. And they want to bring you back to the venue tomorrow to do it specially".

"Awesome. And the bad news?"

"They want to do the interview… in a helicopter".

It would be two years until I'd become a parent, so my desire to get my face in EDC's movie just about edged out my lifelong fear of helicopters. Arriving at the heliport, I was amazed to find it transformed into a nightclub with low lights, a DJ and a free bar. While at the bar, throwing back an ice-cold vodka shot to calm my nerves, Tiesto wandered over.

"Gareth! How you doing man?"

Even though I've been a fairly large DJ for years, I was always a little surprised that he remembered who I was.

"Just trying to get drunk mate. I fucking hate helicopters…"

Jesus, Gaz. *Cheer up, you fucking downer.* But Tiesto just dons his trademark smile.

"You'll be fine man! We do this every year. Enjoy the ride…"

And off he goes.

And so up we went. On our way to the festival, I look out at the lights of the Las Vegas strip at night, and the anxiety fades a little. *This isn't so bad*! Suddenly, the helicopter lurches violently to the side and powers straight towards the Stratosphere hotel. What the fuck is happening!

"It's not responding! Hold on tight! I'm not sure I can control it!"

Ohmygod.

For what feels like minutes, the helicopter powers directly towards the tower. My hands are drenched with sweat. I'm sure we're going to hit it. Then, at the last minute, it swerves away and everyone else in the helicopter pisses themselves laughing – a hilarious in-joke between them and the pilot.

"You absolute cunts. What if I'd had a heart attack?"

Lamborghini Woes: Part 1.
Los Angeles, January 2015.

Taking the Lamborghini was a fucking terrible move.

I'm on my way to Las Vegas for a show, or at least I'm supposed to be, but all that's happened so far is I've sat in traffic. I'm three hours in and I'm barely out of LA.

This is one of these times where reality is completely at odds with my visualization. I'd imagined this trip for a few days, cruising down an empty freeway to Vegas in the Lambo, tunes on as the sun sets, the archetypical picture of a superstar DJ. Getting to Vegas, blasting the Lambo up and down the strip, getting some attention.

It's not worked out that way at all.

To be honest, the car's already feeling like a mistake. What happened was, I moved to Los Angeles, where there were supercars everywhere, and decided I ought to have one too. Why not? I work hard, I was making serious money now. A friend invited me along to the unveiling of the new Lamborghini Huracan – the replacement for the Gallardo, a car I've always loved - and I went along, got talking to the dealer, and plonked down some cash. I was committed.

Now I actually own the car, it's not like I imagined it would be at all. It's low, uncomfortable, and noisy. Kat refuses to ride in it. I've nearly ripped the bottom off reversing out of our drive. I hit the sidewalk in front of about 20 people trying to park in front of a fancy restaurant. It's just incredibly inconvenient. Sure, it looks beautiful, but I could have admired other people's Lamborghinis. I didn't have to bloody well buy one. In short, other than one of my most popular Instagram posts of all time, it's not doing much for me and I'm counting down the days until the lease runs out.

The other thing is, I don't like the attention.

I love being on-stage, but aside from when there's music involved, I don't especially enjoy being the center of attention. I avoid the Los Angeles social scene, and during the day I'll keep a low profile, slinking round in track-pants and only leaving my house if I really have to. It's just how I like my life to be. Perhaps if I'd ever been in a Lamborghini before, or had even test-driven one, I might have realized that owning an attention-grabbing sports car wasn't really for me, but being somewhat impulsive, the first time I ever sat in a supercar in my life was the day mine was delivered.

Still, I own it, so I might as well make the most of it.

It's now three hours since I left home, and I'm still in Los Angeles. I won't get to my hotel in Vegas for at least another five hours, and I'm already fed up with the Lambo. My back hurts because of the seats, the other car's lights are blinding me, and I'm fucking fed up, so I decide to abandon the drive and get a flight instead.

I call Kat whilst I turn the car around and head back. Can she find me a flight from Burbank Airport? I can be there in about an hour. She books me a ticket on Southwest and I'm on my way. Much better.

A few hours later, I arrive at Burbank, dump the Lambo in the parking structure, and head into the airport to find my flight's delayed. An hour later, it's delayed again. And again, and again. From arriving at Burbank at 5pm, it's now 8pm. My flight's now due to take off at 11pm, landing at midnight. My set's at 1am. This is far too close for comfort.

Normally, I'd be a little more relaxed, but this is a major issue, because tonight is my highest paid gig of the year, the flagship show of my new residency at the freshly opened Las Vegas SLS Casino. And I'm going to need this money; Kat and I are expecting our first child, a little girl, in just two months, and I've taken most of the year off heavy touring to focus on being a dad – mainly surviving off the income of my Vegas residency.

Las Vegas, in the space of a few years, had gone from a fun place where I'd do a gig or two and drink, to my primary source of income. My deal at the SLS is a ridiculous amount, and it's a different world to the Vegas I used to play in. These days, I turn up, clean and sober, play the gig and fuck off.

It wasn't always like this.

A Very Vegas Pool Party.
Las Vegas, June 2012.

The party in my suite has been going on at least 12 hours now. Over the night, 50 people have probably come and gone with the hard-core of us keeping it going, but now the last of the animals have finally departed, and I'm left on my own. I survey the damage. The minibar is almost entirely empty: a cool $1000 of drinks at least. There are also a few large bottles of vodka, mostly empty, a load of weed, and what looks like some cocaine. Urgh. I wipe up the powder and head towards the bedroom, my head throbbing.

Last night, I played the legendary Electric Daisy Carnival festival, a victorious set to 15,000 people, but after finishing my set minutes before dawn, there wasn't much time to celebrate, so tonight I wanted to make up for it. However, due to some extreme winds the festival itself was cancelled, so with our plans of going back there blown out, the night turned into a rager in my hotel room instead.

There's a knock at the door. It's Robert Warren, one of my agents.

"Sorry I missed the party last night mate. What's going on?"

"We only just finished. Come on in"

Guess I'm staying up for a while.

Robert and I sit out on the balcony. It's 2pm, but until now I've had the blackout blinds so firmly drawn, it still felt like night. Now, sitting in the unrelenting Las Vegas sun, any remaining pretense that it's still Saturday night disappears. Still, it's a good view.

We shoot the shit for a while. I'm shortly moving agencies, leaving his parent company, so Robert and I haven't got a lot of time left working together. It's not to do with him though, we're good mates and I wish I could take him with me.

"So, you want to head down to the pool now?" he asks.

"What? Nah mate. I'm partied out. I'm going to sleep for 12 hours"

Robert looks faintly amused and a little worried

"Er, you realize you're playing the pool today mate? In an hour? You're closing after Avicii"

"Isn't that tomorrow?"

"No."

Ah.

Shit.

In a moment of hopeless optimism, I wonder if Robert's got the date wrong rather than me. Then I recall that he's stone cold sober, a legitimate boffin with a degree in Maths from Imperial… plus he's an agent. His one single job involves knowing when gigs are.

Whereas I've been up for 30 hours straight.

Yep, even in my current state, it's clear who's wrong. Fuck.

"Ah. All good though. I'm looking forward to the show either way. I'm gonna take a quick shower. See you down there".

I see Robert out, and walk back into the trashed living area and sit on the sofa to figure out how on earth I'm going to manage a two hour set in 100 degree heat. I feel very shaky. It's now 3pm, and I'm due on the decks at 4pm. There's another knock at the door. This time, it's Mayans and Andy. Mayans is my tour manager, and Andy's my manager of sorts.

They were both at the party last night, but given they both look fresh - they must have left at some sort of civil hour. In fact, I recall some vague conversation with Andy as he slipped away, reminding me of a 'big day tomorrow'. It all seems so long ago now.

Mayans takes in my outfit.

"You're wearing the same clothes as last night. Please tell me you've been to bed".

There's little point dressing it up.

"I have not been to bed."

I let them in, and walk off to take a shower. I can't tell if it's the booze, the weed, or the lack of sleep, but I'm starting to feel very, very rough indeed. I'm a professional, though. This is what I do. It's all about small wins at this point. Rack up enough small wins, and I'll win the day. Not passing out in the shower is my first one. Then, I slump on the bed and close my eyes. I overhear hushed conversations between Mayans and Andy.

"Is this the worst state he's ever done a gig in?" Andy asks.

"I've seen worse, I think".

"*Really?*"

"Not really, no. This is definitely the worst."

Before I know it, there's a knock at the door and one of them drifts over to wake me up. It's time. The one godsend about this particular Las Vegas club is that there's a back passage that leads from the artist's hotel rooms on the 17th floor to the pool party. No need to go in via the front door with all the accompanying chaos. We walk down the corridor with a few security guards, and there's Sue B. Doobeedoo– a hard-arsed promoter from New York that runs Marquee with an iron first. Sue has some influence on bookings, and if she gets any idea of how fucked I am, there's a good chance of this stream of cash-cow gigs ending. I avoid small-talk.

All of a sudden we arrive at the pool, and I start to feel very, very claustrophobic. There are about a million people here and the heat is suffocating. The security team force us through the crowd. A few fans shout my name and reach for pictures. I weakly wave back and keep moving. We reach the backstage area. The club is fucking slammed. Avicii is more or less the biggest artist on the planet right now: playing his closing set is a big opportunity that most artists would have prepared well for, ensuring they arrived in an excellent physical and mental state.

All of a sudden, I feel very, very sick – like, I'm going to vomit sick. I desperately look around for something to eat – anything to settle my stomach. I spot some raspberries on a VIP table's fruit platter, grab a handful, shove them into my mouth, and stumble away, the protestations of one of the girls on the VIP table ringing in my ears. *Hey douchebag! That's our food!* Then a security guard. *He's the DJ. He can do what he likes.*

Yes, I can do what I like. And right now, I'd like to be sick.

Within moments, it's clear the berries have had the opposite effect. I am actually going to puke. It's imminent.

I dive into the DJ booth, fall to my knees, and vomit into an empty champagne bucket. Avicii's not noticed me at all, his gaze firmly fixed on the crowd in front of him. I wipe the sick from around my mouth and get up. Nobody seems to have noticed or taken videos. Given there are 5,000 people here, I've dodged a bullet.

"You alright?" asks Sue as I walk out of the booth.

"Yeah. Technical issue," I lie.

For a moment, our eyes meet, and my paranoid brain kicks into overdrive. *She knows how fucked I am!* Luckily, Andy appears at my side to rescue me.

"You want a drink?".

"I don't really know. I'm don't know if I can fucking do this mate. I feel so rough. My heart feels..."

"OK. Drink it is." Andy hands me a bracingly strong vodka cranberry, which I sip pensively.

Then Mayans taps me on the shoulder.

Showtime.

As I enter the booth, some sort of transformation occurs. Having done close to 1000 gigs over the years, some sort of auto-pilot muscle memory takes place, and regardless of my state, I slip into Generic

Superstar DJ Mode. I exchange a few pleasantries with Avicii, some bollocks about how hot it is.

He seems like he's had a few drinks himself, which makes me feel marginally better. I drop my first tune, drink more vodka, and slip into my set. All of a sudden, time starts moving very fast. 30 minutes in, I get a tap on the shoulder. It's Avicii and he's animated.

"Fucking sick remix man, what is it?"

Fuck knows.

"I forget the name. It's a remix of Children though. I'll message it to you on Twitter after the set."

Satisfied, he disappears off with his entourage.

Avicii was enjoying my set? Fuck! I look out over the crowd, and it's as big as it was 20 minutes ago. I would have expected a large quantity of Avicii fans to fuck off when he finished, but no. This is going well. Fuck!

More vodka!

90 minutes later, the set ends, and I have crushed it. I mean, absolutely smashed the fuck out of it. It's fortunate, because that was one of only two outcomes available; the other being a heart-attack behind the decks. I hand over control to the local closing act, take a few pictures, and get the fuck out of there.

We decamp back to my suite with a small entourage. The spirits are high, and I'm ready to go out again. I go to mix myself another vodka Red Bull, but Mayans steps in.

"No, Gaz. No way"

"What? Come on man. I feel great. Let's fucking go out"

"It's 6pm. We're going to go out at 11pm. Take a few hours sleep, get yourself together, and we'll rage tonight. But you need to chill now."

I protest, but before I know it, Mayans has ushered everyone out of my room, and I'm back on my own again.

It's 6.10pm. I consider heading back down to the pool, where I'll still be a hero, but it feels weird. The moment has passed. Instead,

I set my alarm for 10pm, get into bed, and close my eyes. I'm not tired, but I'll try and sleep for a moment.

I'm woken up by my alarm at 10am, 16 hours later.

Avicii.
Los Angeles, April 2018.

"Have you heard the news?".

I'm in the car and Kat's just called me; she's really upset.

"It's Avicii." She says. "He's dead".

I exhale slowly. It's happened. I'm heartbroken, but not shocked. After speaking with Kat, I call Bjorn, a former tour manager of mine who knew Tim too. He's already heard the tragic news.

"I know. It finally happened" he answers.

Tim Berling, Avicii, is dead at 28.

The sad thing us, none of us are that surprised.

Avicii, in my view, was the greatest. I feel like shit that it took me until he was dead to admit that, but he was. I think I'm one of the best melody writers in dance music, with very few people better. Avicii was better - a *lot* better. He was Mozart, I was Salieri. And he was a good fucking dude too. As his career took off, we ended up playing a fair few shows together, and it was clear he was going places fast.

And I was a bit jealous. I can admit that now.

I'd just felt like my career was taking off, and suddenly, there was this 20-year-old kid who made music in a similar style to me, but who was much better. Plus, he'd taken inspiration from trance music, but had slowed it down into house music, avoiding all the commercial toxicity that trance comes with. In short, he was winning. I genuinely loved his music, and was greatly inspired by him, but I never told him, because the world was full of people kissing his ass and I didn't think he needed any more. Now, of course, I wish I had.

A lot has been written about Avicii's brutal touring schedule, and its impact on his early death, and to this day, I still wonder how he was able to slide into such severe physical and mental health issues. Why didn't the people around him intervene sooner? Tim's team were mostly good people, but they must take some responsibility. I only saw Tim a couple of times a year, and as the years went by, he seemed increasingly out of it. Paradoxically, as the Avicii machine became bigger and bigger, Tim himself seemed increasingly fragile. Whether it was alcohol, prescription drugs or illness, he was clearly someone who was being pushed brutally hard.

And whilst Tim was no doubt a workaholic, why wasn't he forced to take real breaks earlier? To focus on his health and his own emotional wellbeing? Even if money was the primary motivation of those around him, they would all have made far more long-term if he'd settled into a sustainable model of touring that could have continued the rest of his life. Instead, it was all over before he turned 30. Utterly tragic.

I've seen first-hand the effects of doing too many gigs. Now, at this point you might be thinking: *come on Gaz, you agreed to do the gigs! You've got nobody to blame but yourself!* And you'd be right. But it's surprisingly easy to be over optimistic when making future plans. The human imagination, whilst a wonderful thing, does have some limits. Have you ever tried grocery shopping, when hungry? It's a disaster. Sure, I might *know* that everything only looks extra-appealing because I'm hungry, but I'm still leaving with Doritos, microwave mac & cheese, and three tubs of Häagen-Dazs. Shopping after a big meal, however, is even worse. Even though I logically know I need a fridgeful of food for the week, absolutely nothing seems appealing.

Overcommitting on gigs is rather like that. Let's say I'm sat in the garden at 11am after nine hours solid sleep and three espressos when my agent emails asking if I want to do a brutal schedule: four countries in four days with long travel in-between and basically no sleep the whole time. I feel fine *now*, so I'll say yes.

Fast forward a few months later and the tour has arrived. My life exists on stage or in transit: clubs, festivals and airports, with a few hours of snatched sleep in a hotel room every few days. I haven't experienced natural light in over a week, and my diet consists of fast food at airports, or the occasional protein bar to 'stay healthy'. Utterly exhausted, I can't face getting on stage without a bracing vodka Red Bull to take the edge off. Friends and family are thousands of miles away so I'm socially isolated, bouncing between the exhilaration of being on stage, to the lonesome anxiety of yet another hotel room for one, and I'm asking: *why the fuck did I agree to this?*

Don't get me wrong: I genuinely love touring, but too much of anything can be a bad thing. And these days, I'm a lot better at predicting when I'm taking too much on. I can do two consecutive nights on a couple of hours sleep: any more than that, and I'm in trouble.

At my peak, I did about 150 shows in a year – and I vowed never to do that many again. Whatever the financial benefits, it wasn't worth it.

Avicii once did 320 shows in a year.

Some friends of mine have asked "why didn't he just push back against his team and cancel more shows?" and it's a valid question.

But it's hard for those outside of the industry to fathom the amount of pressure that would have been on Tim to continue performing. Even when touring is breaking you mentally and physically, cancelling gigs still often feels the harder option. In his documentary, True Stories, he said as much, stating: *"I did not expect that people would try to pressure me into doing more gigs. They have seen how ill I have felt by doing it, but I had a lot of push-back when I wanted to stop doing gigs."* In that same documentary, in a dark premonition about the future, he states: *"I have said, like, I'm going to die. I have said it so many times. And so I don't want to hear that I should entertain the thought of doing another gig."*

I've cancelled a handful of shows during my career when I've been struggling with serious burnout, and it is fucking tough. You're letting down thousands of fans who've bought tickets to see you play, some of whom will have spent thousands on flights and hotels. You're letting down your agents, management and touring crew, all who will lose income over your decision, and which includes some of your closest friends. And you're letting down your own family, who depend on you for income.

Plus, you will be heavily pressured to go through with the show in some way.

In the past when I've had to cancel shows, I faced a grueling 24 hours of questions with those around me desperately trying to make me change my decision. Here's a representative sample of some of the emails and texts I've received in the past trying to make me change my mind.

The promoter can book you a private jet to the local airport, meaning you won't have to do the long four-hour car journey. Will that help?

The venue really don't want you to cancel, and they've offered you only play for an hour, instead of two! Surely, you can manage that? It's only an hour! (plus six flights, four car-rides and 72 hours of non-stop travel without sleep in a bed)

We don't want to worry you, but this is one of the most important promoters in the region. He books all the biggest festivals and likes to talk to all the other promoters. We're worried about the reputational damage to your career if you cancel.

We've booked you a pre-show interview with the local MTV channel, and it will be a very bad look, both for you and us, if you fail to show up for it.

Come on, Gaz. It's just one tour. Knock back some vodka, get through it, and we'll figure out some proper time off when you get back.

Cancelling is fucking hard. Often, the easiest option is just to give in, and play the show, and that's what Tim did many times. I've done the same, although I have cancelled a handful of shows when I knew the alternative – of spiraling into a more serious decline – could be far worse. Sometimes, you just need to stop. But, it took me until my mid-30s to have the strength to push back against the industry machine and demand a time-out for my own health. Avicii never made it that far.

The last time we'd hung out together was around 2013 in a nightclub in Hollywood. We were both in the VIP section and we had a few drinks, chatted a bit. Before long, people recognized Tim, and the VIP area became unbearable, with people pushing and shoving trying to get a picture of him. I wasn't enjoying the scrum so made my excuses and headed home. That was the last time I spoke to him.

But when I saw that he'd retired from touring, after years of major health problems, I was glad. I knew it would have been an incredibly hard decision for him to make, depriving the team that had pushed him so hard of their livelihood, but I was happy that he'd got there eventually.

"Do you think he's OK?" Kat had asked me at the time.

"I imagine he'll either have the most epic comeback in 5-10 years, or he'll be dead within two." I took no joy in this prediction: Tim's death was an utter tragedy, but even for those who didn't know him well, it was all too predictable.

And it still breaks my fucking heart.

He was so fucking talented and should have had a lifetime of songs ahead of him. Songs that we will now never get to hear.

It feels even more unjust because of the army of less talented people who are left behind. The music industry contains many wonderful people, but it also contains lots of bad people – crooks, narcissists, and utter fakes – pretending to make music whilst paying someone else minimum wage to do it. How are they still here and Tim's not?

For a moment I'm almost angry.

Dance music needed you, Tim. We needed you. Your family needed you. I needed you.

Fuck.

I can't justify it in any way, so instead, I throw on some Avicii vocal tracks and feel grateful for the times he gave us. We were still lucky to have had him at all.

Will we learn any lessons from what happened to him? I fucking hope so. But in a world where the stars get younger and younger, many managers and agents are sharks, and we're all operating in the pressure-cooker world of social media.... I don't know. I really don't know.

Lamborghini Woes: Part 2.
Los Angeles, January 2015.

I go to speak to the gate agent.

"Be honest with me. Is there any chance this SouthWest flight to Vegas won't go?"

"I think it will go, but I've also seen them cancelled, when they keep getting pushed back like this."

"How many people are on the plane?"

"Four".

Four fucking people. Shit. I'd say there's a damn good chance of this flight getting cancelled. Time to look at alternatives. I call

Jordi, my tour manager, who's already in Vegas, having not been a total idiot and taken a relaxing flight earlier that day. I explain the situation.

"Think we need to price up a jet, just in case".

"On it.' He tells me. 'I'll call Bruce".

Ten minutes later, Bruce, our private jet contact, has worked miracles. Despite the fact it's January 1st, he's managed to find a plane that can take off from Van Nuys in 45 minutes. Total cost? $8,000.

"OK. Let me keep an eye on this SouthWest, and I'll come back to you in half an hour".

"Sorry, Bruce needs to know now. He's got pilots waiting, but if you want it, they need to confirm. And if we don't take this option, he definitely can't get us another plane tonight"

"Alright, give me five minutes to think".

Fuck. $8,000 is SO MUCH MONEY. Still, if I stick around, I'll potentially lose a lot more money. If I take the jet, I'll spend $8,000 to make $100,000. If I stay with Southwest, I might make the full $100,000, but I might make nothing. The jet seems the safest option. Fuck. I call Jordi back.

"Book the jet. I'm on my way"

I grab the wretched Lambo again and drive over to Van Nuys airport. I'm in a thoroughly shit mood by this point, and as I pull into the private terminal, I think about the glamorous Instagram shots of Lamborghinis next to private jets, and how stressed I am. If you want a lesson about how material things don't make you happy, I am that lesson, right now. Surrounded by luxury, stressed, on my own. Give me a few old mates, a pool table, and some beers any day. A walk in the countryside with the kids. Fuck, I'd take a walk in the neighborhood with my dog over this shite. Point is, material things = overrated.

I board the plane. It's a little old and tatty, and it's freezing cold, one of the coldest days I recall in LA. The pilots are already ready

– they're professional but unfriendly – likely not entirely happy at having to abandon their January 1st plans to fly a DJ to Vegas. I sit back, thinking how much less fun private jets are when you're on your own, and we power off.

Moments into the flight, the cabin fills with smoke, a rancid burning smell filling my nostrils, burning my throat.

Oh fuck. Please, no.

Because of the rather last minute way that I booked this plane, I haven't done any of my usual due diligence into the safety records. I've booked a fucking death trap, and I'm going to die on my own.

The pilots are frantically working up front, presumably figuring out how they land the fucking thing before we explode into a fireball. I've still got service, so I pull out my phone and fire off a text to Kat.

> There's something wrong with this plane. I just want to tell you that I've had the most amazing life with you. The time we spent together were the greatest memories I ever had. You made my life worth living. And whatever happens, you'll be OK. XX

I hit send and try to focus on my breathing, but I'm panicking big time.

A few minutes later, the smoke clears, the smell goes away, and we're on our way to Vegas. What the fuck just happened? The pilots seem relaxed, so I pop up.

"What the hell happened with the burning back there?"

"Oh, the plane was cold and hadn't been used for a while, so when we activated the hot air, it probably burned off a load of the dust in there or something. Not a big deal."

I am beyond relieved. I text Kat that I'm OK, and sit back, the anxiety gone. With a new lease on life, my mind drifts back to another plane, and another time.

An Actual Emergency.
Australia, 2005.

The Virgin Blue 737 powers easily into the sky above Sydney, half empty, and I pop my headphones on and listen to some tunes. This is an hour long flight, easy going, and though I used to be a nervous flier, flying almost every day has managed to knock it out of me. I've got three seats to myself and I'm sitting comfortably in the window seat. I'm on my Australian tour, I've had a great week in Sydney, life is good. And I like this airline. Virgin Blue is a Richard Branson upstart, and the crew, all in their 20s, are livelier and friendlier than those of Qantas, Australia's dominant legacy airline.

"Soon, we'll be taking off. My name's Eliza, and I'm your purser today. Our wonderful crew contains the gorgeous Tom at the back…". We laugh.

The next thirty minutes pass uneventfully, and then in an instant, everything changes. Eliza takes to the PA system again, and within a second of her speaking, I know something's up. As humans we spend a lot of our lives disseminating information. Analysing the words used, predicting future outcomes. But on other occasions, it's pure human instinct, those finely tuned survival systems that have been keeping us alive for millions of years telling us something's not right. I don't need to hear more than one word.

"L-ladies and gentlemen…"

The stutter gives it away. 30 minutes ago, she was confident, laughing, joking, bantering. This wasn't someone who fucking stuttered. Now, before she's even spoken one word, I know something's wrong.

"Please listen carefully to what I'm about to say. In a moment, the captain needs to speak with you all, and after that we'll be showing you procedures for making an emergency landing into Brisbane".

A few gasps. *Well it's happened,* I think. A real-life emergency on a plane. An odd sense of calm washes over me. It's strange how the anxiety of believing there might be a problem, is far worse than actually having one. Rubbish condition, anxiety. I've spent countless flights, sweaty palmed, grasping the seats as my mind raced through all manner of horrible outcomes… the one side of my brain predicting my imminent death in a fiery wreck, the other frantically pleading the reverse, justifying why things are OK.

I've had some form of anxiety as long as I can remember. Now, as far as illnesses go, it's certainly not comparable to losing a leg or similar, but who made it a competition? On a flare up, it's been enough to keep me indoors when I should have been outside. It's led to a few cancelled gigs. Of course, it's also a blessing. The fact that my mind is over-anxious is what makes me very good at my job. I'm not one to think *Ah, no need to prepare well, the gig'll be ok.* I'll assume the worst, and prepare like fuck, thank you very much. This extends to an unhealthy level of perfectionism when it comes to finishing tracks: creating hundreds of versions, spending hours tweaking a single vocal syllable. But no complaints: other than the time taken, there are no downsides to making art better than it needs to be.

Health anxiety is where my anxiety really can be brutal though. When I was a kid, my mum had a thick book on the bedside table: a dictionary of medical symptoms. You'd look through, find your symptoms, and it would tell you how you were going to die. At 11 or 12, keen reader that I was, I'd wander past the book, pick it up, and dive in. There's some information you're just not supposed to have, and this was a book for medical professionals, not civilians, and by reading this book, I was laying the tracks for a lifetime of health-related anxiety.

The advent of the internet made it even worse. Now, I could Google my symptoms in a flash and find out exactly what form of cancer I had today. I became convinced I was going to die young. To most others, this was madness. I was in my 20s, and I was otherwise perfectly healthy. The only thing that would put my mind at rest would be a visit to the doctor, who would always tell me I was fine, often in seconds. There was a running joke in our house that I had a season ticket to the doctors. In reality, I think a season ticket to a therapist might have been what I actually needed, but this was the UK in the early 2000s – mental health just wasn't a thing.

Over the years since then, I've had brain scans, AIDS tests, nerve conduction tests, various MRIs and god knows what else and I am happy to report that I'm still alive. However, the two most useful things I did were seeking out a therapist when things got bad, and learning to meditate. When it comes to anxiety, trying to talk yourself out of it simply doesn't work. Much more effective is to simply observe the anxiety, and be at one with it. Looking the threat directly in the eye this way has a strange way of taking away its power. For any fellow sufferers, the best book I've read on this subject is *Dare* by *Dr Barry McDonagh*.

My mind works fast, and that has a tendency to get me in trouble. Having a brain that operates at 200mph has always struck me as similar to blasting a Formula 1 car around a race track. Great fun when it's going well, but when you lose control, things get ugly fast. I wonder if slow-minded plodders are less affected by things like this. Me? I can hear one unusual noise on a plane and immediately envisage a whole chain of grisly events leading to us crashing. On many occasions, I've gone from enjoying the in-flight peanuts to wondering if my will is up-to-date in a matter of seconds. Again, meditation has been helpful in stopping these self-destructive patterns in their tracks.

Strangely, now we're faced with a real emergency, my anxiety is nowhere to be seen, and a strange calm washes over me. The captain comes on the PA. He sounds relaxed, which is something. He explains that we *might* have a technical problem with our landing gear, and whilst he thinks it's probably nothing, for precaution, we'll be using full emergency procedures to land in Brisbane in 30 minutes time. Alright, then.

For the next 20 minutes, there's not a lot to do. Strangely, nobody's freaking out, nobody's crying, everyone's pretty calm. This is 2005, so there's no in-flight wifi and no way to contact the outside the world. It's just us, in a metal tube, hurtling through the night sky towards our possible death.

I review my life so far and decide it's been pretty decent, and if tonight is my time, I'm OK with it. Then, there's some work to do. The crew frantically prepare the plane, bolting everything down. Then they stop by my seat.

"Sir, are you OK?"

"Er, yeah. Fine"

"Good. Listen, we need someone who's clear headed to come and sit with us at the front of the plane in case we crash and we're incapacitated. The guy who's there is refusing to sit there. Would you be willing to help?"

Social pressure. On one level, I think the guy at the front might be on to something. If the back of the plane's the safest place to be in a crash, I'd really rather be there too. However, I agree to help. I'd love to say it was an act of courage for my fellow passengers, but in reality, I just didn't want to bottle it in front of the young, attractive cabin crew.

"Sure".

I head to the front of the plane. The previous occupant of the front seat pushes past me, head down, on his way to his safe seat at the back, the gutless wimp. I take my seat in Row 1, and the crew, sat opposite me in the jump seats, give me a quick tutorial on how to open the door if I need to.

We're about five minutes from landing now and an icy calm has taken over the plane. Nobody is talking.

"Have you ever had one of these before?" I ask Eliza, who's sat opposite me.

"No", she admits.

"Are you scared?"

"A little. But he's a great pilot. We'll be good."

A few more minutes go by. I suddenly notice my throat is incredibly parched. I really need some fucking water, especially if I'm going to be opening this damn door.

"Mate, any chance of some water?" I ask the male flight attendant.

He jumps up, grabs me a bottle from the galley and hands it to me.

"You can't hold it when we're landing in case it goes flying in the crash, so give it back when you're done and I can stow it".

There's no charge. *Free bottled water, nice.* On this airline, everything costs money, so I appreciate the freebie. Then, I remember that I might be dead in five minutes, courtesy of Team Free Water, and I feel a little less warm towards them. Finally, I decide that in a situation like this you take whatever positives you can. Free water. Yay!

The lights of Brisbane airport appear in the distance. We're close now. The captain comes back on the PA.

"This is the captain, ladies and gentlemen, boys and girls. We're a couple of minutes out. I'll come back on just before we land to ask you to take the brace position. Thank you, I'll see you on the ground, and I hope you're enjoying tonight's flight with Virgin Blue".

The humor gets a few laughs. Eliza shakes her head.

"He didn't just say that..."

A minute later, it's time. This time, there's no joking from the flight deck.

"This is the captain. Brace, Brace. This is the captain. Brace, Brace."

Now, I've flown hundreds of times, and I know exactly what taking the brace position looks like. No problem there. However, what I haven't realized is that the brace position is also accompanied by a chant... a mantra. The crew, shouting at the top of their lungs, repeat it over and over, as we huddle with our heads between our knees.

"HEADS DOWN, STAY DOWN, BRACE! BRACE! HEADS DOWN STAY DOWN, BRACE! BRACE! HEADS DOWN, STAY DOWN, BRACE! BRACE!".

Over and over it goes and in a flash, the surreal becomes real. This is happening. Why did nobody tell me there was a fucking chant?

As we get close to the runway, I notice a few emergency vehicles ready for us, just in case. The captain takes an agonizing amount of time before touching the plane down, presumably in case the airport spot something out of the ordinary and tell him to abort the landing. After what seems like forever, he touches a wheel, then the others, and we land without incident. As it becomes apparent that we're OK, the chant from the crew dies away.

Then, the plane explodes:

... into cheers.

It's like the safety cap has been released. All the pent-up emotion from the past 30 minutes is uncorked. People are hugging each other, crying, calling loved ones. I just sit quietly, thinking, fuck. *Fuck.*

We leave the plane without incident. I hug both crew members who I was at the front of the plane with. And with that, we're off to baggage claim, and I'm struck by how quickly we're back to normality. *Don't we get a debrief? Some explanation? Some more free water?*

Nope, that's it. But I am grateful to be alive. As I walk out and find my driver, I feel utterly numb.

At least it'll be a good story, I think.

"YOU'LL BE OK"

written by Gareth Emery, Anthony Galatis, and Emily Davidson

i was made to live to live this life
and live is what i've done
found the wonder of the night
saw hope where there was none

but i know
the light could fade from my eyes
my plane could fall from the sky
the world could tell me this is my time

count my blessings every day
had more than i deserve
sing this song when i am gone
i'll be in every word

and i know
the light could fade from my eyes
my plane could fall from the sky
the world could tell me this is my time

and if i should die here tonight
darling know that you saved my life
felt your love every day
not a thing i would change
and i know
you'll be ok

MY LIFE IN LASERS

THE PHOTOS

My first 'gig', aged 5. Sarisbury Infant School, Southampton. 1985.

Lord of the Ringtones: figuring out how to extract money from strangers on the early Internet. University of Warwick, 2000. Photo: Joe Timms.

An early 'tones4fones.com' flyer.

No words. 2001. Photo: Alison Cronin.

2003: Perth, Australia. I left my job as a web designer to go on this tour, my first time outside of Europe.

A 2002 Mixmag write-up. Photo: Antonio Petronzio / Mixmag.

Top: flyer for our first ever Manchester event, 2009. Middle: street poster for the Northern Lights Concert, 2010. Bottom: another sold-out night at Sankeys, 2011.

Top: release party for my 2014 album 'Drive' at the Albert Hall, Manchester. Photo: Steven Cunniffe.
Middle: Adam in his private office at Beehive Mill, Manchester.
Bottom: Craig Connelly arrives for his first day of work as Garuda Label Manager.

With Lange, one of my early mentors, and Above & Beyond's Jono Grant.
Ministry of Sound, 2010ish.

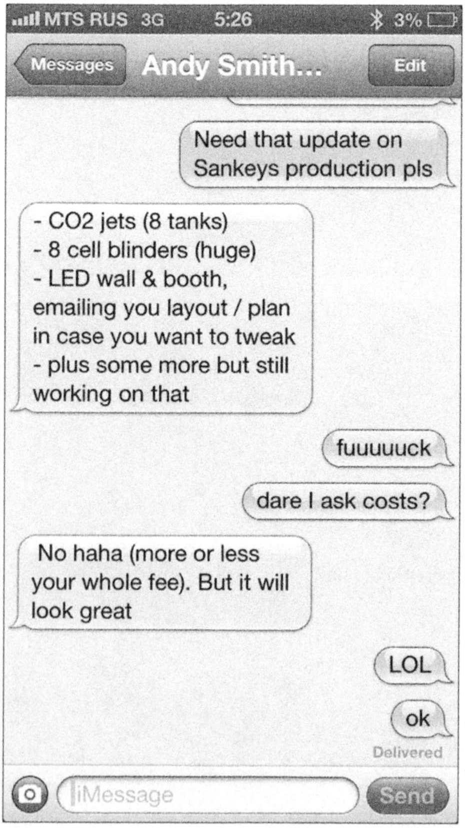

Production is important.
Here I am blowing my whole fee on 'extras'.

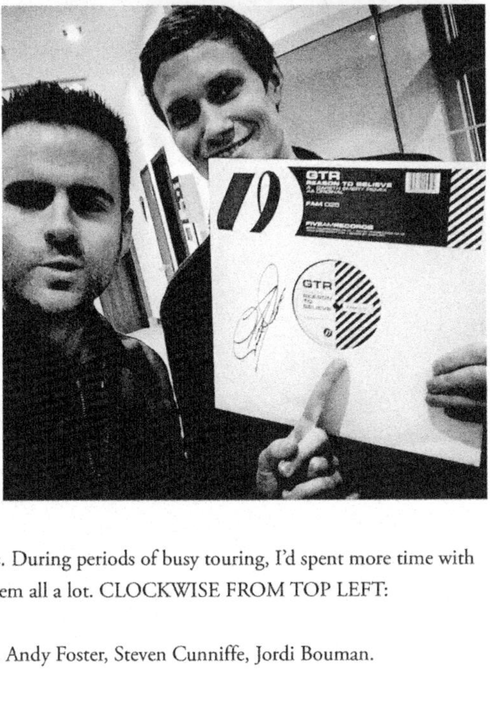

With some of the tour managers I've had over the years. During periods of busy touring, I'd spent more time with these guys than my own family and I owe them all a lot. CLOCKWISE FROM TOP LEFT:

Bjorn Niclas, Dan Peters, Anthony Garcia, Andy Foster, Steven Cunniffe, Jordi Bouman.

One of the most unique shows I've ever played: the closing ceremony of the 2015 European Olympic Games in Baku, Azerbaijan.

Sound checking the stadium before the show.

I've had hundreds of incredible shows over the years, so picking favorites is hard. On some of my most memorable nights, few good photos survived, leaving those nights to live on in memory only, but here are some favorites.

CLOCKWISE FROM TOP LEFT:
EDC Las Vegas (2012, Rukes). EDC New York (2013, Unknown). Coachella (2014, Erick Govea).
Laserface, New York (2019, Eric Cunningham). Global Gathering, UK (2013, Paul Underhill).

Sometimes, it all goes to complete shit. Thousands of people were tuned in for a live stream of my set when the internet went down moments before I took the stage. New York, 2013. Photo: Rukes.

Dad, me and my sister Roxanne on my wedding day. Photo: Mick Cookson.

Billboard at the legendary Hollywood Palladium, 2014.

A few photos of Kat and I over the years. CLOCKWISE FROM TOP LEFT: on an early date / on eve of moving to Los Angeles in 2013 / our wedding day / me seemingly wearing a garbage bag as a jacket.

Billboard in Los Angeles, 2014.

Top: my only helicopter trip, interviewing for the EDC Las Vegas documentary in 2014. Bottom: a very different Las Vegas trip, 2019.

Ashley Wallbridge has been one of my best industry friends and collaborators for a decade. Here he is in a studio looking thoroughly uncomfortable, like a neanderthal man accidentally teleported into a spaceship.

Ashley on a better photographic day. A press shot we took outside Sankeys in Manchester, 2019.

CVNT5 was one of the most fun projects of my life, until it wasn't.
Here, Ashley, Alex and I are on the 'red carpet' shooting one of our online shorts.

CVNT5 was enjoyed by many people, including Armin van Buuren, who kindly featured in our first video.

With collaborators Standerwick and Haliene, celebrating my third A State of Trance 'Tune Of The Year' award for 'Saving Light' in 2018.

Top: an acoustic moment on stage in Vancouver, Canada with Emma Hewitt. 2018. Photo: Keaton Chiu.
Bottom: backstage in London with 'Concrete Angel' Christina Novelli, 2013.

Our 'Laserface' project was one of the most exhilarating and challenging projects I have ever been involved in.
Top: working in the test studio with genius laser designer Anthony Garcia.
Bottom: the finished product is enjoyed by 8,500 people in San Francisco. Photo: Uneak Photography. 2018.

Left: Laserface lands in Ibiza. Right: celebrating a successful Laserface to 15,000 fans in Los Angeles with Andy Foster, Kassy Ruimy, and Anthony Garcia

My manager Kassy with Anthony, checking our Ibiza flyers are suitably well distributed. Ibiza, 2019.

Recording 'THE LASERS' in London with the amazingly talented Annabel Turner.

As 2020 landed and the world went fucking crazy, I shaved my head and delivered a clear message.

Still from the 'You'll Be OK' music video, directed by Lee Jones. 2020.

Looking for innovative places to play during the 2020 pandemic lockdown, we filmed this set in the highest public event space in the Western USA on the 71st floor of the US Bank Tower in Los Angeles.

On the keys during our streamed 'Unplugged' event: another lockdown special.

Top: signing the final copies of 'THE LASERS' and clearly already chinking about what's next.
Bottom: a lovely backstage visit from Sansa & Elise. Anaheim, California, 2020. Photo: Rukes.

ELISE

ISLAND LIFE AND FAMILY STRIFE

Los Angeles, February 2019.

I step out of the United States Citizenship and Immigration office. My new green card is applied for, and I need to get the fuck out of America.

It's 2019, and we've been living in Ibiza, Spain for the first four months of the year. After six years in Los Angeles, I welcomed the change even though it was more for Kat – she badly needed out of LA for a while, so we figured what better way to do it than taking an extended vacation to a beautiful island, whilst sizing it up as a potential future home? And on the surface, there are plenty of reasons why living in Ibiza compared to Los Angeles makes sense. The flight time of just a couple of hours to the UK means the homeland and grandparents are close. There's a great English school that the kids could go to. Both Sansa and Elise will almost definitely end up native-level bilingual, and Kat and I will likely get half-decent too. There are no wildfires, earthquakes or guns. Sounds idyllic.

And, strangely enough, I do really fucking like the Spanish way of life. Spending all day in a country where English isn't the first language has an interesting side-effect of keeping me extremely present, and in the moment. Walking through the village, my mind isn't racing with its usual concoction of anxiety, drive, ideas, but instead I'm just thinking of what I'm going to fucking say next. Shall I use *me gustaría*, or *yo quiero*? What's Spanish for 'witch hazel' again?

And Ibiza is undoubtedly a beautiful place in the winter. The beaches and roads are empty, the locals friendly, and the food's great. Our swimming pool might only be 5c / 41f – which roughly translates as cold as fuck - but I've bought a cheap wetsuit from Decathalon, so I've even been able to keep up swimming. My kids' grandparents seem to be around all the time too, which helps with childcare.

And yet...

I can't get into it.

Despite Ibiza being one of my favorite places on the planet, I find living on an island vaguely oppressive. According to the other ex-pats, whilst most people love the island life, a small minority are afflicted with 'island fever': a curious psychological phenomena of feeling disconnected from the outside world. I appear to be in this minority.

In Los Angeles, I love the infinite possibility. I could jump in a car and drive to New York, or, a little less extreme, to the beach at Malibu, the snow at Big Bear, the casinos of Las Vegas, all in under five hours – and something about having all that expanse at my disposal makes me feel free, even if I don't take advantage of it all that often. The same applies in the UK. Living in Manchester, London was only a couple of hours away. I could drive down to Cardiff for the rugby, to my dad's on the South Coast, whatever.

In Ibiza, all I've got is... more Ibiza. The furthest I can drive is about an hour to the other side of the island, but for what? More beautiful empty beaches. More scenic empty roads. All the same stuff we've got over our side. Can a person have *too* many beautiful empty beaches? It sounds like paradise, but I just miss the rest of the world. Plus, I feel guilty for feeling miserable. What's wrong with me? Everyone else loves this place. I loved this place during my previous

20 visits. But now I'm living here and I'm miserable."Do I just need to man up and get used to it?" I text my friend Gez.

"No mate," he replies. "If you're miserable there, don't discount that. Your feelings count too, you should be thriving there."

And so, for the last six weeks, I've been looking forward to this moment. Getting off the island, getting back to Los Angeles. Getting back home.

The plan was a solid one. Fly back to Los Angeles. Stay at our family home. Apply for a replacement Green Card having lost my former one (which requires a trip to America). Do a few gigs, see some friends, play a game of football (probably the thing I've missed most) then get back. And for the most part, the plan went well. Last night I drove down to Santa Monica – a rare luxury, afforded only because my family are 6,000 miles away, so I've no childcare bedtime obligations – and walked along the beach. As the sun set over the Santa Monica Pier, and I watched the sky turn a multitude of shades of blue as the last couples drifted away, it had never been more clear in my head; California was where it was at. Where I needed to be.

I just wish I had my family with me.

That morning, on my way to the Green Card office, Kat texted me.

It was about Elise.

My youngest daughter was being admitted to hospital.

She was a little sick when I flew out a few days prior, but nothing that would have necessitated me cancelling my travel plans. Just a heavy cough, following a cold that's been doing the rounds on the island.

"Should I go to the States?" I'd asked Kat.

"You should go," she told me. Kat's a lot more relaxed when it comes to health stuff than me, yet another reason why we make a good team. I've got Grade A, fully certified health anxiety, so anything wrong with me or my family involves finding the worst-case scenario on Google within minutes. Kat on the other hand, tends to assume everything's fine, until it's not. Typically it works well, with us eventually finding a sweet spot between my hyper-vigilance and her common sense.

But this time she's actually worried, which means I'm really fucking worried.

Elise is just 18 months old, and that morning had become entirely unresponsive – sleeping constantly with no interest in food, water, or waking up. Thankfully Kat's got her parents with her, so they rushed her in to the doctor, who, through a combination of hand signals and monosyllabic English, informed them that she was being admitted into the emergency wing of the local private hospital, right away. Do not go home, do not pack a bag: hospital, now.

As I drive, my mind's racing with all manner of thoughts. Primarily, I need to get the fuck back to Ibiza. I also feel terrible for now being away from home, an utter failure on my part as a parent. On one level, this isn't rational: Elise was barely sick when I left, and my job involves traveling, plus I needed to get back to attend this notoriously inflexible green card interview. But the fact I'd looked forward to this trip so much is what keeps tripping the guilt switch. I'd looked forward to being away, at a time when my youngest daughter needed me most in her short life. What a shit parent.

My flight's not booked until tomorrow, but I need to get the fuck out tonight. It's 2pm, there should be a way home. It's pissing with rain, uncharacteristic for California, and whilst I'm not particular superstitious, this is as clear a sign as any I need to get out of here. I call the airline most likely to get me home cheaply and at the last minute, and a flight is booked.

Arriving at the airport, my level of anxiety is off the charts. Usually, I can keep it under control via my daily meditation practice, but today is extreme. I self-medicate with a glass of wine. I'm not someone who drinks alone – ever – drinking is purely a social thing for me, so if you see me drinking alone, things are fucking bad.

I board the flight. It's hard to gauge tone over text, but Elise is still pretty unresponsive, and on something called a Nebulizer. From what I can ascertain from Google, it's a steroid inhaler for opening up the airways. They suspect she's got either pneumonia or bronchiolitis, but nobody really seems to know. Kat's struggling with the language barrier, but the hospital seems good.

We power off into the sky.

London Heathrow Airport
May, 2019

I check the departure board. British Airways flight BA269 to Los Angeles is boarding soon, but I take a moment longer to watch the kids playing.

I've flown through this airport hundreds of times, but I never before knew it had a kids' play area hidden in an obscure corner. Never needed to. I watch Elise, still not quite two, but a rough player: bouncing, shouting and wrestling with kids twice her age.

And once I again, my mind goes back to Ibiza and I feel gratitude for how everything worked out. Ten days in hospital, all in all, with Kat and I taking turns doing overnights there, while Elise's grandparents kept our home ticking over. Our elder daughter Sansa, not quite understanding why her little sister wouldn't come home. The first day Elise was back, sitting up, recognizing her dad. The wonderful day we brought her back home.

I'm grateful for the brilliant Spanish health care, and fantastic doctors – their lack of English meaning I'd picked up many Spanish words and phrases I hoped I'll never have to use again. *Ella no puede respirar, necesita oxígeno, urgente.*

I'm grateful to be heading back to Los Angeles. Our home. Could I live in Ibiza, permanently? Maybe. Maybe one day. But not now. I believe there's more for us to do in California first.

One night in the hospital, with Elise sleeping quietly next to me, a melody had started to reverberate around my head. There might be something in it. I'll have to try and work it out in the studio a little more. When I get home...

"ELISE"

by Gareth Emery & Anthony Galatis.

the california sun
has never felt so cold before
with you not waiting for me at the door
six thousand mile away
just keep holding on tight
and i'll fly through the night
to come home

i remember
the day that you were born like yesterday
told you i'd be for there you come what may
and i failed
but if i make this plane, when i land i'll explain, so hold on

you are so much stronger than you know
lax and it's my time to go
sending one last video from my phone

just let me get back home tonight
and we'll all be alright, for forever
just let me get back home tonight
and we'll all be alright, for forever

GUNSHOTS

AMERICA'S GREATEST CONTRADICTIONS

2017.

Another school shooting. I close my phone. Why do I read this shit?

Gun culture is the thing I struggle with most living in the United States.

Not because I'm particularly anti-gun, or pro-gun.

But because it's all so fucking contradictory.

A little confession: I fucking love guns. As a kid, I was obsessed with toy guns, cap guns, water guns, whatever. As a young boy, my dad took me to a gun shop owned by a friend of his where I got to fuck around with all manner of firearms, from the "Dirty Harry" Magnum .44 to a genuine German WWII Luger. It was a good shop, although after the Dunblane school massacre civilian ownership of handguns was entirely banned in the UK, and the place had to close down.

Throughout my life I've done clay pigeon shooting, pheasant hunting, target shooting, you name it. I've shot machine guns in Latvia, AR15s in California and hunting rifles on English farms. I'm also a bizarrely good shot with a light rifle too; strange as my default setting at more or less any sport is 'shit', but for some unexplained reason I'm excellent at target shooting.

None of these mean that I'm pro gun-ownership, though.

When we moved to America, I told Kat:

"Cool, America. I'm getting a gun for the house."

"You most certainly are not," she replied.

To bolster my argument, I took it upon myself to read a little about home invasions, so I could present her with the stats of how much safer we'd be: and was surprised to find the evidence didn't quite seem to be on my side. Instead, having a gun in the house appeared to create all sorts of other additional risks.

Whilst gun ownership still appealed to me, I never could understand the logic behind the public owning military-style assault weapons.

I get the 2nd amendment. I also understand how important the Constitution is to America, but I just can't believe that the founding fathers, wise as they were, penned that amendment imagining military-style assault weapons killing fellow Americans in the numbers that they do. It's fucking tragic. Of course, in 1789, just six years after the British had been kicked out (sorry), I get why it was necessary for the public to stay well armed, given the likelihood of us popping back over to re-establish control at any point. But these days, that ain't happening. We've got enough of our own problems.

Besides, if the 2nd Amendment is really non-negotiable in its current form, why limit it? Allow civilizations to own tanks, rocket launchers, nukes. Why have any limit?

It's the people that kill, of course. Not the guns. And I agree with that.

But look. At my school we had some fucking nutters. Some kids who were borderline mentally ill, who were bullied to fuck every single day (not by me), and whose lives were no doubt so miserable, they would have liked to have taken some serious vengeance. A few times, knifes were brought in. Nobody died. I dread to think what would have happened if these kids, who were utterly desperate and disturbed, could have obtained guns. I think we all know. Perhaps I wouldn't even be writing these words, and you'd never have heard a single piece of music by me. Who knows.

The strangest thing for me to grasp is how out of sync guns are with American life, where a neurotic obsession with safety is part and parcel of living here. Risk is to be avoided at all costs, often in ways that border on the ridiculous. Coffee cups warn you of a 'VERY HOT DRINK INSIDE'. Playing a simple game of football (soccer) requires signing a ten-page waiver. Child seats must have double the amount of harnesses they have in Europe. The amount of insurance you're required to have is mind-boggling (I've currently got health insurance, life insurance, car insurance, earthquake insurance, professional liability insurance, home insurance, business insurance… etc).

On a filming of a TV show we made back in 2017, one of our cast had to jump into a swimming pool, and we were required to have a 'water safety expert present'.

"Why?" I asked him. "Can't you swim or something?"

"Actually, I'm a triathlete," he replied. "The show's insurance requires a water safety officer present even if I'm just sitting in the hot tub."

Nuts.

But look: I also get the other side.

Driving East to West across the USA, you realize how remote large stretches of the country are, especially once you pass Oklahoma. If you look at a satellite image of the USA at night, it's insane how sparsely populated the Western half of the country is.

Back in 2013, Kat and I drove from New York to Los Angeles as part of our honeymoon, taking in the states of New York, Pennsylvania, DC, Virginia, Arkansas, Tennessee, Oklahoma, Texas, New Mexico, Arizona and finally California – spending lots of time on Route 66, an inspired journey that led me to my 2nd artist album

'Drive'. Driving through the deserts of New Mexico and Arizona, we'd see lone ranches, hours from the nearest towns. Trailer parks, desolate outposts where the police would be at least thirty minutes away. If I lived there, I'd own a gun for sure. Who else is going to protect you? Different situation in New York though. And it's clearly challenging to find laws that are as appropriate for the New Mexican desert as they are for the suburbs of Beverly Hills.

As you can tell, I don't really have any answers, so I keep my mouth shut other than to note how fucking sad the senseless killing is. I'm an immigrant and I chose to live here. Any attempt to get political and I'd be told to fuck off back home, and quite rightly so. Imagine an American coming to the UK and telling us why we <u>should</u> own guns? We'd laugh you out of town. So I keep my gob shut.

But it's still heartbreaking, and I hope, at some point either the laws or the culture changes so it ends. The US is too great a country for this shit.

"GUNSHOTS"

written by Gareth Emery & Anthony Galatis

this land is my home
i'm brave and i'm free
nowhere on this earth that i'd rather be
again i read the news
and tears filled my eyes
if he really does exist
then he's on the wrong side

gunshots like church bells all over town
run for your life and keep your head down
i can hear them calling to me
if this is freedom, don't want to be free

your thoughts and your prayers
will fade like the night
but hearts they will break and stay broken for life
another unmarked car
pure evil inside
it was over in a flash
please tell me you tried

gunshots like church bells all over town
run for your life and keep your head down
i can hear them calling to me
if this is freedom, don't want to be free

END OF DAYS

MAKING TELEVISION AND DISCOVERING SONGWRITING

December 2017.

I open the door of my studio to Emma Hewitt. It's my first songwriting session in over five years, and only the second or third songwriting session I've done in the last fifteen years. I am nervous as fuck.

You see, for 20 years, I forgot how to write songs.

Music had always been my *thing.* Unlike sport, I was a natural at it, and while I eschewed formal training as best I could, writing and producing the music I liked was effortless. During my years at University, playing in my band *The Dynamos*, I wrote songs prolifically; probably over 100 in a three year period. For most of my teen years, I'd imagined my career would be playing in a band. I'd play guitar on stage, write songs, and let someone else sing them.

But then I got into dance music, and the songwriting stopped overnight.

The reason wasn't that I'd stopped enjoying it - it was just the culture in the industry. In dance music, almost no DJs write songs. I didn't know this, but after I was able to start working in music full time, I found out quickly.

All of a sudden, everyone I met in the industry wanted to introduce me to 'writers'. If I knew then what I know now, I would have said: "I'm a writer: so by all means find me some mentors, or people to work with, but I'm going to do this myself."

I didn't do that.

Instead, I slipped into the dance music tradition of acquiring what are known in the trade as *toplines*.

I fucking hate the word toplines.

A song, I've come to learn, is a beautiful, organic thing comprised of the music, vocal melody, and lyrics. In order to be any good, to reach that bit of your soul that good songs reach, all three need to work in harmony. They need to come from the same emotional place. Reducing songs to 'the topline and the music' is just bullshit, and part of the reason why so many dance music songs are shit.

Let me explain how it works in dance music.

A record producer makes an instrumental piece of music. At that point, he or she will email it off to writers, to see if anyone can write a decent vocal over it. Often, producers will get a handful of different vocals written for a track – the process can be a bit hit or miss.

Good writers tend to work as teams, rather than individuals, although there are plenty of lone writers out there. But the real pros will often have a team of three or four people, who'll bang out numerous songs in a day.

Ah, what have we today? A new instrumental from David Guetta. Let's write him a song.

Then a few hours later:

What's next? Ooh, an instrumental from Armin van Buuren. Off we go.

99% of the time, the artist isn't even in the room.

In addition, often the final featured vocalist is someone entirely different. So you end up with the team that wrote the music, the team that wrote the vocal, then the singer, who - quite often - not only wrote neither the music nor the vocal, but may not even have met the people who did.

And people wonder why so many dance music vocals are shit.

Well actually, let me rephrase that. 'Shit' suggests incompetency, that the songs are bad, when in reality, most of these are impeccably well-crafted pop-records. Everything happens in the right place, and the songs are written with the cold, clinical precision of seasoned professionals.

However, when it comes to my music, I don't want the cold clinical precision of seasoned professionals. Don't get me wrong – there's a time for that. If I'm going into hospital for a procedure, I want a cold, calm, seasoned professional who's done it a thousand times and knows exactly what she's doing.

But for songs? No. I want someone who's pouring his heart out, weaving every bit of raw emotion into the song and the music, so I feel that way too.

That's not to say the seasoned pros don't write some good songs, because they certainly do. In fact, most dance music hit records come from these sort of 'hit writing teams'. But they're not my sort of thing, and they're certainly not the sort of records people will be playing years from now. Sure, many of them become super successful, racking up hundreds of millions of streams and playing on the radio stations around the world… but that's not my aim. I've got no interest in the casual head-nodding interest of the fair-weather fan, listening along because it's on the radio but without really caring. I want to make songs that change people's lives. Songs that get played at their weddings, and their funerals. Songs that are still being played decades after they've been released. And that requires a different path.

Throughout my career, I'd been lucky to have some of these great songs that live on for years, bring goosebumps to the arm and tears to the eyes, and *have* indeed been played at weddings and funerals. Concrete Angel, U, Reckless, Saving Light… all ticked those boxes, to some extent. But the honest truth is, they weren't really my songs, but the product of my sister Roxanne – an excellent A&R who'd helped me find cracking songs for years.

Now, these songs were good songs, and they were real songs. Christina Novelli really fucking meant Concrete Angel. Bo Bruce really fucking meant U. You can hear the emotion in these songs on the first listen. You can see it in their eyes when they perform them. But if you ask me what they are about?

Fuck knows mate. Like you I can guess, but I didn't write them.

I do have something of a talent when it comes to figuring out how to show songs at their best, though. Working out the correct mix of music to wrap around a great vocal is incredibly natural to me, but it can't be that easy, because almost nobody else manages to get it right. Less is always the key: most producers over-complicate things, whereas with a great vocal, you don't need much. Let the vocal do the talking, and add simple but effective elements that complement it. That's it.

Roxanne's talent was finding these songs in their non-dance music form and spotting their potential. Concrete Angel was handed to her as an acoustic demo. 'U' was a bland rock track by Bo Bruce called 'Alive'. 'Lost' was an acoustic song by Janet Devlin. As these songs already existed, we simply had to agree licensing terms before I could start my work of turning these songs into electronic music bangers.

'Concrete Angel', funnily enough, was the trickiest to produce.

I'd heard the initial demo in August 2011 following the Creamfields festival. I'd had a successful show, and a group of us were back partying hard in my Manchester flat.

"Oh, Gaz, you fucking need to hear this song, by the way," Rox told me. "Christina Novelli's got this new song, and it's absolutely fucking insane. I think you could turn it into a complete anthem."

"Mmmm, really?" I asked, vaguely, pouring myself another wine. Rox had played me a few of Christina's demos in previous years and I'd never seen much potential in either her voice or the songs, and given everyone was wasted, I assumed Roxanne had just had too much wine and was over-excited about yet another average song.

"Can I connect to those speakers over there and play it?" she insisted.

Do we have to? Reluctantly, I let her connect her phone, and the opening bars of 'Concrete Angel' play. It's a simple arrangement, one piano and Christina's demo vocal.

Within seconds of the verse starting, I know it's a smash. There's an insanely chilling, haunting tone to Novelli's vocal that I've never heard before. I'm not even listening to the lyrics, I'm just absorbing the whole thing, and it's making me feel… something. I can't put my finger on it, but this track has something very fucking special about it.

The second verse passes flawlessly, as I sit in silence, I feel a frisson of nerves as I wait for the chorus. *Please don't let them fuck it up*. The chorus arrives and it's incredible – just perfectly written, perfectly sung. Every line is exactly enough. Add or subtract anything and the song would be diminished. I've got goosebumps. Shit. That's a fucking song. I'm choked up.

"Fuck" I manage, eventually.

"So, you want it?" grins Roxanne.

"I definitely fucking want it." I'm already texting Craig, who runs my label. Roxanne introduces us to Christina's manager, and we're negotiating.

The good news is, Christina's up for making it a collaboration with me. She doesn't know much about dance music, but she knows I'm decent at what I do, and I can blow this song - and her - up to a level it wouldn't otherwise reach.

But she's got other songwriters, and they're difficult. The negotiation over who owns what split of the record drags on for weeks. Christina's co-writers claim that I shouldn't have any share of the acoustic version, only my electronic version.

"Fuck that," I tell Craig. "I'm not working on a version for months, blowing the song up, then letting them cash in on the acoustic version when I get nothing. It's not a fucking remix. We're either fully collaborating on it, or we're not."

With Christina's co-writers unwilling to move an inch, eventually Christina finds me a fair percentage from her side. Her co-writers are being extremely unfair, but the sacrifice is the right move – eight years on, Christina's still got a great career launched by 'Concrete Angel', the percentage points she handed to me long offset by the money she's made DJing since that day.

Then I've just got to produce the thing, and for once...I run into trouble.

The weeks go by. Months. Christina and Rob, her manager, are extremely keen to get the track out, but I just can't get it right. Something about the chorus isn't fitting – it's an epic song but I'm struggling to thread a riff around the chorus melody. I listen to the song far too much and start to doubt it. Is it that good anyway? Do I really need it? Every email that Rob sends pisses me off a little more. Eventually, he says that unless I can deliver a demo in a couple of weeks, they're pulling the collab and releasing the track themselves.

Fuck it. I reply back.

> Rob and Christina. I'm so sorry to have wasted your time on this, but after months of trying, I just can't make the record work in a dance music format. Not sure why, but I've really tried. I know you're super keen to get it out, so I'm going to hand it back – you guys go ahead and release it yourselves. Sorry again for wasting your time, but it's a great vocal and I'm sure it'll do really well for you. Gaz

My finger hovers over the send button.

Have I really tried my hardest here?

I mean, *really?*

Do I want give it one more fucking shot?

I've got a two and half hour flight ahead of me, so I decide to give it one more crack on the plane. If I land and haven't made progress, I'm out.

Perhaps it's the fear of losing it, but on the plane everything happens. All of a sudden, things click into place. I figure out I can change the chorus chords for the drop which solves my issue, and all of a sudden I write a fantastic, credible drop riff, which fits perfectly with the chorus. The chords are slightly different, but strangely enough, you can't tell, a surefire sign that it works. Inspired by recent Skrillex records, I add a little arpeggiated flourish at the end of the riff, and boom. The demo's done. There will be many more weeks, months of production, but now, it's just a matter of time. I know how it's going to go.

I land and fire the demo to Craig.

From: **Gareth Emery** <gaz@garuda.nu>
Date: Mon, Oct 31, 2011 at 8:12 PM
Subject: Demo
To: Craig Connelly <craig@garuda.nu>

Dead rough ableton demo, but this sounds like a new Sanctuary to me!

From: **Craig Connelly** <craig@garuda.nu>
Date: Tue, Nov 1, 2011 at 3:56 AM
Subject: Re: Demo
To: Gareth Emery gaz@garuda.nu

It certainly does!
Love it. Everything about it says mature/classy vocal trance, this should be a huge record once finished. Good to come back to something the hardened trance fans will go nuts for. Looking forward to hearing the finished version.

We're off to the races. From there, I hit the studio hard. Within a few weeks, I've got a functional demo, which I play to 15,000 people at the Transmission festival in Prague, its debut play. Immediately it's up on YouTube, and people start guessing what it is.

We work quickly. The next month, we decamp to Los Angeles to shoot the music video, and we release the track in January 2012. Helped by a stunning remix by John O'Callaghan, that year Concrete Angel wins the prestigious 'A State Of Trance Tune Of The Year' poll – the first of three career wins for me – and it becomes a bona-fide trance classic.

And it all happened because of Roxanne.

My lack of songwriting, whilst also following industry norms, was my own fault. In 2016, Roxanne set up a songwriting session at my Los Angeles house during a visit.

"I've got some great writers joining – a vocalist called Haliene and her boyfriend, and a girl called Karra. Are you good for 11am?"

I agree to join the session, but the day arrives and I'm having a bad morning. I'm stressed out with some unrelated business shit, trying to handle my young daughter Sansa's morning routine, and one of the writers leaves the door open, allowing our dog Holly to escape into the street.

"Sorry guys, I'm going to need an hour," I tell them.

I load up a demo that Standerwick and I have been working on so they've got something to make a start on, and disappear off. The first hour of any studio session is usually getting to know one-another so it's unlikely I'm going to miss much. An hour later, Roxanne comes to find me.

"The song's ready" she tells me. In an hour? *This'll be shit.*

I head into the studio. Matt Steeper plays the piano, Haliene sings, and there's Saving Light, written, complete. In an hour. It's insane, and I immediately know it's a smash. I make one change to the vocal melody in the pre-chorus, and congratulate the team. Time to start producing. A year later, another ASOT 'Tune Of The Year' is in the bag.

There's no doubt Roxanne's stellar A&R and songwriting ability accelerated my career when it needed it most. But I never felt like I truly owned these songs, and worse, I often felt the other songwriters didn't really appreciate my contribution either. Sure, I wrote most of the music for Saving Light, including the central riff, whilst Standerwick did the heavy lifting on the production side, but the attitude from the writers seemed to suggest that they felt we were fortunate DJs who'd lucked out by being handed such a bomb of a record. I knew I was better than that, and although I didn't know it yet, I'd soon have to prove it.

Manchester.
December, 2017.

My phone rings again during the meal. This is it – my lawyer calling from the US. Perhaps this is the moment I finally settle this long-standing lawsuit and move on from the brutal conflict that has consumed me for the last six months.

It's Christmas in Manchester and Kat and I are dining out with some old friends. Everyone knows the details of the situation I'm in. This is the third call I've taken to my lawyer in Michigan, who's back and forth with a chain of other lawyers in various places around the globe. There's a lot of money flying around, the majority of it into the pockets of the lawyers.

"Give me the good news Matt," I answer, as I step away from the table.

"They're not taking our offer," he comes back.

"Fuck." I think for a moment. "Should we counter again?"

"Too late now. Their main lawyer has just left his office for his Christmas break. He's not back until January 2nd".

"Are you fucking serious? Doesn't he want to get this done?"

"It doesn't seem an entirely high priority for him, no".

I really wanted to get this deal concluded by Christmas so it didn't drag into the new year. I'd joked that it was one of my New Year's Resolutions: join a gym, lose weight, settle unresolved lawsuits. Hilarious, Gaz.

However, the other side don't appear to be in the same hurry as me, so whilst I don't like it, I'm forced to wait this one out. I return to the table, shake my head at Kat, shovel down some spring rolls, and order another beer. Fuck it.

Spending six months locked in a bitter lawsuit has been one of the most stressful times of my life, and whilst I've got somewhat used to being in a constant state of war, I still feel the cortisol spike in my bloodstream every time a new communication from 'the other side' arrives. But for the most part, I focus on the positive, and remember that things are never quite as bad as they seem.

Looking for the positive in any situation has been a great help to me throughout my life. Sure, I've had bad times, but why dwell on them?

The death of my mother, in 2006, was clearly a pretty fucking bad time, but even as it happened I tried to focus on the positives. She'd died following a long battle with cancer: terrible to watch, but it had given us time to emotionally prepare for what would come next. Plus, as I was still living at home for the bulk of it, we spent a lot of time together. In her last year, I'd run her up to the hospital, the Royal Marsden in London, wait for her to have chemotherapy, and then back home to Southampton. I was grateful to spend this time together towards the end, but even if we hadn't, I wouldn't have felt short-changed by life. I was 26. I'd had an amazing mother for the really important bit of my life, and whilst I was utterly devastated to lose her, I could at least promise her that I'd be OK.

I looked at it as analytically as possible. There are kids who never know their parents. Who lose both parents in a car crash before they even know them. Who have parents who are drug addicts, abusers, criminals. Applying that perspective made me feel very grateful that the first 20 years of my life had been more-or-less picture perfect.

Of course, we all get to choose the perspective we view a situation from.

I could have looked at my circle of school friends, most of whom still have a full set of parents now – 14 years later – but I didn't. Even if life had short-changed me - and I don't believe it did - what would complaining about it ever have accomplished? Ultimately, both positive thoughts and negative thoughts are always available. We get to choose which ones we engage with.

After my mum's death, I got straight back on with my career, heading to Australia for a tour weeks after the funeral.

"Isn't it too soon?" a few family members asked.

No, I don't think so. You think she'd have wanted me moping around the house, feeling sorry for myself? Fuck that. Obviously, I'm going to mourn, but I'd rather mourn on Bondi Beach with 5,000 people in front of me. My mother was one of the most driven workaholics I knew – in fact, a lot of my work ethic comes from her. She'd have wanted me getting on with life.

It may have been coincidental that my career really started to explode after my mum died. Living at home with your parents rent-free in a nice comfortable environment isn't exactly the rocket up your arse you need to go and make something of yourself. After she died, I properly left home and soon had a girlfriend, rent and bills. I had to make things work. Plus, losing a parent reminds you in stark fashion that you aren't going to live forever, either. Life is short. You'd better maximize your own whilst you can.

That's really the extent to which I analyze that period. I hope I've done her proud. I think I have, for the most part. A therapist would probably tell me that I've got some unresolved shit from never really dealing with it, but I'm not sure that's right. I just dealt with it in my own way, and really the only way I knew: work.

My legal issues had all started with **WeAreCVNT5**, a comedy TV show that I created along with my sister and manager, Roxanne. We all thought the show was going to make it big.

It didn't.

Instead, I'd go as far as saying that it ended up being the biggest professional failure of my life.

At the time that infuriated me, but with hindsight, I'm ok with it. Overall, I've had a lot more success than failure, and I learned a lot of lessons. *A hell of a lot of lessons.*

And, it's a fucking good story.

The initial idea was sparked in 2015, in my LA studio with longtime collaborator and close friend Ashley Wallbridge. We were putting the finishing touches on a new track, and were kicking around ideas about how to market it. At the time, a DJ called Mat Zo was on a Twitter rampage, tearing into ghost producers and – in his view – their negative effect on dance music culture. Flicking through his tweets, I asked Ash what he thought.

"He's got a fucking point hasn't he? So many talentless fuckers out there who can't play a single note who just pay someone else to make all their tunes for them".

Ash knew all about this, having been a longtime ghost-producer himself.

"Yeah, it's nuts," I agreed, "but the way Mat's gone about it is all wrong. He's just coming across as angry, bitter, and people are more focused on his meltdown than the issues he's actually talking about."

I thought for a moment. Then came the spark of an idea:

"If you wanted to make people take notice, you'd need to make it... *funny.*"

Dance music was, and still is, a very serious business. We're not an industry full of people that are very good at laughing at themselves, for the most part. Dillon Francis had carved out a unique path by creating a host of alter-egos, acting them out on his Instagram page, with my personal favorite being the uber-purist German techno fanatic DJ Hanzel, but Dillon was one in a million.

Ashley and I had also dipped our toes into comedy back in 2011, with our embarrassingly amateur music video for our track 'Mansion'. Our 'storyline' involved Ashley being jealous of my car, eventually killing me with an axe, and our production value was firmly on the 'high school project' end of the scale. However, as shit as it looked, people seemed to like it, and Ash was up for giving comedy another go.

"How about you and I become a fictitious group?' I asked him. 'The biggest fucking arseholes you can think of. Basically, everything we hate about the industry, rolled into one act, and make a music video where we play them?"

Ash loved it. I made the coffees, and we kicked around an idea for a name. I was determined it would have to be formatted to look a certain way.

"Look," I explained, "every 'cool' act these days has a name all in capitals, mis-spelled. Rehab = R3HAB. Dubbs = DVBBS. It's got to be like that. What else do these acts have in common?" I asked Ash.

"They're cunts," he replied, blunt as ever. "They're all fucking cunts".

I laughed. That was a bit harsh, but Ash had given me an idea.

I wrote it down:

CVNTS.

It looked good, if a bit obvious. I deleted the S and replaced it with a 5, like deadmau5.

CVNT5.

I couldn't stop laughing.

"I think I've got it, mate". I showed Ash the phone, and he was in stitches too.

We had a band. We had a name. We had the song.

We just needed a video.

That night I crashed out knowing there was a good chance CVNT5 would seem like a terrible idea in the morning – often a night's sleep is the perspective you need on whether an 'out-there' idea is good or shit. But, the next day, I was still chuckling over our stupid name, so I fired up Word and blasted out a three-page music video script, or 'treatment', as they're known in the business.

My synopsis of it read:

This parody music video documents the rise of CVNT5 (pronounced 'Cunts'), an ultra-obnoxious, grotesque and talentless DJ duo who become the biggest DJs in the world, without even having to write a single note of their own music, thanks to a talented ghost producer. But eventually, the ghost producer has his revenge...

I sent that and the treatment to my sister and manager Roxanne, and she shot back:

> This is honestly one of the funniest things I have ever read. It's pure genius. One or two additional jokes and script tweaks but seriously I think this is there.

Although she'd never used it outside of a pub environment, Roxanne had an excellent brain for comedy. With a razor-sharp wit and natural taste for controversy, she immediately understood what CVNT5 represented, and the comedic potential behind the group. After a few long brainstorming sessions on the phone, the two of us had hashed out how CVNT5 first few projects would look, starting with the music video.

We soon managed to recruit a director. Tony Yacenda was recommended by a friend of mine. A few years later he would be blowing up thanks to his Netflix show 'American Vandal', but back then, Tony was strictly doing internet shorts. His work got huge view numbers, and he'd made some brilliant music videos for the comedy rapper Lil Dicky - he was definitely who I wanted.

Tony came over to my studio to read the script and give me his take. Having never met a comedy director before, for some reason I expected him to be a bag of laughs, so I was quite surprised to find him serious and softly-spoken. As he listened to my ideas, he never actually laughed, but a few times he nodded his head, saying "That's funny", which to me, seemed like the sort of thing you'd say politely when you didn't actually find something funny. I couldn't really get a read on Tony, but I was happy and surprised when he emailed me later to say that he was interested.

The problem was, Tony thought we needed cameos from big, well known personalities to increase our online reach, and I'd possibly oversold my ability to land them, telling him how easy it would be. After all, I knew every DJ in town. How hard could it be?

But I wasn't accounting for how controversial the material was, and an A-list DJ friend mailed me this in response to my request to have them join us:

> Mate, I fucking love the idea – laughing my arse off – you've actually taken a real problem in our industry and addressed it in a hilarious way – but I just can't do it. I don't want to offend anyone, and you know how vindictive some people can be. Good luck with it, I'll be watching…

Most DJs I knew responded the same way. Even Mat Zo, who's Twitter tirade had started the whole thing, didn't want to be in the video due to being extremely camera shy. The only person who *did* agree was Armin van Buuren, but then he'd gone off-radar and hadn't delivered his cameo after we'd sent him the actual script, so I had no idea if he was actually going to come through or not.

Realizing I'd need to cast the net a bit wider, I decided I was going to get the insta famous playboy Dan Bilzerian to be in the video: an idea that Tony loved.

Nicknamed the 'King of Instagram', Dan's social profile was off the charts, and I had a mutual friend who connected me with his agent. For a period of months, the agent and I went back and forth. Each time, our offers got higher, and each time, the agent dutifully responded with some variant of: "Dan loves it, but he's super busy. Just give me a day and I'm sure I can get this confirmed". This tiresome Hollywood routine dragged on and on. Locking Dan became my #1 priority because if we locked Dan, we'd lock Tony, and if we locked Tony, we'd have a video. By that point, my heart was set on Tony Yacenda, and if I needed Dan Bilzerian to make that happen, I'd get Dan Bilzerian.

We worked our bollocks off to make Dan's offer more and more tempting – with the eventual offer including, at their request, an appearance by me at one of his parties (which, to be fair, I had no issue with).

Then, just as we seemed to be about to get the final go-ahead, Dan pulled out.

Fuck.

With Dan gone, Armin off the radar, and no other decent ideas in-sight, the wind went out of our sails a little.

'Shall we look for some new cameos?' I asked the team, but nobody seemed interested in getting on the phone. Understandably, they were all a little deflated from our failure to land Dan, and knowing Tony wouldn't want to direct the project without at least one solid cameo, it seemed dead in the water. One sad morning, I archived my CVNT5 project file, and started to think about what came next. I was ready to give up.

Then: out of the blue, Armin's cameo landed, and it was brilliant: he'd taken the script, and absolutely nailed it. We HAD to use it. I sent it straight to Tony. Knowing he might waver without a Dan Bilzarian cameo, I piled on the hard sell.

> If you think there may be an issue shooting in January then we may be best to find other options but I 100000% want you to shoot this and although it's a big project my belief in it is bigger than ever - every single person I have told about fkn loves it and it would be a massive shame for us not to do it together!

Tony wrote back confirming that he was down. He'd later tell me that my email arrived as he was out for dinner, a few beers worse for wear, but regardless of his state at the time, he'd said yes.

We were going to shoot.

After we locked dates, things moved fast. With Bilzerian definitely out, we re-wrote the video, which actually led to a better script with an open-ended finish which left the door open for follow-up material. Then, over three very long days, we shot the video in Los Angeles and San Diego. Knowing we'd have some club scenes, we thought hard about how to get them right.

Nightclub scenes are notoriously difficult, and are usually terrible. To try and recreate a nightclub scene, you need background actors, or 'extras' to fill out the crowd. But with every background actor costing over $50 a day, having the sort of numbers that you'd typically get in a real club becomes prohibitively expensive: a real 1,000 crowd of extras would cost well over $50,000, which was north of our entire budget.

Now, being an actual DJ of some note, I had the advantage of being able to shoot at my own gigs, but filming in real, active nightclubs is tough. It's humid, dark, there's sweat dripping off the ceiling, and you have little control of the lights, because the entire production is geared towards giving the crowd a good time, not perfectly lighting a show for your cameras.

Fortunately, we were able to blend the two. I had a gig coming up at the Omnia nightclub in San Diego, one of the best clubs in the US, but close enough to LA for our crew to drive down. The afternoon of the show, we turned the nightclub into a closed set, bringing in lights and cameras, where Tony, with total control of lighting was able to spend hours shooting fantastically lit close-ups of Ash and I. Then, that night, we played the nightclub itself: a real gig. With a sold-out crowd of close to 1,000 through the door, we shot genuine, real footage of the packed crowd full-of-ravers, editing them together in post. It was some of the best, most realistic nightclub footage I'd ever seen in a music video.

For the duration of the CVNT5 project, I was determined that it had to feel real. Sure, our characters were fictitious, grotesque parodies, but I wanted the world they operated in to be entirely authentic. This quest for authenticity caused many arguments over the next few years with people who didn't see it the same way, but I was adamant, and even for this video I was obsessed with every detail, from photoshopping festival flyers (headlined by CVNT5, naturally) to making sure the ghost producer was in realistic clothing (a Moog t-shirt, in case you're wondering).

As we edited the video, adding more and more digital content that required hefty Photoshop or animation work, the budget stretched to north of $40,000, but I didn't care. I was excited and energized, and I believed in the product. Plus, the track was now going to feature on my upcoming album, '100 Reasons To Live' so the unveiling of CVNT5 was going to be a solid bit of a promo.

As I closed in on a final edit, Roxanne and our team worked around the clock to build an entire world around CVNT5 so when the music video dropped, there was a whole CVNT5 universe ready to dig into, for anyone who would look. Knowing that fans would likely Google 'CVNT5', a search term that didn't exist on the internet prior to this point, they created social media accounts, populating them with posts, as well as making sure CVNT5 had their own suitably garish website with a working management email. Anyone who mailed it – and there were quite a few people – received this brilliant auto-response:

> Thank you for your email regarding CVNT5. Due to the large number of emails we are receiving here is our FAQ.
>
> Can I book CVNT5 at my show / festival?
> Yes. Their fee is 5000USD per minute, non-negotiable.
>
> Can I sign a CVNT5 track to my record label?
> If you own Sony, Universal, or Warner, possibly.
>
> Can I interview the CVNT5 for my blog / TV show?
> No.
>
> I am a huge fan, can I please get some signed CVNT5 merchandise?
> No.
>
> KESEF GOLD
> MGMT@CVNT5.COM

On March 10th we dropped the music video. I'd spent all the previous night checking every detail, making sure the launch would be perfect. Having gone over every detail hundreds of times, there was little more for me to do, so the next day, I let the team handle the release, and went walking in the mountains. I didn't want to be sat in front of my computer watching every comment come in. Ultimately, we'd done what we could, and the video was either going to resonate, or it wasn't, so it was better for my mental health to disappear for the day, return once the video had been up a good five or six hours, then get a taste for how the day had gone.

As I returned to the car and turned my phone back on, the news was mostly good. A huge number of blogs had covered the launch and the industry was going nuts: the emails were pouring in. Unfortunately, the video wasn't really popping in terms of views. Those that were seeing it were going bonkers for it, but it wasn't going viral: meaning, we weren't reaching fans outside of the EDM community. That was disappointing, but if it was resonating with the right people, I could take some slightly-worse metrics.

A few weeks after that, the team and I flew to Miami for the annual Miami Music Week, a huge gathering of everyone in our industry, and CVNT5 were the talk of the town – literally everyone in the industry wanted to chat about what we'd created. It didn't matter that the view numbers on YouTube weren't great – the hype for our bastard love-child fake group was off the scale. On every corner, I was stopped by fans or industry who wanted to know what was next for the group. Later in the week, as I played a pool party at the SLS Hotel, we had the 'CVNT5' pop up for a fake stage invasion – and both Armin van Buuren and Michael Woods – who were in the venue at the time, decided to join in on the fun as well. As I looked out over the crowd and watched a slightly tipsy Armin – wearing a CVNT5 hat no less – spraying the crowd with champagne, I realized we'd created something powerful. It didn't take itself too seriously, and that sense of fun made it something that a lot of people wanted to be a part of.

But that didn't mean that everyone saw it that way.

My most awkward moment of the week came on the flight home. Exhausted after staying up all-night, and ready to get back to my family, I was slumped in my business-class window seat with an empty seat next to me. The flight from Miami to LA the Monday after Miami Music Week is typically packed with DJs, so it was inevitable I'd end up having to face people I knew, and I was in no state for that, so I hoped the seat next to me would remain empty.

Then, moments before pushback, Chris 'Chronicles' – a member of DVBBS – appeared in front of me. He took one look at the seat next to me, then turned and walked back the way he'd came, presumably to ask the cabin crew if he could change his seat. However, the flight was full, so a few minutes later he was back – and we'd be sitting next to each other for the next six hours.

A lot of people had speculated the style of CVNT5 had been influenced by DVBBS, and if I'm honest, it had. But that was no bad thing. Personally, I loved their dress sense, and getting to wear those sorts of outrageous clothes – admittedly for a parody project – had been great fun. On the darker side, they'd taken a lot of heat for allegedly using ghost producers, particularly the previous year, where blogs had reported that they'd paid 30,000 euros for two tracks from an accomplished European ghost producer called Maarten Vorwerk. I didn't know whether it was true, and frankly, I didn't give a shit. CVNT5 wasn't about proving anyone wrong, or asserting moral superiority, but instead about relentlessly taking the piss out of an industry that was obsessively self-serious. So what if they used ghost producers? Good for them.

Chris, potentially, didn't see it that way.

We struck up an incredibly awkward conversation.

"Good to see you again mate – it's Gareth Emery, in case you didn't remember..." I started.

"Of course I know who you are," he replied rather mechanically.

I pressed on.

"So, uh, good week? Been up all night myself, rather worse for wear".

"Yeah, it was OK. I've been up late myself."

"Still, I suppose they're the name of the game in our business aren't they… late nights?"

"Yeah, they are."

Jesus. This conversation was killing me. A fan sat behind would have been incredulous. *I once sat behind Gareth Emery and Chris from DVBBS on a plane and they had literally the most boring conversation ever.*

After twenty more minutes of excruciatingly awkward chat, I couldn't take it any longer. Given that throwing myself out of the emergency exit door wasn't an option, I decided it was time to bring up the elephant in the room.

"Look. Mate. So, about the music video…"

Once I'd broached the subject, we were able to have a proper conversation. He'd seen the video – of course he had, and he was genuinely hurt by what he saw as us laughing about his group. I felt a bit mean, if I'm honest. Comedy's fine, until you come face-to-face with your victims, and whilst I stood behind our video, it's never nice to know you've hurt the feelings of another human being who's done absolutely nothing to you. Also, being British, piss taking and banter is a part of our DNA, and it's easy to forget that not every nation sees it in the light that it was intended.

Once I could explain our side of it all to Chris, he warmed up a bit, and we had a pretty good chat in the end.

"To be honest, I first heard about the video the night before it came out", he admitted. "Carnage sent me a text saying that you were about to release a new video where you were tearing us apart, so before I'd even seen it, I was upset".

Carnage, that shit-stirrer.

As we landed in LA, I said farewell to Chris, and headed to the taxi-rank:

where I came face-to-face with his brother – the other member of DVBBS – Alex 'Andre'.

For fucks sake, I thought. Was I about to need to explain the whole fucking thing again? Why couldn't the brothers have been sitting together on the plane?

Turned out though, that Alex's take was totally different.

"Fucking loved the music video bro, pure class. So well produced. Reminds me of a SNL sketch. Seriously well done."

"I've just sat next to your brother on the flight.' I replied. 'Not sure he liked it as much…"

"Ah, fuck that. Chris gets a little sensitive, but he'll be fine. You guys killed it".

Alex and I shared a taxi back to West Hollywood where we both lived, and we had a great chat. He was much more light-hearted about the whole thing, and I felt a bit less guilty for how badly his brother had taken it. As the taxi dropped me off at my house, he clocked the car on the drive, as well as my ancient phone. I'd lost my iPhone during Miami, so was using a much older iPhone as a backup, and it made way for a cheeky diss:

"Brand new Rolls Royce Wraith on the drive, and an iPhone 5 in his hand. You're a man of contradictions, that's for sure".

Alex was actually pretty funny, I thought. I wondered if we could use him in a future video.

As soon as I got back from Miami, we started thinking about how a second CVNT5 piece could look. This time, I didn't want to do a music video: I wanted to do an actual comedy sketch. I downloaded the Final Draft app, used by most Hollywood screenwriters, and knowing it would be hard to accomplish with Roxanne and I alone, I drafted in a few cohorts.

Geraint 'Gez' Jones was a former raving mate of mine, but after leaving the army, he'd become a proper author who had hit the New York Times bestseller list. And, although he was very funny, his own novels were historical Roman fiction, so he jumped at the opportunity to work on something purely comedic.

And finally, Alex Madden joined the team. Alex was a Las Vegas based DJ and music industry type, who'd worked as my tour manager on a few occasions in the past. He was unlikely to match Gez in terms of writing firepower, but we'd fucked around acting out a few scenes in hotel rooms, and I could tell he was an absolutely brilliant actor – far better than me. As well as being very funny, Alex's acting had a certain sadness to it, somewhat like one of my favorite television characters of all time – Tim Canterbury from The Office (Jim Halpert in the US version). Feeling that Alex, as a bumbling, incompetent but well-meaning manager could be the perfect tonic to the unhinged narcissist I was portraying, I decided to bring him in.

With our new writing team of me, Roxanne, Gez and Alex, we put together a 10-minute documentary-style 'short', this time taking aim at DJ Mag's infamously corrupt 'Top 100 Poll'. Again, I saw it as an opportunity to pull back the curtain from some of our industry's darkest secrets.

To that end, we had CVNT5 'visit Vietnam' where they built a 'click-farm': a room full of people voting for them all day long, so they could hopefully capture DJ Mag's prestigious 'Number One DJ In The World' award. In the end (spoiler alert), despite their click farm, they only ended up ranking at #2, as another act had bribed DJ Mag's Editor In Chief.

We dropped the video on the eve of DJ Mag's poll results, and once again, shook the industry to its core. Fans, on the other hand, couldn't believe that it wasn't all fantasy.

What a crazy video, wrote one. *Can you imagine if this was how corrupt DJ Mag's actual poll really is?*

I read it and laughed, shaking my head. In the same video, we'd also taken a truly juvenile shot at Marshmello – something that I'm not especially proud of – and his manager had responded furiously in an email to Roxanne.

If I'm honest, I slightly regretted the video. Making people laugh was one thing, as was ripping into DJ Mag's sham of a poll, but Marshmello hadn't done a thing to me, and I wondered if we had crossed the line. It had also showed some of the risks in running British-style comedy in America: not everyone was as easy-going as Alex from DVBBS, and whilst I had no professional connections with either Marshmello or his manager, I didn't especially want to make enemies unnecessarily, either.

The one good thing that came out of the 2nd video was that there now was some real interest from serious companies about giving us money to make something longer. A few months back, I'd suggested to my agents – WME – that perhaps CVNT5 could be turned into some sort of TV show, and they hadn't shown much interest. However, shortly after that, a rival agency called UTA reached out about representing CVNT5 in the TV world, and once they knew that someone else was interested, WME suddenly decided they liked the idea, against their initial judgment. It turns out that the basic human desire of wanting what we can't have applies to juggernaut Hollywood agencies as well.

We wrote a 'Bible' to pitch the show to the various networks, and it was as shocking and outrageous as everything else about CVNT5 had been so far. In TV land, a 'bible' is a master document for a planned TV show. It lays out the main characters, storylines, and an episode-by-episode guide of what'll happen. It's an invaluable document to sell your show to a network. By now, we had our pitch down. The first page of it stated that:

```
CVNT5 is an eight-episode show shot in
a mockumentary style that chronicles the
```

> antics of electronic music supergroup CVNT5, fronted by Englishman Brandon Bass (Gareth Emery).
>
> CVNT5 is a fish out of water story in many ways. What happens when basement dwelling geeks go from an audience of a cat to 100,000 strong crowds at the world's biggest music festivals?
>
> What happens when the guy who was a virgin at eighteen is sent so many DMs from naked hotties that his Snapchat crashes?
>
> What happens when you take young men with bruised egos and big dreams, and pour millions of dollars into their bank accounts and millions of likes onto their posts?
>
> Well, they become CVNT5.

I had particular fun writing biographies for each of our team. For Gez, a former British soldier, I started his biography like this.

> **Geraint Jones.** Before becoming a writer, Geraint was a soldier. He travelled the world, saw fascinating countries, met hundreds of culturally varied and interesting people... and killed them.

Alex also took a beating.

> **Alex Madden.** Last, and most certainly least, we have Alex Madden. As much of a whipping-boy in real life as his character

```
James is on the show, Alex is fantastic at
writing and playing any character, as long
as that character is a slightly chubby
failed DJ from the East End of London.
```

Armed with our bible, WME had put the word out that we were looking to make a series, and the most interested contender was Verizon, the massive mobile network. At the time, they had just launched a new TV platform called Go90: their own version of Netflix, but primarily designed to be watched on phones. They were dropping serious money programming original shows, and after a few months of flirting, a formal offer arrived.

Verizon Go90, via their sub-network Complex, were willing to offer us just shy of $2.5 million dollars to make an 8 episode TV show.

Fuck. Although most of the money would go on production, I'd get a fair fee per episode (about the same as I'd make in an average night of DJing) as well as being an executive producer, whatever that really meant.

It was at this point that I made an error that would prove to be quite costly. Out of all of the bits of advice that I've given in this book, this one is important. So fucking important in fact that I'm going write it on its own paragraph, underlined for emphasis.

<u>Whenever you 'make something' with other people – be it a TV show, book, company, restaurant, or ANY sort of business or collaborative project – **agree exactly who owns what as early as you possibly can**. Who makes the decisions? Who owns the shares? What happens if you all fall out with each other? Be very fucking clear who's getting paid what, and how you divide up the pie if it all goes tits up.</u>

You might think this will be an awkward conversation, especially if you're in business with friends or family. And you're right. It's not going to be easy, but trust me, it will be much harder years down the line when there's real money involved (which is usually the aim in these sort of things). So do your future self a favor and bite the fucking bullet. Have the hard conversation early. Write down what you're agreeing to, and have all the parties sign off on it. If you're short on cash, it doesn't need to be done properly by a lawyer – just an email that you all reply to staying 'I agree' is much better than nothing. But get it done.

I did not do this, and it came back to bite me. *Hard.*

After over six months of legal wrangling with Verizon and their partners, we got to a point where the deal wasn't signed, but it was close enough that I was given the green light to find a production company. This was where I began to learn how different TV is from music. In music, even when signed to a record label, I was used to a reasonable level of independence. Nobody really told me what my music should sound like, and I was more-or-less free to have creative reign when it came to music videos and associated media.

I was about to discover that TV, by comparison, is a bureaucratic nightmare. This is to be expected, given that you need to hire a small army to create your product, but I was soon to discover that even though I was technically in charge, many other people would be having a say in how the show was put together, and we didn't always agree. Every major decision would have to be run through me, the production company, and the network – all with an army of lawyers and administrators ready to question any decision for licensing, financial, legal, artistic, or political reasons. Getting anything done was going to be very fucking difficult.

However, I didn't know any of this yet, so it was time to choose a production company, and being a complete novice in TV, I had very little idea how the interplay between network and production company worked. Our show had been commissioned by Verizon for their Go90 network, but this had been done via the media company Complex, who were technically our network. I'd met Justin Killion, who headed up operations over there, and he was a great dude: definitely someone I could work with. However, Complex would now need to bring in a production company. Once I'd chosen a production company, Complex would be stepping back to allow our new producers to do almost all of the heavy lifting, so it was an important choice. Soon, they'd sent me a shortlist, and I started shopping.

My first meeting was the one I was most excited about: Avalon. They had a great list of credits, including John Oliver's Last Week Tonight, a hugely successful comedy/news show, but from the moment I walked in the door, the vibe was off. The producer who I was meeting with immediately launched into a fairly passive-aggressive line of questioning: strange, I thought, given this company was supposed to be pitching for our business.

"So you're from the music industry, but you're getting into TV. Why? Do you think there's more money in television? Because, let me tell you: there isn't" was his contemptuous opening gambit.

I laughed it off, and continued to tell them where my head was at. Naturally, I'm self-deprecating – a typically British trait – and even though I'd just landed a $2.5m budget TV show, I played down my own talents.

"To be honest, I don't know much about TV but I'm excited to make the show," I told them. "I think we can deliver something really amazing here, although as you can imagine, I was surprised to be given this much money to make a show".

"I'm surprised, too", Dan replied. "But that's TV these days. Real writers can't catch a break, yet the networks will throw money at 'influencers' who haven't got a clue what they're doing, to be honest".

Influencers like me, I wondered? I didn't know whether I'd just caught him on a bad day, or whether he genuinely resented the fact Verizon were handing us cash. Either way, there was little good energy or positivity in the entire meeting, so I moved on.

Every other production company was more friendly, and all seemed to have a decent reason why they should produce the show. The problem was, my radar was off. In music, after 15 years of having companies pitch for our business, I have a good radar: I can catch a vibe of who really believes in the project, and who's bullshitting. In TV, I just couldn't tell. I didn't know the telltale signs, the giveaways, and with hindsight, I should have brought someone who knew a bit more about TV than me along.

Eventually, one New York based company – Acres – sent me a glossy, well-written ten-page pitch document that nudged them ahead of the pack.

> *In my experience working in the writers' room on Entourage — along with working on Jimmy Kimmel and Ugly Betty — I got to see how comedic television is made at the highest level. With the right team around you, there's no reason CVNT5 can't evolve into a great series. We think, if given the opportunity, Acres can put you and your team in a position for success.*

Sounds good. And they seemed to get the characters.

> *We need to see Brandon and Chad get undercut badly, again and again, so that no matter how absurdly they behave we maintain the audience's sincere love for them. In essence, they need to be the cunts we love, the douchebags that still somehow give us the warm-and-fuzzies regardless of their behavior. Even if their ultimate goal is really just to be rich and famous for the sake of being rich and famous, the viewer will care about them because we've set them up to be more complex characters than even they're aware of themselves.*

It's a glossy document filled with imagery from many of my favorite shows and films: The Office, People Just Do Nothing, Peep Show, Ali G, Spinal Tap. It ends with a picture of Paul Kaye as Frankie Wilde, the protagonist from 'It's All Gone Pete Tong' pulling a Jesus pose.

'These guys get it.' I thought to myself.

I decided, based off this one glossy sales piece, that I wanted Acres, but Justin over at Complex wasn't too sure. Sitting in his Los Angeles office, he gently questioned me.

"I get that you like them, but these guys are based out in New York, and they've never really done anything on this scale before..."

"I know, Justin, but these are the guys. I'm sure of it."

"OK, then. You're the boss..."

We hire Acres, and soon enough, I'm not the boss any more. I soon realize that as a show creator, when you hire a production company and director, you're essentially *hiring your own boss,* which is fucking madness. One minute someone is pitching for your business, the next, they're locked in contractually, you can't fire them, and they're entrusted with spending the money, and telling you what you can and can't do. *Bonkers.*

Acres – who now seemed to be in charge – rented a plush Hollywood Hills mansion for us to attend a 'writing camp', where we'd take our skeleton ideas and flesh them out into full, scripted episodes.

And so, in November of 2016, we rolled up at a hillside house, high over Hollywood, with sweeping views over the whole of the LA basin. The road was called Grand View Drive, and it was aptly named: due to the amount of hills, Los Angeles is a good city for views, but Grand View Drive really was exceptional, with a stunning night-time vista of millions of twinkling city lights from Downtown LA to the Pacific Ocean. God knows how much the place was costing – but with millions of dollars of network money to spend, Acres weren't going to be slumming it, accommodations wise.

Soon, our small team arrived at the house, and the writing began. On my side, I was joined by Roxanne, Alex, and Gez. From Acres, we were joined by Harrison and Adam - two writer / producers who we hoped would have the knowledge and experience to guide us to where we needed to go.

Things started out well enough. Before long, Harrison and Adam had huge whiteboards up, and we brainstormed all manner of ideas. We dug into the plotlines and crafted a season 'arc'. We thought long and hard about the characters: where they'd come from, what their goals, dreams, and aspirations were, and I was quickly realizing this was going to be more difficult than I thought, particularly when it came to structure. As well as a 'main story arc' that would progress through the eight episodes, each episode would need its own self-contained story arc, *plus* a few sub-plot lines specific to that episode too. Fortunately, everyone else was better at this than me, and soon we had the rough shape of a season down.

Even in the first few days, it was clear that Harrison had strong opinions, which overflowed during a conversation about race, as he shot down a proposed Gez storyline.

"Ah, hang on. No, that story makes no sense. As a white man, you can't experience racism. That's not possible".

"Eh?" Gez replied. "Surely, racism is any sort of discrimination based on race?"

"That's where you're wrong". Harrison replied. "Racism is the subjugation of a race. As a white man, you've never been subjugated, therefore: it's not possible for you to experience racism".

We pondered for a moment.

"What about this," Gez pipes up. "What happens if Alex here, goes for a walk later tonight, and a bunch of – let's say – Indian kids decide to beat the shit out of him whilst calling him a fat white fuck. Would that be racist?"

"No, not racist!" Harrison persists.

"What would it be then?" I ask.

"That would be an, er… *an unfortunate incident*".

Silence.

Alex then pipes up.

"Firstly, I don't think it's likely some kids could beat me up, and secondly, they probably wouldn't call me fat".

"They could, and they would", Roxanne replies, and on that, everyone agrees. We ignore Alex's protestations and move on.

Soon after that, we hit the first real bumps in the road.

"Alright, so we've got rough plotlines for all eight episodes,' Harrison told us, 'so it's time to team off and write them. Let's split into three groups of two."

"I'll write with Gez", Alex piped up. This made sense: he was the shittest writer out of all us, so his best hope of leveling up his own meager skillset was to shotgun the best writer in the room. Gez shrugged.

"Fine with me. Although I don't really need him."

"Great." Harrison continued. "So, Gareth and Roxanne will write together, as will Adam and I…"

"Hang on…" I interjected. "You guys are the experienced ones, you've done this shit before. Rox and I are total newbies at this. Wouldn't it make sense to pair one of you with one of us?"

"Ah yeah, the thing is, Adam and I have been writing together for over 10 years. We've really got a flow, you know. Our methods are pretty locked in. Best if we stick together, as do you, and we'll tidy up your work later".

This didn't feel within the collaborative spirit of the writing camp, but I agreed anyway. Next up, it was time to allocate episode numbers, and again, Harrison had a plan. This time, I didn't even get an opinion: instead, after coming back from taking a piss, it all seemed to be decided.

"So, Adam and I will take Episode 1, and Episode 8… we feel those are where we can best add value. Gez and Alex want to do 5 and 6, so you and Roxanne can choose out of what's left".

The two other groups drifted off to start writing, leaving Rox and I. Frowning slightly, I chew on my pen, and mull over what's just happened.

"Does this seem a bit… off… to you?" I venture.

"How do you mean?" she replies.

"Well, this is our fucking show. We're supposed to be the writers. Yet these two, who are meant to be here to help us, appear to have grabbed the pilot and the finale – the two most important episodes – leaving us with the sloppy seconds?"

"God, you're right." She thinks for a moment. "Fuck it. Let's not have any negativity this early. Everyone can write their episodes, and we'll figure it out".

A few hours later, and we're about half-way done with our episode. I go inside to make a coffee, and find Alex lounging on the sofa watching football, sipping on an ice-cold Corona.

"Er, what the fuck are you doing?" I ask.

"We're finished mate!" he chortles, delighted. "Gez is on the phone to his bird, so I'm just chilling here. Nothing else to do until the team read!"

I grit my teeth. *It had better be fucking brilliant*, I think.

A few hours later, Roxanne and I finish our episode too. The next step is to print off all three episodes, but we have a problem: the professionals still haven't finished, and aren't anywhere close.

"How much longer until you're ready?" I ask, sticking my head around the door.

Another hour or so, comes the answer.

And now, I wonder if *we* were too fast.

For a moment, I feel like I'm back in school again. During exams, I'd often see a question was an easy one, and I'd blast through it, done and dusted, thank you, piece of piss. Then, on popping my pen down, I'd look over and notice a classmate frantically scribbling away. Minutes and minutes go by. *Why the fuck is she still writing when I've finished ages ago? Was it a trick question? Does she know something I don't? Did I miss something really important?* So I'd frantically go back over my work, looking for what I'd missed, but invariably, I hadn't. The question was indeed easy, and some people just aren't that bright.

Hours later, the professionals have finished, and Adam has made a FedEx trip whilst the rest of us scoffed sushi. Then, it's time to read our scripts.

Roxanne and I go first, and our script is... *solid.* We get a few laughs from Gez and Alex. Harrison and Adam give little away. We've definitely nailed the emotional tone: the characters feel developed and three-dimensional, but it's clear when reading the whole thing out loud that some of the conversations go on way too long, and the structure is a bit linear. Still, a solid start. First test, passed.

Next up, Gez and Alex's script. They finished theirs extremely quickly, so I'm not sure what to except, but it is *fucking brilliant*. It's a masterclass in structure and flow. The whole thing slots together like a Swiss watch, allowing the various intertwined plotlines to unfold at a rapid pace. The characters are brilliantly acted by Alex, and we're all laughing out loud numerous times.

I'm fucking glad we went first, because following this would not have been easy.

Finally, it's Harrison and Adam's turn, and their script is... *something.*

The structure's solid, but something's missing. The writing is perfectly competent, grammatically fine, and compared to Rox and my script, it's probably more professional. But it's soulless. Robotic. And that's not a surprise. These were our characters, our creations: born out of years in the dance music industry – is it any surprise that people from outside our world couldn't deliver them in an authentic way? I get ready to deliver this bombshell, but then...

"Great script!" Alex pipes up. "Let's do the next one!"

I desperately look at Gez and Rox to see if they feel the same, but it's too late.

"Cool" responds Harrison. "On to the next!"

A few days like this go by, until I'm sat outside on my own, and Roxanne comes out.

"Gaz, can I talk to you?"

"Sure."

"What do you think of Adam and Harrison's scripts?' She says. 'I mean, what do you *really* think about them?"

It all comes out.

"Honestly? I hate them. This is our thing, our show, our characters… and they're being written by people that don't know us, and that don't know the characters, and they're not from the world of dance music so the scripts have no relation to how people actually act in our world. Plus, they're not funny, and they've lost all the British vibe. This was a pure British style comedy, and it's turned into a bad American sitcom, dumbed down for the masses".

Rox nodded. "I feel exactly the same."

"What?" I don't believe it. "Fuck! Really? I thought I was the only one…"

I'm not.

"Yep," Roxanne confirms. "And Gez feels the same way too." *Fuck.*

I'm not a naturally a confrontational person, and I hate rocking the boat. However, after nearly two decades in the music industry, I've realized that it's a necessary evil. Of course, you choose your battles: nobody wants to work with someone who's always kicking off. But, when your art is at stake, you need to saddle up and have tough conversations, so I request an audience with Harrison, and we both sit down outside.

"Listen, mate. No offence. Don't take this the wrong way. But at the end of the day..."

Jesus, Gaz, enough with the banal platitudes. Just say it.

"... I don't think the stuff you and Adam are writing is working. I mean it's good, surely, but it's not *my* sort of good. And, you know, this is kind of my show, so it has to be my sort of good, you know..."

Crazy, really, that I have to explain why my show should be something I like, but here we are.

"... and whilst I think the show you're writing would do great, this show is super personal to me, and it's vital that it feels authentic to my own life, my own experiences, and what you're writing doesn't do that. I'm sorry".

Up until now, Harrison's been the person in charge at this writing camp, and any attempts by me to change direction have been shot down in seconds, so this feels like a full-scale rebellion. I'm now about to see how much influence I really have here. For all I know, he might shut the whole thing down, cancel the show, or worse, tell me I'm fired and continue without me (*can he fire me? Shit! I should have checked if he could!*).

But instead, I get an apology of sorts, admittedly veiled in typical corporate media-American therapist-speak.

"I'm sorry I made you feel that way. It certainly wasn't my intention. This is your show, and it's got to represent your experiences, and my role here is to make sure that happens, so let's talk about how we can fix this".

Well that was easy! We're back in fucking charge. *We got this.*

After usurping the usurpers, the rest of the writing camp passes uneventfully, if awkwardly, and if I'm honest, I don't really blame Harrison and Adam. They'd been writing scripts for over a decade together without any real bites, as far as I could tell. To see that we'd been handed our own show off a music video no less, with no real idea of what we were doing must have been galling, and whilst it wouldn't have been my approach, I understand why taking over must have seemed an interesting opportunity.

On returning home, I review the scripts. There's some solid stuff there, but given I plan on binning almost everything that Adam and Harrison wrote, there's a lot more work to be done.

Christmas comes and goes, and as we enter the new year, I throw myself into the writing process. Kicking Harrison and Adam off the writing team might have been necessary, but it now means the task of delivering eight completed scripts - nearly 200 pages - is entirely on my team. There's an awful lot of work to be done, and much of it falls on me. Alex is more of an actor than a writer. Roxanne and Gez, whilst both brilliant in their own ways, are both spread across multiple projects and are working in a different time-zone.

And so I throw myself into the process. It's now my full-time job.

One thing that life has taught me many times is that if you practice something really fucking intensely you'll make great strides, very quickly. As the first quarter of the year tends to be fairly quiet for dance music, I have plenty of time to sharpen my craft as a writer, and I ferociously attack the process. I read numerous books on screenwriting, along with interviews of some of my favorite writers. I consume the blog of screenwriter John August daily, and listen to podcasts by Billions writer Brian Koppelman. I download scripts for some of my favorite shows, and watch them, script-in-hand, trying to reverse-engineer the process as best I can.

Most importantly, I write, every single day.

And soon, I improve.

Before long, my new enthusiasm for writing spreads to the rest of the team, and both Gez and Rox are working on the show daily too. Scripts fly back and forth every morning, and each day I wake up excited to see what the pair of them have written whilst I was sleeping.

Soon, we have a show.

Eight episodes.

And it's good. *Very good.*

Realizing that the show's really quite special, I start to get cold feet about our deal. My gut instinct tells me it's a bad idea to go forward. Currently, our main deal with Go90 still isn't signed, so if I wanted to back out and take the show elsewhere, I could, and I start having second thoughts.

Whilst I appreciate their faith in us, Go90 had signed the show off the back of a music video – a skit - but it's now turned into something far bigger, better, and with more potential. I truly believe that what we've written could be a brilliant show that could run for years: are we screwing ourselves by releasing on a brand-new platform? Plus, things have been very awkward with Harrison since the writing camp: do I want to have to work with him for another six months, after he'd essentially tried to take over our show and failed? I'm no military expert, but there's a reason why the generals of failed *coup d'états* aren't usually offered jobs in the victorious government.

In fact, during the six months in which we were going back and forth with Go90, Tony Yacenda – our original CVNT5 director – had written, pitched, sold, and wrapped a show for Netflix, which would be released in the summer. I have a catch up with Tony, and it sounds like Netflix work fast, support program creators, and have huge numbers of viewers. Am I missing a trick by not even pitching the show there?

Plus, horrible rumors about Go90 are swirling around. If the news articles are true, the network's hemorrhaging money, hardly attracting any viewers, and might be cancelled at any time. Now we've written the show, do I want to spend the next six months working my arse off on something nobody might end up seeing? I look to see what shows are currently playing on Go90. The top shows seem to be one about social media called 'T@gged', and an action show by YouTube star Hayes Grier called 'Top Grier'. Not the ideal material to be sharing a platform with.

On the other hand, we wouldn't have written the thing in the first place without their belief and support, so perhaps I owe them the show, based upon that? One of our team optimistically suggests that we can be the show that turns their fortunes around. There are arguments on both sides.

I call Joel Zimmerman, head of electronic music at WME, and ask for his advice.

"So let me get this straight… you wrote the script based on a Go90 deal, but that deal isn't yet signed, and you think you might be selling the show short?".

"Exactly".

Joel offers to help me sell the show elsewhere, and promises to put me in touch with the WME TV department, so I shoot him a few scripts and our show bible so he can he send it around for feedback. However, the weeks tick by, and I hear nothing back, with my follow-up emails ignored.

With Joel MIA, the pressure starts to build. Alexandra, my agent at WME who set the show up, puts serious pressure on me to do the deal. Her motives are entirely transparent: it's obvious that she wants the deal done for *her* standing within WME rather than my career – a good agent would have framed the benefits to me – but the constant pressure does affect me. Plus, our own Alex is desperate to do a deal, and piles on the pressure too. Eventually, Alexandra tells me that by pulling out, even though we haven't signed a deal, I'd be risking lawsuits. I write to my current lawyer:

> I am moving towards just getting this deal done.
>
> Got a few other ideas for shows which we could sell the regular way with none of the drama required from backpedaling on this one.

Soon enough, the pressure gets too great, and I settle. Telling myself *it just wasn't meant to be* (a very well-used phrase by anyone abandoning their ambitions), I forget my dreams of Netflix and HBO, and just sign the fucking Go90 deal. It'll do.

With a signed deal in place, everyone celebrates, but I'm not quite feeling it. I'm glad to have a deal done, but something felt wrong, as it indeed should have done.

I'd just made one of the biggest professional mistakes of my entire life.

Telling the full story of the three months we spent shooting WeAreCVNT5 would likely be a book in itself, so as much as I'd love to write about the many wonderful people who helped us make the show, it will have to wait for another time. Suffice to say, it was one of the most intensive experiences of my life. We laughed. We cried. We occasionally cried with laughter. We pulled 18-hour days on set. Every day seemed to bring the most intense challenges: not only creative challenges, of trying to make the show I wanted, but challenges of holding my own team together.

By failing to clearly set out the ownership of our show months previously, I'd established the fault lines for a future earthquake – and that happened on set, as our own small team fell apart over disagreements about who owned the show and who should be paid what. Points of contention which likely could have been resolved easily enough during normal times became weaponised in the pressure-cooker environment of a TV set with over 50 people working on it. Professional and personal relationships fell apart as a result. Having come so far together, it was a heartbreaking way for CVNT5 to end, but I kept my head down, and finished the show. I didn't know what else to do.

But after three months of filming and another six months of post-production work, we had a show. In many ways, it felt like a pyrrhic victory. Roxanne and I had ended our management relationship during the show, so when I got my head back into the music business, I was going to need to find new management and re-build some sort of team around me. It was fair to say my music career was in a bit of a mess.

But, on the upside, the show was good. Really fucking good.

'WeAreCVNT5' finally premiered in June 2018, and despite Go90 being on life support, the reactions were good, and the show seemed to be gaining popularity with the right sort of names. Mark Gillespie, manager of Calvin Harris and one of my oldest friends in the industry shot me a text: *Your show is brilliant! Can definitely gain a cult following. We should see if we could pick it up for a bigger platform.* The Daily Beast website declared: *'We Are CVNT5' Is a Bonkers, Must-See EDM Mockumentary*', concluding the following:

> ...Chad may be a vacuous playboy, James an amateurish pushover, and Brandon a vain neurotic, but deep down, they're all good guys, and as a team, it's hard not to root for them. Though currently housed in LA mansions, the three men all hail from small towns in Britain, and the utter earnestness that derives from these humble origins—no matter how much they try and hide it—is endearing.
>
> It's difficult to tell whether they have any actual talent—"Those that can do, do. Those that can't, blog," Brandon yells at a roomful of music critics in one scene—but by the end, it hardly matters. We're not here to moralize. "Have I learned anything from this experience?" Brandon ponders, seemingly sincerely, after a major flub. "No," he decides. We haven't either, but a light laugh is more than enough.

It's all going well.

Then, just weeks after the show launches, a distraught Alex sends me a Deadline article confirming my worst fears: **Verizon Pulls The Plug On Go90 Video App**.

Go90 disappears with immediate effect, and with it, so does our show, never to return. I relentlessly hustle Complex to find a new home for the show, but my fears from over 18 months ago are well and truly confirmed. Hundreds of Go90 shows are looking for new homes, and rather than us being able to pitch CVNT5 in earnest, it's being sold in a fire-sale alongside the rest of Go90's utterly shite catalog.

Anyone want to buy Go90's sloppy seconds? Including Top Grier, T@gged, and WeAreCVNT5?

Obviously not.

Complex tell us that nobody's interested, and that's that.

And at the time of writing – June 2020 – the show has never returned, and frankly, I doubt it ever will. I chased up every angle, from trying to find direct contacts at Netflix etc., to offering to buy back the show myself to run it on my YouTube. By this point of course, any expectations of CVNT5 repaying its investment to me were long gone – and to be honest, I was done with making TV for a long time. But, I wanted the show out there for everyone who had worked so fucking hard on it. We had actors who thought the show was their big break, including Alex, who was genuinely brilliant on-screen, and the fact it hadn't even seen the light of day broke my heart.

But, now, I accept that it's done. CVNT5 was a product of its time. When we started writing the show, Barack Obama was president, and the United Kingdom was still in the European Union, and whilst the world was far from perfect, it felt like a time when you could still have a laugh. And our show was brutal. Nobody escaped our comedic wrath, and whilst it worked at the time, I'm not sure how it would fare in the hyper-sensitive environment of 2020. The world feels more divided than ever, and with an angry internet mob ready to 'cancel' people, often for tiny slights, in a way I'm almost glad we never made it to air. We would have made a lot of people laugh, but there are many people looking to be offended in 2020, and you can be sure they would have found that offence in us. In a way, whilst I'm gutted our amazing art never saw the light of day, I'm glad not to have been a lightning rod for all that.

In many ways, the whole thing felt like one extended midlife crisis. Did I really plan on giving up music for acting, when I'm clearly a lot better at music? My only conclusion is that it was a period where I wasn't particularly inspired by the world of electronic music, so putting together a TV show that made fun of that world was my response: and as that show gained a life of its own, it ended up taking up far more of my life than I had ever anticipated.

It was time to go back to music. With CVNT5 completed, I could finally move on with my life and in my work - often the same thing - but there was one issue.

I no longer had any songs.

Our break-up has forced mine and Roxanne's mutual contacts to take sides, and naturally, almost all of the songwriters are on hers. The 'Saving Light' team get back together – all five other writers apart from me – to work on a follow up as a Standerwick solo record, and whilst it doesn't quite manage the heights of 'Saving Light', it's better than anything I've done in years.

A few months later I release my own comeback single, my first release of the post-Roxanne era. 'Call To Arms' is a song that felt like it had real potential: co-written by Snow Patrol, defiant themes, great vocalist. However, our big-budget $20,000 music video languishes on a few hundred thousand views, and the record fails to make it out of the underground.

Yep, I definitely have a songs problem.

My experience with WeAreCVNT5 has shown me that TV isn't where I want to be. Music was my thing, but without Roxanne, I had no idea where the good songs would come from. We solicited a few toplines, and everything we received was distinctly average. That was no surprise. Topline writing teams save their best efforts for the most commercially viable acts: Guetta, Garrix, Snake. I was getting C or B list vocals at best.

Then, the embryo of an idea formed in my mind.

I'd written songs. Admittedly, a long time ago - and I never wrote lyrics - but I used to be able to write songs. Could I do it again?

I booked a songwriting session with Emma Hewitt in Los Angeles. Emma's not only one of the best vocalists in electronic music, but a truly lovely person too. If what I contributed was shit, she'd tell me in a way that would spare my feelings. Writing with her felt safe and, so far out of my comfort zone, safe was what I needed to feel.

Emma showed up at the studio, and on the first day we wrote the vocal melodies to 'Take Everything'. We didn't have lyrics yet, but I'd had some melodies floating around my head for a while which worked pretty well. Emma sung along in tongues – nonsense speak – placeholder stuff until we wrote actual lyrics.

That night, whilst Emma was back at her hotel, I had some lyric ideas. I'd never written a single lyric in my life, and I was convinced what I'd written was terrible, but I had an idea for the song: a defiant message to the world that I was still fucking standing after the Roxanne battles. Using as much language as possible to talk down what I'd written, I sent an email to Emma.

---------- Forwarded message ---------
From: **Gareth Emery**
Date: Tue, Oct 10, 2017 at 6:12 PM
Subject: lyrics and shit
To: Emma Hewitt

Very literal, and I am shit at lyrics, just a load of lines in my head to the vague theme, but could be useful for mood board etc.

CHORUS:

so go ahead and take everything
when it's over i'll still be standing
because i was here from the start
you've won but you've still lost my heart

Emma writes back:

"So your lyrics are bloody awesome and fit super well, I just worked on some revisions to make the singing flow... let me know your thoughts on below."

What the actual fuck? Emma – a proper, accomplished songwriter - likes my lyrics? Shit.

We finish Take Everything using 80% of my lyrics, I produce the song, and we throw it out… and amazingly, nobody comments on my cringeworthy, newbie lyrics, and instead people just seem to enjoy the song. It's not my biggest hit, not by a long way, but it's also not a total bust, and I'm feeling empowered.

Inspired, I decide to throw myself into songwriting; are you noticing a theme here? I start to learn about the craft, read some books, and listen to interviews with accomplished songwriters. I start to realize that - rather than the mystical dark art I've believed it to be all these years - it's something anyone can do, including me.

Kassy, a member of my team, is starting to fill the gap left by Roxanne, and is pushing me hard creatively. A long-time fan, we worked together on a blockchain project before she joined my team properly, and we're establishing a great working relationship. However, rather than finding me songs, she's instead pushing me to write them. To dig into my own creativity. With her encouragement, I'm finding creative depth that I didn't think I was capable of. And this strategy, surely, will serve us better in the long-term. I jokingly paraphrase the old Navajo proverb:

Give an artist a song, and you'll be giving him songs for ever.

Teach an artist to write songs, and he'll be writing his own songs for ever.

Initially, we agree that any new songs are for an alias, a side project, perhaps titled 'GE'. I'm nervous as fuck writing them, but knowing that they won't be released with all the pressures that come with a Gareth Emery release allows me to be creatively free.

And so, I start writing.

I write about my family.

I write about dying.

In Manchester, memories of my years in the city overflowing, I write about how fucking strange it is to be back there now.

I write about relationships, old and new.

I write about America, my love for the country, as well as the things I don't love.

I write about the most recent love of my life, my new daughter Elise, just turned 1.

And, in a song called 'End Of Days', I write about Roxanne, our break up, and how I fear it'll affect my dad if we don't make up at some point. I don't want the next time I see her to be his funeral.

That's my worst fear of all.

And so eventually, Roxanne and I talk on the phone, and agree to see each other. In Los Angeles, we take breakfast at one of my favorite cafes – Toast, on Melrose. Regardless of everything that's happened, the one positive of this whole situation has been learning how to write songs which I know for sure will be the next chapter in my career.

Always look for the positive. Always the positive.

LONDON, April 2019.

I'm still new to this all, and my writing is rough around the edges, but it's real, raw, from the heart. These songs mean everything to me, and that usually means they'll at least mean *something* to someone else.

As I start to hit a wall on some of the songs, I reach out to Anthony Galatis - a superb London-based songwriter - and in his West London studio, he helps me get past the creative roadblocks. Lyrics are still an area where I can get stuck, and Ant helps me punch them up: making them sharper, cleaner, more effective, whilst still retaining the emotional firepower. As we put the finishing touches on 'End Of Days', it's time to find someone to actually sing it. He suggests a vocalist he's been working with – Annabel Turner – and she turns up shortly after:

Straight from the school classroom.

It's hard to quantify Annabel's voice, but after a few sessions, I don't want anyone else other than her singing these songs. With many highly personal lyric sets, I expected it to be difficult to find a singer, but Annabel takes each one and infuses more emotion than I ever could have imagined, her voice the perfect blend of melancholy and euphoria. I've got an idea.

"Guys, fuck finding other vocalists. Annabel, how do you feel about doing the whole album? Singing every fucking one of these songs? I don't think anyone else can do them better".

I've written the songs. Now, I've found the singer.

A few weeks later, back in Los Angeles, I sit down with Kassy to discuss our plans for the GE band, and she breaks it to me.

"Do you think these are the best records you've ever made?"

"Yes, by a mile…"

"Then it's simple. This music isn't for a side project. It's for you. Don't hide behind an alias. Put them under your own name. I think we're listening to the new Gareth Emery album right now."

She's got me.

Writing these songs, believing them to be for a side project, was what I needed to be creatively honest: to get out of my own head.

After over 15 years of releasing music, fans have certain expectations of how they expect your records to sound. If you decide to break with past tradition, the reactions can be brutal, and the common criticism usually goes:

"You've changed your sound for the money."

The actual reality is very different – if money were the primary goal, I would never change my sound. Giving people exactly what they want and expect is a reliable way to make great money, but not necessarily great art. I can't enjoy the process of writing music unless I'm constantly evolving and discovering new things, so if anything, the main motivator behind my changing sound is a selfish desire to make my own creative life more fun.

The point is, making music as 'Gareth Emery' comes with baggage, so imagining I was going to hide behind an alias was a great way to avoid that baggage.

If the music does well, great. If it fails, ah well, it was under an alias anyway.

But, it turns out, just believing this music was destined to be hidden under an alias was all I needed. With the baggage stripped away, I was able to write the music I wanted to write, free of worries about how the public would respond. And then at the end of it all, I realized that actually, I quite liked what I'd written.

And it was still me.

With these songs, this knowledge about how far I can go, there's no going back. My old life, of having other people write my music for me, will never be something I can go back to.

What else will change?

"END OF DAYS"

written by Gareth Emery & Anthony Galatis

it's the last day of the year
the battle lines have disappeared
but we're still standing here
i've got to walk this road alone
if only we'd tried face to face
not writing on the phone

how did we fall so far?
from reaching for the stars

when the words run out
nothing more to say
i'll still love you
to the end of days
you can break my heart
in a thousand ways
but i'll still love you
to the end of days

we were the greatest team on earth
we could solve a million problems
except how to fix this hurt
it isn't just the two of us
all those other hearts left broken
all those other dreams we crushed

how did we fall so far?
from reaching for the stars

when the words run out
nothing more to say
i'll still love you
to the end of days
you can break my heart
in a thousand ways
but i'll still love you
to the end of days

when the ashes fall
from a blood red sky
we'll be forced to stand
at each other's side

as the water flows
to wash our pain away
we'll make our peace
just a day too late

so we'll turn around
go our separate ways
and we'll say goodbye
until the end of days

THIS IS YOUR NEW LIFE

RECORD LABELS, SOCIAL MEDIA, AND THE ROAD ALONE

December, 2019
30,000 feet over Utah.

As the jet climbs to altitude, I think about my new album and how different it is to anything that's come before, and I wonder, not for the first time, if I'm making the right move. It feels such a radical step away from anything I've done, but in reality, it really shouldn't be.

It's not like I'm releasing a Peruvian pan-pipe album. This is dance music. There are great songs. The melodies are really strong. Musically, it's as classically 'me' as it could possibly be.

But, the vast majority of the record is not *trance*, and that's a problem. You see, for almost the entirety of my professional career up to this point, I sat squarely in a neat pigeon hole. 'Gareth Emery is a Trance DJ', Wikipedia will tell you. And I'm fine with that. At about 20 years old, I decided I wanted to be a famous trance DJ, and nearly two decades on, it's safe to say I achieved my goal.

By more or less anyone's definition, whether they like me or not, I'm one of the most well-known and successful trance DJs in the history of the genre. Not the most successful, but anywhere from top three to top ten, depending on the country in the world, and who you're asking. And that's not bad. I've done alright. Now, being a trance DJ isn't quite as popular a career choice as, say, becoming a professional footballer, but to become one of the top ten people in the world at *anything,* out of the 7,700,000,000 people currently on the planet, would be pretty good going, even if you'd just managed it once. I've been here for about 15 years.

And yet, I need to try something new.

The problem with being very well-known for a particular thing, is that there are certain rules and regulations that you're then expected to live by. There are certain things almost all trance DJs do without fail: they make music between 130-145 beats per minute, designed to be blended seamlessly with other trance music. They do not release records that sit outside of this usual BPM range, because that would mean that other trance DJs can't play them. They have radio shows where they play the most popular trance releases of that week or month. They do not, typically, decide to abandon the decks for live instruments.

And they certainly don't fancy themselves as songwriters or storytellers.

And yet, these are all things I'm doing. What the fuck am I thinking?

It's not that I don't love trance music: I do. So much. It's just that, after nearly two decades doing the same thing, I need to try something different. I need to push myself, and if I'm honest, I feel like I'm holding myself back by operating in the same small sub-genre of dance music where I've done more or less everything there is to do; I've won the genre's most prestigious award ('A State Of Trance Tune Of The Year') three times, and finished second twice. I've made some of the most influential classics in the genre. Played the largest festivals. Had three albums, each of which was an iTunes #1 in over 20 countries. What's left now? Where is there to go?

I have unfulfilled ambitions in music. Deep, dark, secretive ambitions that have long been forgotten. Ambitions that go back a lot further than my love affair with trance music.

As a 15-year old in Southampton, England, I wanted it all. I wanted chart hits. I wanted to sell-out Wembley Stadium. I wanted to be fucking Oasis. Then, a few years later, I discovered trance, and instead, I decided that I wanted to become a famous trance DJ instead. Well, two decades on, it's time for an update. Mission accomplished. What comes next, 15 year old Gaz?

The problem is, the things I want to accomplish at this point in my life aren't going to happen in the world of trance. Much as I love it, it's an aging genre with its heyday some years in the past, and every year the fanbase gets a little older. Now, I'm fortunate in that I've always straddled the line between trance and *just good dance music* to ensure I wasn't too attached to the fortunes of trance, and that I always retained a young fanbase. Other friends and former colleagues weren't so fortunate. I've seen numerous trance artists watch their fanbase get older and older, the attendance at their shows gradually diminishing until one day they realize that in a decade they've gone from 10,000 ravers at a festival, to playing classics for 10 forty-somethings in a pub.

Me? I'm a lot more fortunate. A recent survey of my fans showed that just 25% of them defined themselves as 'trance fans' with the other 75% just liking 'good electronic music in general'. My biggest ever solo show happened in 2018, selling 8,500 tickets at San Francisco's legendary Bill Graham Civic Auditorium… at the age of 37, to crowd with an average age far younger. So, the fact I've been around for a while doesn't seem to be too much of an issue.

There are of course days when I wonder if I'm fucking mad for even daring to believe I'm capable of more. This is likely due to some deep-down psychological fucked up shit from childhood. Imposter syndrome, or whatever it's called these days. That said, it's got me this far, so there must be something going for it too. Do

I wish I'd left childhood with zero baggage, trauma, or shoulder-chips? Nah. In my experience, super well-adjusted, confident kids tend not to make very 'successful' adults (although they're likely happier). And whilst I'd never wish a genuinely crappy childhood on anyone, a few tough moments do appear to be part of the recipe for shaping success from the music studio to the sports field. The fact is, hitting the top level of *anything* is extremely fucking difficult. Becoming a famous musician, sportsperson, actor, artist, politician, entrepreneur or anything similar takes a level of dedication bordering on the psychotic. You have to face public rejection and ridicule on a daily basis. Continue fighting even when every inch of your being is telling you to give up. Watch your job consume your entire life for decades. I've seen plenty of happy, well-adjusted artists who each day would spend a few leisurely hours in the studio before popping off for another game of tennis and a spa treatment, but where are they now? Nowhere to be seen.

Don't get me wrong: workaholism has plenty of downside, and I've worked very hard to find a balance in my life, especially since becoming a parent, but to pretend you can achieve anything difficult without superhuman levels of dedication would be a lie.

Plus, there's nothing remotely normal about live performances. What motivates people to want to play football in front of 100,000 people, or to get on stage and play music to similar numbers? These are not *normal* things to do. If your time on earth so far has been utterly idyllic and secure, with no anxieties or chips on your shoulder, you're quite unlikely to decide to dedicate your entire life to achieving insane goals. That said, my upbringing was, for the most part, pretty good. I had a great family, and came out of it with just the right level of fucked-up-ness to drive me to accomplish the things I have:

Perfect.

This is why it does bug me a little when I see artists getting shit for finally making a bit of cash. These people have gambled their whole lives on the belief that they'd make it. Taken paths with zero job safety or security and absolutely no guarantee of success – and even if you are successful, it can end at any time. For the handful that do make it, surely they deserve some financial reward after running the gauntlet?

On tougher days, I do worry that I'm too old. Not because I worry that I'm past my best – in terms of my ability to create music, I'm better than I ever have been - but the vast majority of artists seem to achieve their greatest moments early in life. For me to achieve my greatest moments in the next decade would be severely bucking that trend. But it wouldn't be the first time.

So, yes; I want to play Glastonbury; have hit records; win awards. But I don't want to do these things for ego, or to post on fucking social media. The rewards are not the goal - they're a nod that I've hit the heights I wanted for my own self-imposed idea of accomplishment, and because I don't want to give my supporters - YOU! - anything less than my abso-lute-fucking best. That's what you deserve - my blood, sweat, and tears. (OK, I may not bleed in this job, but I promise you that I lose sleep, and sweat, over worrying that I'm giving you back what you give to me.)

I want to make this record because I've made music that changed people's lives, and for me to continue to do that, I need absolute creative freedom. I can't write the songs I need to within the context of trance music, and that means, in many ways, this record feels like my first album.

Of course, I'm anxious about how the fans will react.

The weight of expectation has weighed heavily on me in the past, and this time I deliberately try to avoid getting sucked into it. A year ago, I released a collaborative album with Ashley Wallbridge. We called it 'Kingdom United', and it was something of a retro album for me: a record closer to the music I'd made when I was just starting out.

I'm not sure why I decided a throwback album was a good idea, but I put some of the blame on one thing:

I was reading the YouTube comments.

Every month or so, I'd find myself in a 1am YouTube session, and often I'd end up checking out my old tracks. Usually this was just to remember how they sounded – I don't keep good records of the music I've released, and without YouTube many of my tracks would simply be lost in time, victims of my poor organization.

Of course, once I'd loaded up the video of, say, 'Exposure', it was near-impossible not to scroll down for a cheeky look at the comments, and you can guess which ones got my attention. Yep. The ones bemoaning how much I'd changed, and how much better I used to be.

> "It all went downhill after this for Gareth, hard to believe he made this classic when you listen to the cheesy shit he's making today."

> "Gareth Emery is such a sellout. I bet someone else actually made this because there's no way Gareth would have made it."

> "If only Gareth still made music like this today, I'd be in the front row of all his gigs again."

Now you – as the reader – can probably see through this sort of nonsense, but at that time in my life I couldn't, so I decided to give the people what they apparently wanted. Ashley and I crafted a beautiful album that felt like the direct competitor to Northern Lights, my 2010 debut which is so heavily revered by my former fans. Hardly any vocals, full of stunning trance melodies.

I imagined, naively, that the YouTube Comment Crew would all be back to enjoy it, celebrate it, and tell me how grateful they were that I'd made something for them again.

The album was released, and the result?

Tumbleweed.

It wasn't that Kingdom United got bad feedback, it just got *no feedback.* Nobody really seemed to give a shit. My current fans rather liked it, but none of the old ones returned. I asked an assistant to look through the comments, to see if any of the '*Gareth Should Return To His Old Sound*' crew had commented, and nobody had. They just didn't care.

The album ended up streaming modestly, but the UK tour was the worst selling I've ever done. YouTube Comment Crew, where were you?

Kingdom United hadn't really worked, but why?

Soon, the answer dawned on me.

The problem was, YouTube Comment Crew didn't actually want me to make music like Exposure (2009) again. They actually wanted me to be making *Exposure* itself again, and for it to be *2009* again. Confused? Let me explain.

Music is more than just music. It's *memories.* And any old song is intricately tied to the memories at the time, and that's as important as the music itself. Where you were when you first heard it. The friends you had. The clubs you raved at. The daily commute you played it on.

And I'm no exception. Whilst on the surface, I might think "I'd love it if Oasis released music like Wonderwall again", I don't really mean it. Fuck, I didn't even bother listening to the last two Oasis albums – they might be full of Wonderwalls for all I know. But it's not really about Wonderwall, as much as it is a great song. It's about 1995. It's about me leaving school, learning to play guitar, and starting a band. It's about discovering alcohol, meeting girls, and going to my first ever house parties - where, without fail, Wonderwall would always be played. How on earth could anything Oasis made today compare to all that?

So, sure. I can make music like Exposure again, but I can't make it 2009 again. And I certainly can't make the YouTube Comment

Crew ten years younger – to bring back an era when they didn't have kids, mortgages and beer-bellies, and when Sankeys was still open. It's an impossible task.

I'm now resolved to only make music based on who I am now. No longer will I try and ride off the memories of the past: we'll leave them just where they belong:

in the fucking past.

All those old songs are still unchanged on Spotify or YouTube, and anyone who wants to reminisce about 2009 can go back there any time with a few taps of a phone.

But I won't be listening myself.

I'm busy making music for 2020.

For people who are living in the present, and who want to make new memories.

Los Angeles, December 2020.

Over sushi, Kassy and I review the various record label offers. They're good, very good. I knew these songs were solid, but the label reactions have been insane. But, rather than jumping, we're holding fire and carefully considering the implications of every deal.

Doing an album right requires investment – either by the label or the artist. My first two albums were entirely independent, but each time we had to hire a small army in order to get the job done. Each part of the album process requires money, from the obvious stuff like music, artwork, and mastering, to the less obvious stuff like radio plugging, playlist promotion, and digital marketing.

In the early days, social media was an easy short-cut: a guaranteed way to reach huge numbers of people with zero investment. But these days, reaching people has become extremely expensive. In many ways, Facebook – the first social platform to really scale – tricked everyone with a massive bait and switch. From 2008 (when Facebook launched Artist Pages) to about 2012, almost every artist on the plane directed people to their Facebook page first and foremost. Many new artists starting out didn't even bother with a website: a Facebook page was all you needed.

Facebook numbers became a very fucking big deal – particularly hitting that first million fans - with artists using a multitude of strategies to grow their Facebook audiences. Later, when Facebook introduced in-house advertising to allow artists to further promote their pages, many artists - including me - jumped on it, often spending tens of thousands (and, in some unlucky cases, hundreds of thousands) of dollars to grow their Facebook fan count.

We all got more fans. Facebook got more visitors. We felt this was a mutually beneficial arrangement. Us and Facebook, helping each other out. But, in reality, we'd taken the bait.

And then came the switch.

All of a sudden, we all noticed that our 'numbers' were going down. You'd post the biggest record of your career, which was going viral on YouTube, but on Facebook, you'd only get half the likes and comments compared to an average track you released a year ago… despite having more fans. *What the fuck was going on?*

The explanations were long, complex, and came with lots of smoke and mirrors about algorithms, but there was one clear fact underlying it all.

Facebook would no longer show your content to all your audience, unless you paid for it.

This was a massive fucking slap in the face.

For years, we'd invested in building our Facebook followings, often at high cost, whilst promoting the platform, with the assumption that *we'd be able to connect with the people who'd voluntarily liked our pages* and all of a sudden, that wasn't true any longer.

Over the next few years, Facebook gradually squashed 'organic' (i.e.: unpaid) reach to the extent where a non-promoted post would reach less than 1% of people who'd liked your page.

So, either you paid up, or you watched the tumbleweed roll past your posts. If I wanted a post to reach any more than a tiny fraction of my fans, I'd have to pay well over $10,000 (it's likely a lot more expensive now). What a fucking con.

To further rub salt in the wounds, anyone else could also pay the fee, and target a post to my fans. So, if Joe Bloggs decided he wanted to send a post to people who liked Gareth Emery, he'd be able to do it for the exact the same cost as me, despite the fact I'd spent years building up my audience. So fuck Facebook.

I should note that this isn't unique to me, or even to music – all sorts of businesses around the world, from local village cake shops to leisure centers, spent years endorsing Facebook and we all got equally fucked.

Instagram's a little better, but being owned by Facebook, we can be sure the same principles are at play. If you want to start a social network, this is the process:

a) Provide access for free.
b) Trick artists and businesses into building up audiences on your free platform.
c) Once they're locked in and too invested to leave, deny them access to their audience unless they pay for it.

Urgh.

Personally, I equally love and hate social media. On one level, there's no doubt that its impact has allowed my music to spread further and wider than it would have done otherwise. I've no doubt I wouldn't have performed in countries like Azerbaijan, Syria, Qatar and Moldova without social media. And having a direct line to supporters and fans is very valuable - receiving feedback in real time and not having to rely on traditional press to get the word out.

But these platforms are also designed to be addictive as fuck, and they do that job very well. There's been many interesting articles and documentaries written about this so I'm not going to repeat what's out there, but the fact is, if you figure out how addictive these platforms are, and take measures to protect yourself, there's a major competitive advantage to be had, because 99% of people are hopelessly addicted to this shit and they don't even know it. You'll see them every day, zombies stumbling around, unable to look up from their phones, even as they cross the street. If you're part of the 1% that realizes that unfettered access to highly addictive applications might come with unintended consequences, then congratulations. You're already doing better than most people.

Much of the last five years of my life has been about winning the battle against social media. Time is our most precious resource, but social media is a highly addictive time-suck which'll eat up every available minute of my day, if I allow myself unencumbered access. Whilst I have *somewhat* of an addictive personality anyway, social media networks are very fucking good at keeping you around – and so they should be – it's what pays their bills.

As you can probably tell, I can bore on about this subject endlessly. So I don't end up down a rabbit hole talking about dopamine and reward pathways which will no doubt leave you finishing this book early, instead, here's a simple question I like to ask friends to illuminate how this works.

Imagine this. One day, you open Facebook and it pops up with a message that says:

> *Hey! We'd like to offer you a new version of the Facebook News Feed. It's full of content you're going to enjoy even more. You'll find this new content so compelling that you'll never want to leave! If you accept, we project you'll spend twice as much time on Facebook as you currently do. Do you accept?*

> "No way, I use Facebook enough already" is the usual reply.
> Well, my friends, they don't need to ask you.
> They'll just fucking do it.

About five years ago, realizing social media was taking up a disproportionate amount of my time, I knew I needed some systems in place. Quitting social media altogether wasn't an option: but I did need to figure out a way that I could use social media for its professional benefits, whilst avoiding the biggest pitfalls, like reading Instagram at dinner instead of listening to my kids tell me about their day, something I'm ashamed to admit has happened once or twice. However, after years of testing various strategies, I've got things pretty well under control now, and here's how.

Firstly, I don't have emails on my phone. At all. The Gmail app is long gone, and access to email is blocked in almost every way. Emails often feel urgent, but unless you're the president, they likely can wait. However, when I used to have emails on my phone, I'd constantly be getting sucked into work-based 'problems' during studio sessions, playtime with my kids, country walks, etc. These days, I believe that unless I'm able to respond in that moment, reading an email serves no purpose. If I receive emails during dinner, and they contain problems (as they invariably do), unless I leave dinner to handle them I'll sit there ignoring the rest of the table as the problems swirl ominously around my head. I'm not fixing the problems, and yet I'm a worse guest at dinner, my attention elsewhere. No thanks. So these days, my email is accessed on a computer when I'm sat with a cup of tea in front of me, ready to respond to everything and solve any necessary problems.

Secondly, I'm a big fan of Apple's new Screen Time app. Being able to block apps on your phone a few years ago was extremely challenging, but Screen Time makes it easy. As my album deadline approached, I limited Instagram and Safari to a spartan 5 minutes each per day. To ensure I couldn't break this limit (as I no doubt would try), I had my wife set a password which she then wrote down and locked in a cabinet in the house.

Extreme? Sure.

Successful? *Very.*

The result? During the album process, I used both very sparingly: popping into Instagram to check all was well on my professional account, and keeping Safari for emergency searches, whilst delivering the album before the deadline.

On my phone, I tend to block anything that has the possibility to distract me from work, my kids, or the present moment, but other apps I'll allow at any times. For utilities like Uber and Maps, and 'positive' apps like meditation apps, or Spanish learning apps, I can use them as much as I like.

However, when I really need a time-out, I'll revert to my old Blackberry Bold 9000. A decade-old relic (but still utterly solid, and not just for drug dealers), it'll make calls, text, take notes and nothing else. There's no apps, and accessing the internet is so painstakingly slow, it's not really worth it. On a recent trip to Hawaii, I left the iPhone at home and rolled with the Blackberry only – giving my team instructions that whilst I wasn't checking texts, I'd be more than happy to take a phone call any time in case of emergency. The happy result of this? I didn't receive a single phone call during my trip. Instead, the team found a way to solve any emergencies without involving me, and I enjoyed a thoroughly restful four days with virtually no internet usage at all.

My third strategy involves keeping most work-based messaging separate. On my iPhone, I'll keep iMessage for close friends and family only. So whilst I do have iMessage notifications enabled, I receive very few messages, and those that I do receive are important enough to interrupt my day. Everyone else, however, contacts me via WhatsApp, which includes all my industry friends, groups within our company, and general chit-chat. On WhatsApp, I have no notifications, so there's no possibility of a studio session being interrupted. Instead, I'll choose when I'm ready to jump into the mayhem.

Finally, I make myself deliberately hard to contact. I'll change my email address and phone number every couple of years. So, if you've tried to contact me in the past and got no reply – I'm sorry, but you probably mailed an old address. If we ever actually do become friends or colleagues, you'll find me most responsive.

Do I occasionally miss out on stuff? Sure. I've no doubt my lack of contactability has led me to miss out on the occasional cool opportunity over the years, but it's a cost well worth the hours a day I've claimed back for studio and family time.

You might think at this point that all these rules and systems sound a bit weird: and you're right, they are. I regularly get incredulous looks from people when I explain I don't use email on my phone, or I can't look something up because I've maxed out my daily limit on web browsing.

And yep, of course: these sort of extreme rules aren't 'normal' – but if 'normal' today involves being hopelessly addicted to a litany of apps, neglecting friends, family and work for mindless hours-long Instagram binges, then I'll pass, thank you very much.

Anyway, back to the album.

As my team and I evaluate the record label deals, we seriously discuss the prospect of releasing the record independently. My first two albums were entirely independent, so I know the lie of the land, and for the first time in decades there's finally some money in music streaming again.

For my last album, 2016's *100 Reasons To Live*, I signed off on the deal without giving the figures much thought: *Who gives a shit? Touring is where I make my money.* That was my mantra. But recently I've taken more of an interest in these matters, and realized that the deals that artists usually get are great for the short term, but over a career you can do a lot better by backing yourself.

The more I learn, the more I start to realize the power of owning my own music. Although the royalties don't seem like much (100,000 streams on Spotify currently pays about $400 - yep, really! Now you know why it's so hard for new talent to make it), if you stack enough records over time, it starts to add up, and I can see that owning my own music can become a great investment.

Kassy chats to the various record labels, explaining that we're considering all offers, and the independent route. After giving it some more thought, however, I decide to 'burn the boats.'

I love that phrase, which refers to a famous incident where a commander, having landed in a hostile country, ordered his men to destroy their ships so that they would have to conquer the country or be killed.

We're going independent.

It's probably one of the biggest decisions of my career, but my gut tells me that it's the right call.

Putting your success - and by that, your happiness - in the hands of others is a recipe for misery. Win or lose, it's in our hands now, and that's where it should be.

After all, if you can't back your own work, why should you expect anyone else to love it?

The End.
London, December 2019.

I leave the studio, bid farewell to Ant, Annabel and Kassy, and walk into the street. The album's done, titled 'THE LASERS', the videos are shot, and in a few short months we'll be released. It's by far my greatest work to-date and that gives me a strange feeling. I feel accomplished, but I also wonder what's next? Where do we go now? I never felt like this with my previous albums, always feeling as if I was holding something back. With this one, I've given my all, left nothing out. Fuck it. I can analyze it later. Right now, it's time to celebrate.

It's Christmas in London, always a beautiful time of year in the UK, so I pull on my scarf and head towards the restaurant where I'm meeting my old friends, the Christmas lights and general good vibes helping my mood. It's been a long hard year and I'm ready for a beer.

Strangely enough, I'm not nervous about the release of this album.

I should be. It's the most risky project I've ever done. Only a handful of songs are in the trance style I'm known for, and I'm accompanying it with a book, in 2020, a year when hardly anyone reads.

But it feels right. Nine songs, nine stories.

And even if it tanks, I don't mind, because it's pure me. The most honest art I could possibly make at this point in my life, and I know I've left it all on the field. There's nothing more I could have asked of myself, and when you've given your all, the result doesn't matter.

I take a rare moment to reflect on everything that brought me here. The places and people, the journeys and destinations all forming a part of the fabric of my life.

My bedroom in Southampton. Sankeys in Manchester. Sunset Boulevard in Los Angeles. More airports, hotels and crowds than I can remember. The good times, bad times, celebrations, fights, wins and losses. The people I shared it with. Those that I still share it with today. Those that have moved on.

It's all a part of me, and for a brief moment, I embrace my history. All of it. And for once, I feel at one with the person I am and the path I've taken to get here.

And then, as ever, my thoughts shift to the future.

What comes next?

What art will I make next?

And more important, who will I become?

Eventually, I find the present, and with my mind neither in the past or future, I notice the chill of the London air, the hint of a raindrop on my skin, the festive streetlights, the good sounds of London at Christmas.

And I savour the moment. Here. Now. Me.

Because all we really have is the present, and it's the only state that creates our memories. Our life. Our stories.

What is there left to do?

Everything.

WELCOME TO YOUR LIFE

written by Gareth Emery and Anthony Galatis

one more hour till morning comes
faded lights, the sound of drums
too far along, to turn back now
and save ourselves.
we'll forge our swords from lessons past
promises that this will last
in your eyes i see what this will take
though we may fall, we'll take it all

this is your new life
it's made by you
welcome to your life
you'll feel brand new
this is your new life
what you gonna do?
welcome to your life
have you thought this through?

they burned the boats, we're on our own
a thousand places we could go
past the bones of those who've gone before
we'll live as long as we deserve

this is your new life
it's made by you
welcome to your life
you'll feel brand new
this is your new life
what you gonna do?
welcome to your life
have you thought this through?

EPILOGUE

THE GREAT PANDEMIC AND A FUTURE UNCERTAIN

"Right now, we have two large, complex systems. The first is a virus sweeping through the global population and our combined efforts to mitigate it. The second is a declining global economy. Both systems are incredibly difficult to measure and understand, much less predict. Both are so large and unruly that we struggle to even comprehend them in their entirety. And so far, pretty much everything we've thought about either has been utterly wrong"

Mark Manson – Nobody Knows What Is Going On

This book was supposed to end here.

However, we're well into the second half of 2020, and humanity is currently facing the biggest crisis of my lifetime. This is very much an ongoing situation with no real end in sight, but given it will be the defining moment of many of our lives, it would be remiss for me to exclude it from this book.

I have no epidemiological qualifications – in fact, science was my worst subject at school – so I'll stay well away from topics where I am clearly not qualified. I will, however, try to document the effects that I have witnessed first-hand on our industry, and offer some thoughts about where we may end up in the future.

But first: another virus, and another time.

April 2009: China

As the pilot deployed the landing gear and we approached Shanghai, I shifted around in my seat nervously, and applied hand-sanitizer for what must be the 50th time that day. H1N1/09, also known as swine flu, was sweeping the globe, and rather than choosing to sit it out at home, I was on a Dragonair flight from Hong Kong to Shanghai, where I was booked to play a show that night. I'd spent most of the short flight reading newspapers about the growing pandemic, and the more I read, the more fearful I felt.

Terrifying new illnesses had been in the news for some years, with Asia ground-zero for most of them, so as a frequent traveler to the continent, and lifelong germaphobe, I paid attention. For the last couple of years, the news had been focused on H5N1, better known as bird flu. Bird flu had experienced sporadic outbreaks throughout Asia during my trips there. This strain didn't generally transmit between humans – you had to have contact with sick birds in some way – but its terrifyingly high mortality rate of 60%+ made sure we took notice. Walking through crowded, humid Asian cities with my tour guides, I'd give a very wide berth to the ubiquitous caged chickens which could be remarkably common in some countries. Of course, after alcohol I wasn't so cautious. One morning I'd experienced a full anxiety attack, waking up hungover, and getting a horrible flashback of scoffing some sort of chicken skewers from the street market, post club; vague memories of my fellow European DJ shaking his head; *not a chance Gaz, haven't you heard of bird flu?* Me laughing it off; Fuck. My old hypochondriac tendencies coming out to play; was that a tickle in the back of my throat?

Bird flu had never really managed human-to-human transmission, so whilst it was deadly, it wasn't that much of a problem as long as you avoided sick birds. That didn't stop plenty of terrifying headlines about it, though: "*Bird flu pandemic 'could kill 150m*'" reported the Guardian[1], showing modeling by a then-obscure professor at Imperial College in London by the name of Neil Ferguson. Terrifying doomsday scenarios aside, eventual worldwide deaths were less than 1,000, but it wasn't the last time I'd be hearing Neil Ferguson's name.

Swine flu, on the other hand, was a different beast. It was extremely good at jumping from person-to-person, and whilst its mortality rate was far lower, it was spreading fast, and countries were nervous. Newspapers also covered the possibility of the true doomsday scenario: where swine flu and bird flu somehow merged, creating a new hybrid with the infectiousness of swine flu, but the mortality rate of bird flu, which didn't help the general sense of panic.

China was taking swine flu extremely fucking seriously. Unlike many similar illnesses, swine flu had started outside of Asia – in Mexico most likely – and it was not an import the Chinese were keen on. This meant that every flight arriving into China was subject to temperature checks on-board the plane immediately after landing. It was usual to walk through temperature check-points arriving in Asian airports, but checks on the plane were another matter, particularly given the consequences for anyone with symptoms.

It was hard to get concrete information about what was happening in China, but it seemed that on arriving, the entire plane

---

1 As of August 2020, this article remains online, and starts like this: 'A global influenza pandemic is imminent and will kill up to 150 million people, the UN official in charge of coordinating the worldwide response to an outbreak has warned'. Although bird flu eventually killed less than 1,000 people worldwide, reading historical 'panic porn' like this can be helpful in providing perspective.

would be checked for flu-like symptoms. Anyone exhibiting them would be taken to quarantine in a Chinese hospital. This wasn't voluntary– if you had symptoms, you were going. I wasn't especially nervous about swine flu itself – I was 29 and reasonably healthy – but missing my gig because I was getting carted off to a Chinese hospital against my will did not sound fun, so I was taking every precaution I could to avoid getting it.

Now, I'd never really heard of hand sanitizer prior to swine flu. That sounds bonkers today, but it just wasn't widespread in the world prior to that point, outside of hospital environments. Sure, I'd used it in hospitals, but likely couldn't have even told you its name. You wash your hands, then you use that other stuff. What's it called? Fuck knows. But now, medical advice on avoiding swine flu recommended using an alcohol hand sanitizer, so I'd picked up a few bottles at the airport, and I was addicted. Flying can be a grimy, germy experience at the best of times, so a lovely bug-killing alcohol gel I could use to ward off nasties was right up my alley.

"Everyone, please remain seated. Do not stand up. I repeat, do not stand up. The Chinese authorities will be entering the plane to perform a health check and it is important you remain seated and calm".

Here we go, then. The moment of truth.

Moments later, Chinese agents entered the plane, dressed head-to-toe in what I'd later describe as 'hazmat suits' – which in reality I know now was full PPE. I'm not sure what it is about a full-body protective suit that's so fucking terrifying but the situation immediately felt far more serious and frightening than it had a moment ago. I felt my heart rate elevate, and tried to dry my clammy palms on my jeans, whilst my mind went into overdrive. Could I give myself a temperature from extreme anxiety? *Shut up Gaz, that's ridiculous*. But maybe it is possible. *Well, if anything, the more you think about it, the more chance you've got of it happening.* STOP THINKING ABOUT HAVING A TEMPERATURE.

I tried to breathe slowly.

The hazmat-suit crew checked my temperature with some sort of gun looking device, which gave a small beep, then they continued down the plane.

Well, it's done now. Ten minutes to get the results.

My last ten minutes of freedom, my anxiety mocked me.

Shut up, Gaz.

We waited.

Some time later, the pilot came back onto the intercom.

"So, ladies and gentlemen, some not-so-great news I'm afraid. We have three suspected swine flu cases on-board the plane, so we'll need to wait here a little longer whilst the Chinese authorities work out what to do with us."

Whilst we waited, chatter broke out in business class amongst anyone who spoke English. Nobody seemed overly bothered, which helped my nerves.

"I've been through all this last week", the portly Australian businessman sat next to me told me. We'd chatted a bit throughout the flight, and he'd handed me his business card. What was his fucking name again? I snuck a look at the card. Joshua, that was it. He had the look of a true road-warrior: mid 50s, battered Tumi luggage, huge belly cultivated after thousands of business-class dinners and lounge-snacks. Josh continued.

"What happens is, they'll check everyone's seat numbers when they come off the plane. Then, they'll quarantine anyone within two rows of the people with the flu".

"Three rows?" I replied. "Are you fucking joking?"

"No, mate. So if someone in Row 17 has the flu, all of Row 15, 16, 17, 18 and 19 are off to quarantine".

This was a worrying development. If someone near me had the flu, all of my diligent hand sanitizing would be for nothing. It hardly seemed fair. I looked at the floor. Josh must have detected my discomfort.

"Look on the bright side though mate, as least you're up here in biz. Much less people up here to be sick. Better chance for all us".

Josh was right. We deplaned, and an agonizing 30 seconds followed while Chinese officials studied my boarding pass and cross-checked my seat number. Over his shoulder, I spotted a list of seat numbers of the unfortunate individuals who'd be on the quarantine bus. I was allowed to go, as was Josh.

'Knock 'em dead mate!', he shouted at me as we parted entering the airport concourse.

A great fucking show awaited, and I played with the energy of someone who had just avoided a prison sentence.

February 2020: Los Angeles

"Have you heard about this coronavirus thing?" Kat asks me over breakfast.

"I've not heard of it, no."

"You might want to check and see if it has any effect on your tour".

For a few months now, I've been on a self-imposed news blackout, consuming no news whatsoever, which has led to all-time-low levels of anxiety, and a remarkably productive run in the studio. I figured, if there was something I really needed to know about, Kat, who occasionally dips in, would probably tell me.

In a week, I'm due to head for a tour of Australia and Asia, taking in a 15,000 person concert in Sydney alongside clubs in Singapore and Jakarta. I haven't travelled since the Christmas break, and when you constantly are on the road, six weeks off is a long, long time, so it's fair to say I've been excited, and I'm not best pleased about a stupid new virus apparently named after a Mexican beer causing problems.

"It'll be fine," I tell her. "I've travelled throughout the swine flu pandemic, so I know the drill. All good."

"You might want to read a little into this one," she cautions, "just to make sure."

I break my no-news rule and do a little reading. Nothing at this point seems overly concerning, but I chat with the touring party, and we decide to take a few extra precautions, just in case. We're not travelling to China, but I was due to be connecting in Hong Kong. With restrictions on flights from China on the rise, I decide to give Hong Kong a wide berth. Sure, a ban on Chinese flights *shouldn't* apply to Hong Kong which is its own administrative region, but I didn't fancy having a debate over East Asian politics with a US immigration guard on my return.

I also text Andy, our tour manager, and ask him to pick up some masks. I don't intend to wear one, but I'd rather we're equipped, just in case.

They've got to be N95 masks, whatever the fuck those are, I text him. He goes shopping the next day and easily picks up a pack.

The next week, we fly out.

My manager, Kassy and I stroll through the Tom Bradley Terminal of Los Angeles International Airport, and it is *dead.* I've never seen it so quiet. More disturbingly, a good 50% of passengers are wearing masks. Masks have been very common traveling in Asia for as long as I can remember, but almost nonexistent on flights in the US or Europe, but for the first time in my life, large amounts of Americans seem to be masked-up. Something here does feel different. But then we head upstairs to the first-class lounge, where there's not a mask in sight – the frequent travelers are clearly a lot more relaxed about this than the population at large.

We transit uneventfully and soon arrive in Sydney, where nobody's talking about the virus. On Feb 8th, I take to the stage at Transmission Sydney to perform to close to 20,000 people at an epic concert. I don't realize it at the time, but this will be my final large performance for some time. As I walk off stage, a member of the production crew shows me his laptop.

"Over a million people in China watched your set on the live stream. These numbers are insane, we've never seen anything like it. Of course, they're all quarantined because of the virus, so that helps".

The rest of the week in Australia is uneventful. Uncharacteristically for the Australian summer, it's pouring with rain every day, so my days are spent in my room. With our tourist plans for Bondi Beach, the Sydney Harbour Bridge climb, and ferries to Manley cancelled, I decide that now's a decent time to learn a new skill, and spend most of the week locked in my hotel room, learning the Final Cut video editing program and creating promo videos for the new album. On our final day in Sydney, the rain clouds finally lift. Chatting about business, Kassy and I take advantage of the improved weather and walk for hours: from Sydney's CBD, under the Harbour Bridge, and away from the crowds, strolling around the bay until the path finally runs out.

Our next show was in Jakarta. Indonesia – at this point – was reporting zero coronavirus cases, a figure which was doubted by most of the Western media. With little idea what we were getting into, as we landed in Jakarta, our small crew of myself, my tour manager Andy and his fiancée Steph, decided it was time.

We were masking up.

I'd never worn an N95 mask before in my life, but it was clear within minutes that these were masks designed for fairly stationary use, not for walking miles through huge Asian airports.

"Fucking hell" I remarked, "I can barely breathe. Can't wait to get this fucking thing off."

Masks aside, our show in Jakarta went without a hitch. Panic hadn't set in here yet, with the club sold out, packed wall-to-wall with excited Indonesian fans.

Donning our masks, we headed back to Singapore to close out the tour. Here, we were immediately much more conscious of the virus. Although the tiny city-state had experienced less than 100 cases at that point, the city was on high alert, with hand sanitizers everywhere, and masks on almost every face. Still, life was normal enough, and with better weather we were able to explore the city a little. I walked for hours up and down the Singapore river: one of my favorite places in the world, before catching up with our crew to eat Korean BBQ, finishing up with cocktails on a rooftop looking over the city.

We ended the tour at the legendary Zouk nightclub. The local promoter informed us that people in the city were starting to get a little nervous about the virus, and to expect the venue quieter than my previous visit, but it was hard to tell. The place was still packed, and the night went off without a hitch. Singapore has some of the best electronic music fans in the world, and it's always a pleasure to play for them, but as enjoyable as the gig was, I hardly appreciated what it was. What it represented.

This was to be my final gig for a very long time.

We left Singapore early the next morning. Whilst the number of cases in the city were still less than 100, there was a general feeling of panic setting in, and whether it was justified or not, we were glad to be heading home. As we headed to the airport, Andy informed me that hand sanitizer was entirely sold out in the city – my first taste of the shortages that would define much of the next few months – but he'd creatively managed to re-fill our bottles from the sanitizing stations dotted around the hotel.

Transiting through Japan on my way back to Los Angeles, almost every passenger was wearing a mask. I also decided to play it safe and avoid food on the plane. At a small Japanese shop, I picked up enough pre-packaged sushi and protein bars to last the eleven-hour flight[2], as well as some insanely colorful Japanese magazines for the kids. It was time to go home.

2 There is absolutely no evidence suggesting you can catch COVID-19 from food, so this level of caution was unnecessary. Since returning home and learning this, I have continued to order delivery food as often as possible in order to support our local restaurants.

The arrivals procedure back at LAX felt like a masterclass on how to spread a virus. Compared to Asia, there were no temperature checks, no forms to fill in: just a brutally overcrowded arrivals hall. Even most of my fellow passengers from the Tokyo flight removed their masks: perhaps thinking they were safe now that they were on US soil. I kept mine on: the arrivals hall was even more packed than Zouk's dancefloor, and with passengers from all over the world waiting to enter the US, it felt this was likely the highest risk environment of the entire trip. After an hour's wait, I finally stood face-to-face with an immigration official.

"Have you been to China on your trip?" he asked.

"No." I replied.

"Welcome home."

It was now mid-February, and back in Los Angeles, life was strangely normal. My kids were in school. Coffee shops were open. People chatted on sidewalks to their neighbors without masks. Cases in the US were few, but now I was tuned in, I couldn't help but feel this would be short-lived. That weekend, Kat and I headed to one of our favorite sushi restaurants in town. We didn't have a reservation, and usually that would mean a thirty-minute wait for the sushi bar, but instead, we were ushered straight to a prime table. It was clear what was happening: people were starting to stay in.

The weeks ticked by, March arrived, and the panic started to spread. I'd never seen panic-buying in seven years living in the US, but in the UK we're seasoned pros, with any potential crisis leading to a run on the nation's supplies of toilet paper and bread. Now, the US jumped on the panic-buying craze in a big way. Hand sanitizer and bleach were entirely sold out – which made sense with a horrible virus on the loose – but toilet paper and basic food staples were running low too, which made less sense to me, based on my reading of the symptoms of the virus. Things took a darker turn when our children's nanny Patty arrived back in tears after going shopping: she'd been racially abused and attacked for taking the last pack of vegan sausages: utterly sickening on every level (although, if I can inject a little humor into a horrible situation, personally I'd only fight *not* to eat vegan sausages).

The media played a big part in fueling this panic, a trend that would increase dramatically over the coming weeks. I'd seen this in effect in the UK before, and the US was no different. Whilst panic-buying was a problem, and somewhat newsworthy, I couldn't get on board with news outlets running wall-to-wall sensationalist coverage, endlessly panning the empty shelves, and sometimes going as far as to portray stores as war zones. Naturally, anyone reading about basic supplies running out would be more likely to rush to the stores themselves, compounding the problem, and creating even more juicy headlines for the media. Personally, I avoided the stores when I could, instead picking other methods to contribute to our household: like making home-made hand sanitizer, using isopropyl alcohol and aloe vera gel[3].

With a fully-stocked house, my mind turned to shows. Our next show was Ultra Music Festival, three weeks away, and I was beyond excited for it. Ultra had always been a tough sell for me: for whatever reason, the festival had never quite 'got' me as an artist and what few offers we received were always terrible. '*This is all he's worth: take it or leave it*' would be the feedback my agent would pass on yearly, and yearly, I'd politely decline. Initially, I took it personally, but as the years ticked on, it bothered me less and less. I was doing well, and if Ultra didn't see that, fine. I'd just carry on doing my thing. They were just one festival out of hundreds, after all.

The year previously, 2019, I decided we'd throw our own show in Miami. Laserface Miami was a huge success, selling over 3,000 tickets in a Wynwood warehouse, during Ultra's opening hours. That last part really got the festival's attention. If we could shift that many

3 I do not recommend doing this, but if you must, please find a credible set of instructions online. Having too little alcohol in your final hand sanitizer mix will render it useless.

tickets competing with them, what could we do if we teamed up? So, for 2020, the first non-shit Ultra offer I'd received in nearly a decade arrived. Proper money, headline billing, great stage, sweet set time. I couldn't wait for the set. Miami during Music Week is always a great time, and the Ultra set was going to be the final victory in a battle I'd been fighting for years: also, vindication of my strategy that not selling myself short was the right move. I'd certainly doubted it enough times.

It was going to be epic.

However, the virus had landed in Miami. I woke up to a barrage of messages from Anthony Garcia, my Laserface partner. Over a flurry of frenetic WhatsApp messages sent in the middle of the night, I deduced that whilst nothing concrete had happened yet, there were serious rumors about the festival's future, and Garcia was in a spin. This was bad news. Whilst cancellation at this point was clearly possible – if unlikely – until we heard anything concrete, it was best if both of us kept to our jobs. For me, that was planning the music, and for him, that was programming the lasers. After a chat, we agreed that until we heard anything concrete, we'd continue preparation as if the show was 100% happening.

I got back to trying to create my best festival set of all time.

Garcia got back to programming the greatest lasers of all time.

All was good.

Then, the fucking festival was cancelled.

With Ultra gone, we considered our options in Miami. A big promoter in the city was looking to put on an alternative program of events titled 'Miami Flusic Week'. Despite the rather crass name, the offers rolled in, and for a few days, we carefully considered our options. Was it safe? Maybe. Were our flights refundable? Nope. Was it worth taking the risk, and potential public backlash for a handful of club shows? Not sure. However, once again, the virus made the decision for us: in a matter of days, the United States banned all flights from Europe, just as the City of Miami placed a 200-person limit on shows. With most DJs ruled out, and capacities severely limited, Miami 2020 was finished.

Over the next few weeks, the cards fell quickly. Event after event was cancelled, with major restrictions being imposed on live music around the world. I felt lucky that Sansa, our eldest daughter, was able to enjoy her 5th birthday party just days before Los Angeles was hit with a lockdown order, which would still be in place months later, but it was a rare bright spot in a world that was in crisis.

I should note at this point, that although my analysis of the pandemic is somewhat focused on its effects on my own industry, that doesn't mean I'm imperious to the devastation the virus itself has caused. With one parent and two parents-in-laws over 70, I've been worried about them, as I have about friends who work on the front lines of the medical service. Friends have lost parents to the virus, and it's more than likely that I'll be affected personally in the future. However, the effects of the virus itself have been widely circulated in the mainstream media, and I see little mileage in repeating narratives that have already been well covered. However, the effects on our industry have been brutal, with many people working behind the scenes in live music forgotten – and I feel I'm better using my platform to shine a light on these areas.

Initially, I was broadly supportive of the lockdown. There was so much still unknown about the virus, and if the initial WHO mortality rate of 3.4% had turned out to be accurate, drastic action was indeed merited. As I read about 'flattening the curve' the science seemed to make sense. Even with a far lower mortality rate, this was a virus that, until late 2019, not a single human being on planet earth had had. With no immunity, even a fairly mild virus would sweep the global population, quickly causing massive hospital overwhelm: a brutal situation that it was clear had to be avoided.

Regardless of that, I was facing real issues. Live shows, which represented upwards of 95% of my income, were gone. My wife's art gallery, which usually could have kept us afloat, was forced to close by the LA County lockdown. Our family income, for the foreseeable future, was zero.

Financially, I was a bit fucked.

Again.

July, 2015.
Manchester, UK.

This cannot be right.

My pulse races and my throat dries up, as the full extent of the massive shit I am in starts to hit home. I ask the question again.

"So… the total debt we need to repay is, just in case I didn't hear you correctly?"

"Just over $750,000, in total. Due in the next year."

I'm part-terrified, part-angry. I'm in my small flat in Manchester – which no doubt will soon be getting repossessed unless something very fucking drastic happens.

I am so fucked. And I'm angry.

I'm angry at my accountants for getting me into this mess, with no real idea of how I'd get out of it.

I'm angry at my family, for never giving me a proper financial education.

But most of all, and most appropriately, I'm angry at myself.

I am FUCKED.

Let's rewind a few decades.

I didn't start in music because of money: it was simply never a major motivation of mine growing up. Money was more of a necessary evil: I wanted to do cool shit, so I needed to earn the money to do it. I never had much of an interest in stacking the stuff up in the bank. I still don't, if I'm honest. You can't take it with you, and I'm not especially keen for my daughters to inherit huge sums. Warren

Buffet stated that he wanted to leave his kids '*enough to do anything, but not enough to do nothing*', and whilst our definition of 'enough' likely varies, that sounds about right to me. I've met various people in my life who've come into massive inheritances, and few of them have turned out well.

Growing up, money wasn't talked about a lot in our household. My dad, who grew up to a coal-mining family in the Welsh valleys, is extremely careful with his cash – and constantly received abuse in our household for the contents of his weekly shop. We'd never enjoyed Heinz Ketchup, or any other premium brand, due to his insistence on only ever buying items that were on a 2-for-1 sale; the kitchen cupboard a revolving door of off-brand discount groceries.

My dad's extreme frugality was balanced out well by my mother, who preferred to spend whatever she wanted with little thought for the consequences. Together though, they made a good team. If my dad was in charge, family holidays would have been whatever war zone was on sale at the travel agency, but instead, thanks to Mum, we ventured to the South of France where we'd stay in lovely little villas with swimming pools. We were still frugal, only eating out a few times during the vacation as a treat, but it was a good life.

My own financial tendencies tended towards my mother's side.

As I started to achieve success as a DJ, all of a sudden, money did come into the fold. It was simply impossible not to be influenced by your peers; any junior, professional DJ, will undoubtedly notice their more senior colleagues seem to be way, way, richer.

Leaving a festival in Poland, miserably standing in a seemingly endless airport security line, I watched as the likes of Sasha, Pete Tong and Sven Vath strolled past me, happily chatting away as they entered the lane marked 'Business Class Only'. Later, boarding the plane, as I trudged down to the back of the bus, I noticed the business class cabin was almost entirely full of DJs, gossiping away as flight attendants fussed around them, handing out ice-cold champagne and complimentary canapés. Fuck, man. Business class was where it was at. Imagine the deals that were getting done up there, while I was wedged into the back row between two people who, judging by their size, were only interested in deals that involved 2 for 1 at Dominos.

I soon decided that my next goal was to earn enough money to fly business class. I appreciate that as a goal, it's fairly crass, but I was travelling every week and it was killing me. Long-haul economy is fine a couple of times a year on holiday, but do it every week, and it'll start to grind you down. And long-haul is where business class really comes into its own: with lounges where you can work before the flights, and full beds on board the plane, so you can actually arrive fully rested before your show. Business class wouldn't just be more comfortable: it'd be better for my health and career, too.

And that goal was achieved quickly. By 2008, I was flying exclusively business class. Of course, I still wasn't happy. (Have you noticed a trend yet?)

At that point, although I could afford to travel the world in the business-class cabin, I didn't look like I could afford to sit there, and each time I shambled up to board a plane wearing a Ben Sherman shirt with a shit wooden necklace and chunky DJ backpack, I'd inevitably be stopped in my tracks.

"Sir, this is the business class lane only. Please join the economy line."

At this point, I'd fumble for my business class boarding card with as much indignation as I could muster, and after some sort of half-arsed apology, I'd be on my way.

But I was sure Pete Tong and Sasha weren't getting stopped at every check point. I just didn't look the part, and so I started burning cash on clothes and accessories. Out went the old backpack, to be replaced by a smart £500 Tumi roll-on suitcase – the luggage of choice for any discerning road warrior. I stopped shopping at Top Shop and River Island, and went exclusively to Harvey Nichols. At this point, my outgoings were still fairly low – the flat I was renting cost £650 a month – so I had more money than I knew what to do with. I'd walk into Harvey Nichols, pile up a stack of designer clothes and sunglasses, and be on my way.

As my earnings increased, so did my reliance on material tendencies. I bought a BMW Z4, then a top-of-the-line Supercharged Range Rover Sport. I bought a Rolex. And plenty more stupid items, each one delivering a short-lived burst of fleeting joy, before the longing for something else took over.

However, these material possessions weren't just to ease my passage into the business class lounge. On a deeper level, they were my defense against the world. My profile had exploded over the last few years, and I was getting major attention online – not all of it positive. This was the early years of Facebook and Twitter, and 'haters' had just arrived on the scene. Today, after over a decade of social media use, I've developed a fairly thick skin, but the first time anyone finds people that they don't know online telling them that they're shit, talentless, and should die, it's fucking tough, and it's fair to say I didn't quite know how to deal with it.

My dad was never much of a 'turn the other cheek' sort. By his book, if someone comes at you – with an insult or otherwise – you hit them back twice as hard. And this was a good strategy when it came to dealing with school bullies, who rarely bothered me after the first encounter. Unfortunately, online trolls are a different breed. They live for the attention – it's their oxygen – and the more attention you give them, the more they come alive.

I was learning this the hard way. One Miami Music Week, on Ocean Drive at dusk, after a few too many B-52 shots, I idly checked Twitter. As usual, my timeline was full of people singing my praises, all of whom I entirely ignored. No, I was looking for something else. And then I found it.

> **arsenalfanboyx99**
> I hate @garethemery the weedy arrogant little shit. Gonna break his fucking nose if I see him around Miami this week.

Woah, there. Immediately, I felt my cortisol spike as my body went into defense mode and I tried to figure out what I'd done to offend this particular character. It didn't seem we'd had any prior interaction, so this unpleasant attack had come out of nowhere.

"You alright Gaz?" Adam asked. He'd seen this look before.

"Yeah, fine", I told him, still buried in my phone.

I blocked him, and got back on with my conversation, but the tweet kept niggling at the back of my mind. All I had to do was do nothing, and I'd never hear from him again. But, due to the alcohol, ego, or something else, I couldn't help myself.

In the next lull in conversation, I grabbed my phone again, and checked out the picture of my would-be assailant to see who I might be dealing with. Short, squat, weedy looking. He might be ruining my night, but he wasn't particularly threatening in a physical sense.

I fired back.

> **garethemery @arsenalfanboyx99**
> At the Breakwater on Ocean Drive mate. Come down and have a go.

I know, I know, but I'm trying to be real with you here, and that means showing the dickhead in me, too.

For the next ten minutes, I drifted in and out of the conversation with my mates, furiously refreshing Twitter every 30 seconds or so. Here I was, in the prime of life, in one of the greatest cities in the world, with some of my favorite people, and I was focused on some idiot on the internet.

Eventually, he replied:

> **arsenalfanboyx99**
> Unbelievable @garethemery has actually just threatened me with physical violence. Reporting this tweet to Twitter.
>
> **arsenalfanboyx99**
> So unprofessional @garethemery you have just shown the whole world why you have never taken your career to the next level and never will.

What the fuck? He was the one that said he was going to punch me!

I look for his original tweet, to find he'd deleted it, leaving only my reply for the world to see. And before long, a few of his mates were replying saying the same thing:

I was aggressive, out-of-order, unprofessional and they'd never be listening to my music ever again.

I deleted my own tweet, and blocked the lot of them. If only it was so easy to block my feelings of anger, towards the troll, and myself.

I did learn a valuable lesson that day though. Until then, I'd tried to be liked by everyone – and if I couldn't be liked, I'd at least beat them in an argument. But this user's insane U-turn showed me a few things.

Firstly, some people will never like you, and you're best off not wasting your time with them.

And secondly, well-practiced trolls were better at this than me.

Although I stopped engaging, the haters were still in the back of my mind. I was in my late 20s at the time, and whilst in hindsight the music I was making was pretty good, I had no confidence in it. I was plagued by perfectionism, fears of not being good enough, and every negative online comment cut to the bone. However, I hadn't learnt how to be honest and vulnerable yet – so my only tool was fighting back – which I did with money. In a way, it was my shield against the haters. The unspoken picture would say: *you might hate me, but I'm sat in an Emirates First Class suite, wearing a watch that cost what you'd make in a year.*

I know: what a completely knobbish attitude to have. I'm sure it wound up the haters, but it also would have turned off many genuine fans, who wondered why their favorite artist was suddenly acting like a rapper.

However, all this was nothing compared to the mess I was about to get myself in, by moving to the capitol city of knobbish behaviour:

Los Angeles.

Watching the likes of Sasha and Pete Tong in business class had an effect on me, but at least I was still living in Manchester – a reasonably unpretentious place where it was hard to really spend serious money. Sure, there were a few places where you could burn cash, like the footballer-hotspot Panacea, but living large in Manchester, I still couldn't spend the cash I was making.

In Los Angeles though, everything was different. We rented a house in the hills above Sunset Boulevard in West Hollywood – an incredible, buzzy area, but the center of Californian materialism. The houses cost a fortune. Everyone was driving insanely expensive cars: Lamborghinis and Ferraris on every corner.

And I was about to totally lose control of my money.

Moving to America, I had little idea how the American financial system worked. I'd never had a bank account in the US, and when I asked about setting one up, a sleazy lawyer who'd been helping me at the time gave me the solution.

"Bank account? G, don't be silly. You need a *business manager.* Anyone who's anyone in LA has a business manager. I know all the top guys. Let me know when you arrive, and I'll get you introduced."

Before long, I'd met a few business managers and chose my favorite – let's call them MBM ('Music Business Managers') and what a sweet deal it seemed. The MBM guys would do all the usual boring stuff which my UK accountants did – pay taxes, run payroll for staff, submit tax returns – but they'd also do everything else: set up my mobile phone accounts, arrange for internet at my house, return my Amazon packages. Basically, they'd do all the shit I really hated doing (who likes waiting on hold?) for an hourly fee.

When I asked about bank account access, they laughed.

"Well, of course, we *can* give you access to the accounts, but you're the artist. Much better for you to spend your time making music than worrying about money. Just pop into the office a few times a year for an update and we'll handle everything else".

It sounded a good plan to me. These guys had a flash office with the walls covered in gold discs and magazine covers of the artists they represented. All manner of A-list musicians and movie stars also used them, so I felt like I was in good company. So, I got down to the task of making music, with very little thought about money. I'd rack up costs, send the invoices to MBM, and never hear another word about it.

Of course, I'd occasionally get updates. A few times a year, we'd meet in the MBM boardroom where we'd receive incomprehensive financial reports in thick binders compromised of 'inverse-budgets', 'touring-reconciliations' and other things that seemed too much like real work, so I assumed that the MBM boffins had a good handle on things and carried on spending on designer clothes, fancy meals out, and leased sports cars.

Little to my knowledge, I was in deep shit, and it was about to get deeper.

A few months later, Kat and I were preparing for some extensive renovations on the house that we'd purchased. At an MBM meeting, we presented the budget, and were met with a few raised eyebrows, before some murmuring about a 'home equity line of credit', then a conclusion along the lines of *don't worry, you'll have the cash.*

A few weeks later, I signed a thick stack of paper for a loan from the bank so the building work could begin. MBM were hazy on the details, but had assured us it was a very easy, standard thing that everyone did, and there wasn't even any interest to pay. What a great deal!

At this point, what I really needed was an email written in capital letters saying:

YOU ARE SPENDING WAY MORE MONEY THAN YOU HAVE!!!!!

STOP SPENDING MONEY YOU FUCKING IDIOT!!!!!!

Instead, I had facilitators.

A year or so later, this epic mistake was hitting home. Wandering around my Manchester flat on a trip back to the UK, MBM called me, and for the first time in our relationship, they had chosen to give me the bad news.

"So, a small issue. As you didn't pay back the home equity line of credit in time, it's now switching to a fairly high interest rate, and needs to be paid back every month".

"Eh? I thought the thing was interest free?" I'd clearly remembered something, at least.

"It was, but only for the first year. So we'd have needed to pay it all back over the last year for that to happen."

"Why did nobody tell me that? How much have we paid back so far?"

"None."

"What the fuck? Why not?"

"Well, we've not had the funds. Your new studio went over-budget, and then of course there was the Lamborghini, the Rolls-Royce…"

"Jesus Christ. And how much did we borrow again?"

"Well, let me just check – we took a few different loans so the grand total is – seven-five-eight-one-oh-nine."

"Seventy-five thousand dollars?"

"No. Seven hundred and fifty-eight thousand. $758,109 to be precise."

I instantly felt nauseous. "Fuck."

I stumbled away from the phone, thinking: this cannot possibly be right. After a few hours of going through forms with Kat, it turned out that it was.

I was close to tears. Somehow, I'd managed to rack up nearly a million dollars of debt.

This would *never* have happened in Manchester.

The next two years was largely spent getting control of our finances back. Kat, who was always much better at money than me, took a much bigger role, helping me see all the money I was wasting, and just how out of control things had become. In a shock, it turned out my biggest cost was MBM themselves. Yep, as well as facilitating my own insane spending, we realized that each month they were charging anything from $15,000 to $35,000 for their services – and as they were in control of the accounts, I never got to approve these amounts – they were simply deducted. Their huge invoices were calculated on an hourly basis on a model where simple tasks could trigger huge cascading charges.

I forget the exact model, but let's say our main business manager cost $500 an hour. I'd sent him an email, which might only take him a minute to read, but that would be billed, and as the company billed in quarter-hour increments, that one minute, reading my one email would cost me $125. It was insane.

I soon fired MBM, moving to a new firm that cost a fraction of the price, and were more than happy for me to be actively involved in my own finances. I sold the cars: I was hardly at home anyway due to touring, so it was madness keeping them. Whilst I took a huge hit financially ending the various leases early, I was surprised to find my happiness level didn't change at all – in fact, I felt rather liberated to have gotten rid of a huge pile of debt. Then, slowly but surely, we started the process of getting out of the rest of our debt – initially, paying off the insane home-equity loan that MBM had got us into, and then getting rid of credit cards and other lines of credit.

AMA wasn't my only problem. I was also staffed up to the max, with managers, day-to-day managers, interns, assistants – all working out of a pricy office in a tower above Sunset Boulevard, and all doing their best to spend the money that I was making.

A friend visiting from the UK – he's a jeweler, and one of the few people I know who really understands money – was shocked as we drove from the airport to my house, and I told him about the insanity of my personal finances.

"Fucking hell Gaz. This is absolute madness mate," he told me.

And he was right. I needed a way out.

I'd find it in education.

I realized that my total mismanagement of money wasn't down to any real fundamental character flaw. I'd simply never had any training on how to correctly handle large amounts of cash. I had to get educated.

Over a period of a few years, I threw myself into finance books, with my favorites written by Dave Ramsey. Ramsey felt like an unlikely place for me to find salvation: a devout evangelical Christian talk-show host from Nashville, Tennessee, but his books on personal finance were game changers for me. He did a great job of explaining why complex financial products are often the last thing you want, and how the management of money can actually be very simple.

Eventually, quite recently, after seriously cutting spending, we'd managed to get in a much more stable position with very little debt. My current lifestyle is surprisingly frugal: I haven't owned a car for over three years, borrowing Kat's when I need to or taking Ubers instead. I spend almost nothing on clothes, instead owning a pile of Uniqlo V-Necks that cost less than $10 each. I don't really give a shit about flexing on the internet, or impressing strangers that I don't know anymore. And overall, I feel happier, more content, and far less encumbered than I did when I had hundreds of thousands of pounds of gleaming metal sat on the driveway.

Did I need to buy a succession of unnecessary material possessions and take myself to the verge of bankruptcy to get to this point?

Maybe.

I'd been told growing up many times that 'money doesn't make you happy', but that was usually by people who didn't have a lot of money. Would they have felt differently sipping a cocktail onboard a private jet as it powered off from Las Vegas? I had to find out.

Plus, we live in a very materialistic world. Sure, the gurus can tell us that money won't make you happy, but in the modern world, we see over 5,000 advertisements every single day. That's nearly two million ads per year, and most of them are based on telling us that we'll be happier if we buy whatever they're selling. With so much conditioning, you can see why most people do indeed think that *more stuff = more happiness.*

Of course, not having enough money for the basics does bring unhappiness, and for people struggling to put food on the table, feed their families, or gain an education, money for these things will have a real difference on happiness. However, the benefits taper off: studies show that happiness only increases with income up to about $105,000 in the US, with people actually getting *less* happy after that![4]. That's insane right? Someone earning $105,000 is actually likely to be happier than Jeff Bezos.

Once enough money is earned to cover basic needs, new purchases, whilst exhilarating at the time, quickly become part of our

4 'Money not linked to happiness past $105,000 in U.S., study suggests'. USA Today, Feb 26th, 2018.

baseline expectations of life. Whether it's a new car, house, clothes: they soon lose their novelty and just become *normal.*

That said, this is a lesson best learnt first-hand. Almost all wealthy people that I know splurged a lot of cash when they first acquired it, before settling down into two broad groups. The first group quickly realized that money wasn't the key to happiness: and instead shifted their focus to living a fulfilling life. Plenty of these people still make lots of money, but they don't base their happiness or self-worth from money in the bank or a car on the drive. The other group simply continue looking for larger material goals. More expensive watches, bigger houses, fancier cars, private jets, private islands. True happiness seems to elude these people: instead, it's always around the corner, if they can just buy that 'next' thing. Many rich people live life this way, and they are some of the saddest, emptiest people on the planet.

Me? I think I learned my lesson fairly early on. I thought – as many do – that money would make me happy, but I was able to thoroughly test that hypothesis and find my experience didn't agree.

And I guess I did have some fun along the way, too.

August, 2020.

With no end in sight to the pandemic, my mind turns to my own industry, and how it'll be affected long-term. Will we get to perform live again at some stage? Sure. But it'll be in a new world, not a return to one we all enjoyed up to February 2020.

The fact is, the music industry has been irreparably damaged by the lockdown. This is an extinction-level event for many promoters and venues, plenty of whom lived month-to-month at the best of times. When we return, venues will have closed, promoters will have gone bankrupt, and essential personnel that we relied upon like production crew and agents will have left the industry.

In fact, much of this is quietly happening behind the scenes already. Major agencies have already instituted drastic moves ranging from culling hundreds of jobs, to 50% pay cuts for those who remain: and agency employees are much better prepared to handle the upcoming crisis than VJs (video jockeys), tour managers, bar staff, security, cleaners, and many others who work on a contract basis with no guaranteed salary or health insurance.

Even when we do get back on the road, it isn't going to be easy. Initially, there will be severe restrictions on venues, with empowered local authorities shutting down nights at a moment's notice based on local outbreaks, making planning anything in the future difficult. There will be international travel restrictions. Some countries may require vaccinations for visitors, if one even exists. The Netherlands has already decided that no large-scale live events will be happening until a vaccine is found – and even if a vaccine is found quickly, getting it into production, and vaccinating basically *the entire fucking world* is going to take a while. Besides, do I really want to take a rushed-out, bodge job vaccine? Actually, if it meant touring again, sure. If you've got a vaccine, hit me up.

However, as grim as things currently are, I do believe we'll see mass gatherings again: they're simply too integral to the human experience. Early in the pandemic, I worried that the audience might not return even when things were deemed 'safe', but after witnessing Black Lives Matter protests around the world, it's clear that this is not the case.

On the eve of the largest protest in Los Angeles, in the Pan Pacific Park, I opened Twitter to get a sense of the mood. And to my surprise, I didn't find anger and fury, but instead, young adults excited for the event. *Who can help me make a sign for tomorrow? Is anyone driving from Palmdale? What's the best thing to wear to a protest?* If I hadn't known otherwise, I could have been reading a stream of people attending EDC or Coachella. With sport and music removed, protests were the only remaining pressure valve for society to release some of the pent-up anger it felt.

And this gave me hope. Not only was I happy to see a focus on real issues affecting the United States – such as the brutal murders of Breonna Taylor, George Floyd and many others – but seeing the need of the younger generation to gather together against the odds gave me real hope for our own industry.

Still, things will take time. The vast, *vast* majority of humans are unlikely to seek out the raw data on their own risk profile to this virus – instead, they're led by the environment created in mainstream and social media, which currently is one of panic. Human beings are inherently suspicious of other humans, and there needs to be significant social changes before live music returns. Presently, in Los Angeles County, masks are required: you can't even leave your house without one. There are an awful lot of rungs of the ladder to climb down to get from here to standing shoulder-to-shoulder with tens of thousands of others at a concert.

For me though, life is indeed inherently risky, and that's part of its beauty. Playing team sports outside carries the risk of skin cancer, broken bones, and heart attacks. Swimming in the ocean exposes you to the risk of shark attacks or, much more likely, drowning after being washed out to sea in a riptide. Taking a long-haul flight, giving someone a hug or – yes - attending a concert will increase your chances of picking up a variety of killer diseases, from the flu to meningitis. Shit, even driving your car is risky.

But many of these things aren't optional add-ons to the human experience: they are the human experience itself.

Ultimately, each of us needs to make decisions about the level of risk we're prepared to accept in life. There are no doubt people who avoid swimming in the ocean, long haul flights, and team sports because of the risk, whereas I do all of those things and strongly believe my life has been better for them. However, I also draw the line somewhere, and avoid more extreme activities like bungee-jumping, racing cars, and skydiving, where the risk/reward ratio is a little out of my comfort zone, particularly as a parent to two young children. As live events start to reopen, citizens of the world will need to start thinking about the level of risk they're prepared to accept for a rich and fulfilling life.

As the lockdown proliferated throughout 2020, many DJs began playing free sets online. Various online 'festivals' were set up, and the offers of unpaid sets flooded in. I declined them all. I wasn't against DJing online, per se, but something didn't feel quite right. With no idea where things were going, I didn't want to rush to give away my life's work for free.

Some of the most popular platforms for DJs to play on were Instagram Live, which paid no money to the artist (but certainly helped the profitability of Instagram itself), and Twitch, which had a much better model, but left artists relying on subscriptions and tips from the audience. Neither felt quite right to me. I'm certainly not above asking for tips (if you want my PayPal just ask) but I didn't want my sets to become request-based, which was how you made the best money on Twitch. Crafting a set is an art form, and I wanted to be able to do that without a stream of real-time feedback – otherwise, I'd just feel like a glorified jukebox.

The other thing that didn't sit well for me was that almost all of these online festivals were for charity. I've done a lot of charity when times were good. When I bowed out of the DJ Mag poll a few years back, I donated my entire usual marketing budget of $15,000 to charity, conducting my own 'poll' with fans on my Facebook page deciding which charities would benefit. I've raised similar amounts in one-off charity events, including a fundraiser for the Greater Vancouver Food Bank where we raised $15,000 in one night. Over the last year, I've supported a variety of causes close to my heart, including major world events like the Australian wildfires, to industry-specific causes, like a fundraiser much-loved industry photographer

Rukes held for his parents, who had accumulated severe medical debt following a car accident.

There are times to give to charity, but the moment you've just lost 95% of your income isn't one of them.

Chatting to a close DJ friend who I knew was struggling, I asked him why he was playing all these charity events.

"Dude, you told me last week you were worried about making rent. No joke, but you're kind of the charity right now – it's you that needs the money," I told him, phrasing it like a joke, although I was deadly serious.

"I know man," he replied "but everyone else is doing the charity thing. I don't want to rock the boat – I just need to remain as relevant as possible for when the gigs come back."

On my side, I didn't particularly care about rocking the boat. In my view, the *only* reason why most artists in our industry were giving their art away for free was because, in their view, the return of gigs was just around the corner. When they realized the gigs weren't coming back, they'd all soon have to work out a way to remain in the business. Much better to start now.

Plus, every other business was already one step ahead. My daughter's school had already shifted their learning to Zoom classes – like the school itself, the classes weren't free. A personal-trainer friend of mine shifted her classes to online: again, she continued to charge. Every other industry who could go virtual and continue to charge fair prices was doing it. Shit, even other areas of the music industry were doing it, with theatre, classical, and rock swiftly gravitating towards pay-per-view concerts. Yet in dance music – typically a genre that's ahead of the curve – we were giving away our finest work for free, and stigmatizing even the suggestion of the opposite. How had we got it so wrong?

As I mentioned, charity in 2020 was never an option – instead, my priorities were my family and staff: the people that really fucking depended on me. Obviously, I needed cash for the mortgage and to keep the kids in school, but also I needed to keep as many of our staff on payroll as possible. Running a small business means employing numerous others, many of whom have families of their own, and I was acutely aware of the knock-on effects if I had to let people go, particularly in a brutal job market where they'd not be able to find new jobs.

There was no question: I had to keep making money.

I had to buck the trend of our industry and continue to charge for performances.

And so in April, we announced the Decade Concert. Decade was originally a tour that would have taken in 10 North American cities during March and April. The first ever 'classics' tour I'd done, it was a show that had sold well when tickets went on sale. With every show cancelled due to the virus, this felt like a good opportunity to dip our toes into the waters of pay-per-view.

We decided to make the Decade Concert free to anyone who'd bought a ticket for the original tour, even though their tickets had since been refunded. Not only was it the right thing to do, but the goodwill of thousands of ticket-buyers would likely help with any backlash. For anyone else, the cost was $10. For this, I'd play a four hour set of all of my classics, with real, festival-style production. I wouldn't be streaming from my bedroom with piles of dirty laundry behind me, no: this would look and feel like a proper night out.

We invested close to $10,000 in the production of the show, and I felt good about that. Even if we just broke even, we would be creating work for people in an industry who had almost no work at the time: our laser vendor, production crew, cameras, driver, management, and more. And even with my basic knowledge of economics, I could see the flow of that money back into the economy. By putting on a show that left just ten people with real money in their pockets, they could then go and spend on other companies that badly needed their business – for instance, ordering takeout from a struggling local restaurant. No need for charity: instead, we were injecting real money back into the economy, and allowing people to do their real jobs with their heads held high.

As we announced the show, I felt prepared for a little backlash. As the first pay-per-view concert to take place in dance music, I was more than prepared to take a little flak, but I was comfortable enough with the economics of it all to defend our decision. I strongly believed we were doing the right thing, and also believed that others would soon join me, so everyone would forget who was first anyway. As it happened though, my worries were barely necessary. Feedback was 99.9% positive, and our ticket sales far surpassed our expectations, selling over 2,000 tickets for both Decade and its follow up concert Unplugged. Reading thousands of happy comments post-show, I realized we were onto a good thing.

As the year ticked on, with live income still non-existent, I was forced to become an expert at finding alternative income streams: transforming our merchandise business from a four-figure to a six-figure business annually. My team and I worked hard to deliver items with real value: from beautiful '*we'll be ok*' clothing, to signed CDs, vinyls, and yes: the book you're currently reading. In short, I realized that not being able to tour wasn't the end of the world. Make great products that are worth more than they cost, and people will buy them.

My advice to fellow artists: there has never been a better time to focus on your core supporters. Make things better than you need to. Know their names. Bounce messages on DM. Create amazing experiences for them that nobody else is. When you go the extra mile, you'd be amazed how supportive people are. The era of accumulating millions of fair-weather fans is over, at least for a while. Instead, it's time to do more than ever before for your biggest supporters, who will have your back in the upcoming years.

Aside from my own industry, it was a time where I felt fairly concerned about the state of the world. As the months went by, and the virus failed to become the anticipated plague, my support for an endless lockdown ebbed away. The lockdown also became highly politicized, and I was thoroughly disappointed to see what should have been a bipartisan public health issue, become a highly polarized political wrestling match.

Locally though, the effects were real, and as a family of small businesses owners, we felt for those who were wiped out. Within weeks of the lockdown, vacant shop fronts started popping up on our local high-street as LA's notoriously brutal landlords evicted shops and restaurants by the dozen. As the FOR LEASE signs multiplied in front of our eyes, I couldn't help but feel for the business owners, and the people previously employed by them. Where were they now? Did they have children? Were they getting evicted? I texted a friend who owned a chain of restaurants to ask how he was getting on, and he replied that he'd been forced to lay off 500 people. It broke my heart.

Chatting to friends, I found an array of different opinions. Clearly, any small business owners understood how serious this was, being well aware of how income flows back into an economy, and how devastating it can be when that stops. Other friends of mine were less understanding.

"It's just JOBS, and that does not compare to DEATH!" my friend Karla texted me back, as we chatted one day. "People just need to deal with it!"

I was just canvassing opinion so I didn't disagree, but I did wonder if her own situation – happily working from home in a stable £60,000 a year government job – meant she lacked a little empathy for the millions out of work. The previous week she'd informed me how much money she was saving by not commuting due to the lockdown, and I wondered if she'd feel differently if she was being evicted from her house.

And whilst her narrative of 'death is the most important' feels compelling, as a political science student, I learnt that the realities are often far more nuanced and complex. Of course, death mattered to me: losing my mother in my mid-20s had shown me the brutal reality of the loss of an immediate family member.

But statistics should guide us more than personal experience: and poverty causes death, too. The UK's austerity program, a series of public-service cost cuts which were implemented from 2012, were estimated to have caused 130,000 deaths[5], primarily due to cuts in health care. It scared me to think that the recession we were about to enter into in the US would make the UK's austerity years look like a walk in the park – and the US has much less of a social safety net. Reuters covered a UN report, which warned that the global economic downtown could '*kill hundreds of thousands of children in 2020'* due to tens of millions of children falling into extreme poverty: a terrifying prediction from a credible source, yet almost no news outlets covered the story.

This bothered me deeply. Deaths from the virus were clearly news, but so should be the deaths of hundreds of thousands of children – even if they occurred in a much more insidious, behind-the-scenes way. I wondered how deeply the real effects of the lockdown were truly understood. Yes: we seemed to be flattening the curve, but at what cost? What would happen to cancer patients, missing vital screenings or chemotherapy sessions due to not wanting to visit hospitals, for instance? What about domestic abuse victims?

I read more and more, but found few concrete answers. The terrifying projections which had led most governments around the world to lockdown had come from my old friend Neil Ferguson, notorious for his prediction that bird flu would kill 150m people. And as the months ticked by, his terrifying simulations which had predicted 2.2 million Americans would die of the virus – a number that absolutely would have justified what the country was going through - started to look increasingly inaccurate.

---

5 'Austerity to blame for 130,000 'preventable' UK deaths'. The Guardian, June 1st, 2019.

Soon enough, my head spinning, I lost faith in the news. The mainstream news outlets had a clear narrative: hundreds of thousands of kids dying from poverty didn't fit in, but deaths from the virus merited constant updates and snazzy graphics. But the alternative news wasn't much better: with the other side of the spectrum a hodge-podge of anti-vaxxers, conspiracy theorists, crackpots, and the occasional bit of sense. I couldn't get on board with an endless shutdown – that was clear – but watching anti-lockdown protestors who were wearing 'Jesus Is My Vaccine' t-shirts turned me off too. Those weren't my people, either.

Getting nowhere, I realized I was missing something very important.

Perspective.

I had to break up with the news again.

Sure, there was plenty to make me angry: but wasn't that always the case? In reality, little of note was happening each day, and I had Kat to inform me of the latest lockdown rules

Instead, I used my reading time to seek out perspective, consuming an all-you-can-eat diet of history. History's quite a wonderful hobby: there's something about reading about major events in the past that really helps you to zoom out and get a 10,000 foot view on modern-day crises, without all the noise you experience reading the news daily.

Rejecting my previous diet of mainstream news websites, I read books on past pandemics, the outbreak of World War 1, the creation of the modern Middle East, and the age-old Israeli-Palestinian conflict: all topics I've had a decades-long fascination with, and my mood shifted from anger, to gratitude. Compared to what many of these people had suffered, and were still suffering, having to stay home for a few months – or even a few years – suddenly seemed far less of a big deal. As I finished Leon's McCarron's 'The Land Beyond' - an incredible journal of an Irish adventurer's 1,000 mile walk though Israel, Palestine, Jordan and Egypt – and I sunk back into my comfortable bed in an air-conditioned house in peacetime California, I felt at peace with the world again.

I was very fucking fortunate.

There's no neat, tidy end to this part of the story, I'm afraid. Perhaps in a future edition, I can look back on how things eventually played out, but right now, I feel grateful for all that's good in my life.

Despite facing more uncertainty than I've had in my life so far, I feel good. I'm healthy, as are my family, and that's my main priority. I'm also fortunate that Kat's business has been a bright star throughout all this, providing a life-line for our family. Many others in music have no such fortune, and my heart breaks for them, but going forward, I'm ready for the challenge.

I'm not expecting things to 'go back to normal' – for me, uncertainty *is* normal, now, and I believe that happiness and fulfillment will be found by learning to thrive in it, rather than by waiting for it to pass.

And so, I'm ready to adapt.

To explore new technologies.

To engage deeply with my core fan base and serve them better than before.

And I'm confident that by the end, we'll come out of it better, together.

Wishing you and those closest to you good health. May you live life to the fullest.

See you in the lasers.

Gareth Emery
Los Angeles, August 2020

A special thanks to our Kickstarter backers. Over 800 people pledged $50,000 to bring this book to life, and I'm truly grateful to each and every one of you.

AAKAASH BHOWAN. AARON BARLOW. AARON BEAVEN. AARON CHONG. AARON DUGGER. AARON MCNAY. AARON STEFANSKY. ADALI TAPIA. ADAM BUDD. ADAM CLARK. ADAM EXCESS. ADAM HALL. ADEN LEE. AIDA ARZEROUNIAN. AINI SURVO. ALAN LLOYD. ALBERT NGUYEN. ALEC PATINO. ALEJANDRA URIBE. ALEJANDRO. ALESSANDRO DI ROBERTO. ALEX & SOPHIA. ALEX DUGGER. ALEX ENGELMANN. ALEX GLASBERGEN. ALEX HEYES. ALEX HU. ALEX MIRABELLI. ALEX MULLANS. ALEX NEIL. ALEX PEREZ. ALEX PIETROCARLO. ALEX THIESSEN. ALEX WELCH. ALEXANDER CABALLERO. ALEXANDER SHERMAN. ALEXIS OSTRANDER. ALFREDO MARTINEZ. ALICE MALONE. ALISON VANBECK. ALLEN C. LIEU. ALVIN LOONG. ALVIN TIN. ALYSA BORELLI. AMANDA FOON. AMIR URSANI. AMY KING. AMY MASON. ANAHID VASSILIAN. ANDREA DUTTO. ANDREA HENDRICKS. ANDREA SAGEN. ANDREAS SALVESEN. ANDREI HORGA. ANDREW BARRIE. ANDREW C ALFIERI. ANDREW KROPP. ANDREW KUEBLER. ANDREW NORCOM. ANDREY SHULZHENKO. ANDY EMRICK. ANDY HATHAWAY. ANDY LEE. ANDY LEE. ANDY ROEHRS. ANDY VAN DEN ENDE. ANGIE SUPHANTHUCHAT. ANGUS SIU. ANGUS WILLIAMS. ANIL PRAKASH. ANNA RODRIGUEZ. ANNIE QUINTY. ANTHONY FREDIANI. ANTOINE BEYET. ANTONI MARI TUR. ARMANDO SOSA. ARTHUR LEJTKOWSKI. ASHIQ AHAMED. ASHLEY & CHRIS STAKE. ASHLEY BRAIN. ASHLEY MATEJEWSKI. ATLE BJUSTVEIT. AUSTIN KELLAR. AXEL RÄNTILÄ. BÁLINT KLÉRI. BECKY FAIRWEATHER. BEN CANNINGS. BEN DAO. BEN KREBS. BENJAMIN CHOU. BENJAMIN SMITH. BENJAMIN TROOST. BJÖRG PRODAN. BL HOLTER. BLAKE CROSBY. BRAD EICHEN. BRANDON GAZA. BRANDON MAXWELL. BRANDON NIXON. BRANDON STEGMAIER. BRENNEN BAKER. BRET TIDERMAN. BRETT GWINN. BRETT MOORE. BRIAN CUTHBERT. BRIAN FAHMIE. BRIAN KATZ. BRIAN KIBLER. BRIAN MCDONALD. BRIAN MORTON. BRIAN NG. BRIAN SWIFT. BRIAN TAI. BRIAN VETROVEC. BRIAN VU.

BRITT MEADOR. BRITTANY BISHOP. BROOKE SUGAMELE.
BRYAN FEGLEY. BRYAN WASHINGTON. BRYCE DENIS. CALIE SPENCE.
CARLO PRONE. CARLOS CORREA. CARMEL HOPKINS. CARMEN FUNG.
CASPER PLOUG. CASSANDRA SWANSON. CASSIDY VILLEGAS. CASSIE C.
CATALIN NICANOV. CATE CATO NEUHAUSER. CATHY KADOOKA.
CÉDRIC CARLIER. CHAD TEHINI. CHARITY LOPEZ.
CHARLES WARCZINSKY II. CHARLIE BOYLE. CHARLIE SMITH.
CHELSEA & EVAN REDMOND. CHELSEA COWLEY. CHELSEA DAVIS.
CHELSEA JAMES. CHRIS CORNISH. CHRIS DALTON.
CHRIS ERLANDSON. CHRIS HAMILTON. CHRIS HAVILEY. CHRIS LI.
CHRIS MEDLOCK. CHRIS MOFFITT. CHRIS WALKER.
CHRISSY ATHERHOLT. CHRISTIAN FORD. CHRISTIAN LAZZARINI.
CHRISTIN DUNLOP. CHRISTINA & KYLE HAIG.
CHRISTINA ALEXIA ROEHRICHT. CHRISTINA NG. CHRISTINA SAY.
CHRISTINE KEARNEY. CHRISTOPHER. CHRISTOPHER CALAMBI.
CHRISTOPHER KWONG. CHRISTOPHER MICHAEL DIROMA.
CHRISTOPHER SLIVKA. CHRISTOPHER STEPHENSON.
CHRISTOPHER WONG. CHUKK NIELSON. CINDY MARTINEZ.
CLAIRE PARTYHARD HARVEY-BEAVIS. CLAIRE STANFORD.
CLIFFORD RICHMOND. COLIN EHNEBUSKE. COREY DOCKEN.
COREY GILBERT. CORI YODER. CRAIG FRISBIE. CRAIG MCDONALD.
CRAIG NORTHCOTT. CURT ROTHERT. CURTIS TING.
CYNTHIA MERCADO. CYNTHIA REYES. D SCOTT GERK.
DAMON CHANDLER. DAN BROPHY. DAN LAUGHLIN. DAN LE.
DAN MCCABE. DAN SINNREICH. DAN WILSON. DANA REINHART.
DANIEL BRUCE. DANIEL CARRARO. DANIEL CLARK. DANIEL CORNEL.
DANIEL HARRIS. DANIEL MAYESHIBA. DANIEL MOULTON.
DANIEL VOINEA. DANIEL ZUMBRO. DANIELA DISILVIO.
DANIELLE GLEIT. DANNA PETERSON. DANNY SWÄLAS. DANNY YANES.
DAVE CURRY. DAVID BOCEK. DAVID CALDER. DAVID CALL.
DAVID CHORVINSKY. DAVID HARMAN. DAVID HORTON.
DAVID MATTHEW KERN. DAVID OEHME. DAVID PEREIRA.
DAVID PRICE. DAVID SCHACHNER. DAVID SEGAL.
DAVID SPYKZ NGUYEN. DAVID THAI. DEAN BROWN. DEAN C HARRIS.
DEDE LOUIE. DEHVID NGUYEN. DELANEY THOMPSON.
DEREK BUMRUNGSIRI. DEVIN DOYLE. DHRU BEE. DIEGO GARCIA.
DION RODRIGUES. DJ OLE. DOBY DOBERSON DIXON. DON FOSTER.

DONALD SEAGREAVES. DOUG HAMAMOTO. DYLAN SCHRODE.
ED CODA. ED COOK. ED KAY. ED LANNIGAN. EDDIE WU.
EDGAR GARCÍA VARGAS. EDRIC TOM. EDUARDO HERRERA.
EDWARD EWEN. EFI G. EGBERT VAN DER ES. EI LEEN WONG.
EIGOR MALDONADO. ELEANOR YAP. ELIOT GORE.
ELIZABETH HANCHETT. ELLEN N. ELLIE BOWMAN ELLIOT TIERNAY.
EMILY WONG. EMMA BAIN. ERIC APRILL. ERIC DIXON.
ERIC LAPLACE. ERIC LIU. ERIC STILLWAY. ERICK GOVEA.
ERIK PUTRYCZ. ERIKA GRIGGS. ERIN CARANTZA. ERIN SIEGMUND.
ERLEND S. ERVIK. ERWIN HERKELMAN. EVIL DRE. EZEQUIEL H.
FAUVE TAPPENDEN. FEDERICO HOLSTE. FION LIU.
FIONA MONTALDO. FLORA SHALDJIAN. FORTINO MENDOZA.
FOUAD ISSA. FRANCESCO GARASSINO. FRANCIS LEONG.
FRANK RYMAN. FRANK VAN 'T ENDE. GABRIEL PAPPALARDO.
GABRIELLE FERRARE. GARETH JONES. GARETH ROYLE.
GARETH WAGG. GARY NEWE. GAZ JONES. GEOF GREENWAY.
GEOFF HATCHER. GIANCARLO D'AGNILLO. GLEENA THOMAS.
GRAEME STEWART. GREG BOUIN. GREG PORTER. GREG SANDY.
GREGORY SHAPIRO. GARY NG. GUILLAUME LUSSIER. HALEY GANT.
HARRISON TSAI. HAYDN YEO. HEATHER KANTOR.
HEATHER TSICOURIS. HECTOR DELGADO. HECTOR MENDOZA.
HEIDI CAREY. HELEN RO. HELENE CHAN. HENRI MONFLIER.
HENRY PHAN. HUNTER HAYES. IAIN FRASER. IAIN ROWLANDS.
IAN CHUNG. IAN FLORO. IGNACIO GONZALEZ GONZALEZ.
IRENE PETERS. JACK CHEN. JACK HILTON. JACK MARKEE.
JACK PETERS. JACK WATSON. JACKSON ALEXANDER ZERBY.
JACOB CUMMINGS. JACOB WACHMAN. JACQUELINE UGALINO.
JAIME LALIBERTE. JAMES CROFT. JAMES DUPREY. JAMES ELLINGTON.
JAMES JOSLIN. JAMES PIWORSKI. JAMES PRUE. JAMES WALTON.
JANE ANDERSEN. JANELLE WONG. JANICE LEE. JASON CHEN.
JASON HUFFER. JASON LAI. JASON LENNARD. JASON PAQUETTE.
JASSMINE YUMUL. JAXC ROSÉN. JAZMIN MARLENE GARCIA.
JEFF KAMMEYER. JEFF TUPPER. JEFFIELD MAK. JEFFREY KUO.
JENN MARTINEZ. JENNIFER DESTEFANO. JENNIFER GENTRY.
JENNIFER NAKAZONO. JÉRÉMIE ANDRÉ. JEREMY INGRAHAM.
JEREMY SCOTT. JEROEN VAN WERKHOVEN. JEROME NEITA.
JERRY EMERY. JESPER DAHLGREN. JESS NASH. JESS NASH. JESSE DAY.
JESSE RICO. JESSICA DOBBS. JESSICA ESTRELLA. JESSICA HO.

JESUS MENDIOLA. JI-SOOK YIM. JILLIAN KOLUPANOWICH.
JIM MITCHELL. JO BETHELL. JO SFAKIOTAKIS. JOE PALOMERA.
JOE TYSKO. JOHN DOLAN. JOHN FERNIE. JOHN FRIMML.
JOHN GRANDE. JOHN KOSIOR. JOHN MIYASATO. JOHN MOWERY.
JOHN NEERDAEL & JUN ANN SIA. JOHN P LILLIS. JOHN PENNY.
JONATHAN AVIDAN. JONATHAN IVENS-BROWN. JONATHAN NOBLE.
JONATHAN THIELMANN. JONATHAN VILLEGAS.
JONATHAN ZESLAWSKI. JOONO PARK. JORDAN FITZGIBBON.
JORDAN LIENHARD. JORIS BERGMAN. JORN WITTEVEEN.
JOSÉ ANTONIO REY. JOSE JARDON. JOSÉ LUIS REYES. JOSE VARELA.
JOSEPH ALSTON. JOSEPH MALLON. JOSEPH RAYA-ELLIS.
JOSH HUMPHREY. JOSHUA KRAFT. JOSHUA MEYERS. JUAN GARCIA.
JUAN KARMY. JUDD GOLDRICH. JUDIT DOJCSAK. JUKKA TENO.
JULIA YIU. JULIAN CHALMERS. JULIANA JOHNSON. JULIE YI.
JURIS REMESS. JUSTICE HSIUNG. JUSTIN ANTHONY. JUSTIN BRAND.
JUSTIN DUKE. JUSTIN MARM. JUSTIN TOY. JUSTIN WANG.
KAELIN MANOA. KAITLYN HEM. KANOELANI AHINA.
KAREY MARQUART. KARIM HAMASNI. KARL ANNETT. KATE KOVACS.
KATHERINE LEE. KATHY MARIE MCNEAL. KAYLA HENDRICKSON.
KEIKO KAWANA. KEITH BOWDEN. KEITH LEE. KELLY CORREA.
KELLY COULTRUP. KEN BERGMANN. KEN EMERY. KENDRA KLEINER.
KENNETH NG. KETIL STEINE. KEVIN HIGGINS. KEVIN SMET.
KEVIN VALENCIA. KEVIN WU. KEVIN YUEN. KHOI TRINH.
KHRISTOPHER CARTER. KRISTEN SKILLMAN. KRISTINA BRODEUR.
KRISTINE HILLE. KRISTOFER JAXNE. KRISTY WONG.
KRISTYN KARPINCHICK. KTAM. KURT LINKE. KYLE EVAN.
KYLE GETZ. KYLE SANTOS. LANCE TOBIAS. LARS ANCION.
LARS MADSEN & ROSE ANN VIRAY. LAURA MUNSON. LAURA STOW.
LAURA WAGGONER. LAUREN ELSTONE. LAUREN MAGNESS.
LAUREN MCPHERSON. LAUREN VEZZOSI. LAUREN WONG.
LAURIN BRUENIGER. LEAH BERG. LEANNE NEWELL.
LEESA (SAMANTHA LEE). LEILA SOUNDS. LEONARD KUANG.
LEONARDO OLIVEIRA. LESLIE OKAZAKI. LEXI LYSENKO.
LIAM MACNAUGHTON. LIANA COOPER. LIESBETH GEBUIJS.
LILLIAN CALLER. LINA & ADAM BORDEN. LINDSAY MCMAHON.
LINDSEY MORIYAMA. LINH LAM. LISA JOHNSSON. LISA MANSFIELD.
LLYWELYN LEHNERT. LONDON LAROUX. LOTUS O. LUCAS ACHTEM.

LUCIA PURAC. LUKAS VOGLER. LUKE TEO. LYNDSAY LYON.
LYUBOMIR MARINOV. MADS VON QUALEN. MANVIR SOHI.
MARA SAYNES. MARC SCHNEIDER. MARCEL THIES. MARCO PM.
MARCO SEALS. MARIAN MESIA. MARIANE CHOW.
MARIANNE VOELLINGER. MARILYN VICENTE. MARISOL BALABAN.
MARK CORSI. MARK GOODYEAR. MARK KOVIC. MARK LOEWEN.
MARK PETTS. MARLON CHESTERMAN. MAROŠ KOVÁČ.
MARTIN CRAMPEN. MARTIN MICHNIAK. MARTIN SÖDERLUND EK.
MARTINE GALLARDO. MARTYN FRASER. MARTYN PIDDOCK.
MASON GALLOWAY. MÁTÉ BOKOR. MATHEW CARLE.
MATT BARTLETT. MATT BORUCKI. MATT DEKENS. MATT FATTORE.
MATT GUENTHER. MATT ROBERTS. MATT WATSON.
MATTHEW ROLLINS. MATTHEW ALLSOP. MATTHEW BELLEGHEM.
MATTHEW GOODYEAR. MATTHEW HOLGATE. MATTHIEU BOURLAUD.
MAURA FITZGERALD. MAX COLLOPY. MELISSA DESORMEAUX.
MELODY YORK. MELVIN KUANG. MICHAEL "NEWTELLUR" BAÑOS.
MICHAEL (A. SCUSAY) MELNYCHUK. MICHAEL CHAS WHITEHEAD.
MICHAEL CLEGG. MICHAEL FLORES. MICHAEL FLYNN.
MICHAEL HERNANDEZ. MICHAEL MIKOVICH. MICHAEL PIPER.
MICHAEL REVELL. MICHAEL SAECHAO. MICHAEL SAGE.
MICHAEL SILVERSTEIN. MICHAEL STEVENS. MICHAEL WOLFE.
MICHAL STOKLASA. MICHELE & GREGORY KUS. MICHELLE CASANOVA.
MICHELLE MOSMAN. MICHIEL ROOK. MIGUEL G.
MIKE AND JANELL "OLD AF SQUAD" STURDIVANT. MIKE MCCLATCHEY.
MIKE SAHAGUN. MIKE SCHIAVONE. MIKE TROTTER. MIKE WAN.
MILLA TUOMINEN. MIMMI BERGDAHL. MIRKA GARLAND.
MISSY DAVIS. MITCH DUGGAN. MITCH SMITH. MONICA HUERTA.
MONYREYNOSO. NANCY GOV. NANCY LUONG. NATE ORR.
NATHAN MILLER. NATHANAEL HUESO. NATHANIEL LEE HAMMOND.
NEORXNAWANGE (SARA SCHMID). NGA DOAN. NHOMSTER.
NICHOLAS A BOLD. NICHOLAS BACCHUS. NICHOLAS KENNING.
NICHOLAS PAINTER. NICHOLAS VERRAS. NICK DAWES.
NICK LAWSON. NICK SHERMAN. NIHAR SHAH. NISSIN STEINBERG.
NOAH GIBBON. NONGNAPAT AREEVIJITTRAKOON.
NORMAN CHUCHER. OHAD KANNE. OLIVER GILBERT. ORR KOTZKY.
ÓSCAR GIL. OWEN PARRISH. PAIGE FULLBRIGHT. PALMA TOTH.
PAMELA GRIFFIN. PASCAL ROY. PASCUAL REGINIO. PATRIC GEGOR.

PATRICK DONEGAN. PATRICK LONG. PATRICK MCNULTY.
PATRICK MEEHAN. PATRICK WEI. PATRICK WILLETT. PAUL BUCKLEY.
PAUL DAVIS. PAUL GARDNER. PAUL GONGAWARE. PAUL HOBSON.
PAUL LEYSHON. PAUL RICKLI. PAUL ROBERTS. PAUL SPEGELAERE.
PAULINA LIWSKI. PAULINE P. NGO. PETER DIEP. PETER HARRISON.
PETER HAWKINS. PETER HELLBERG. PETER SWANSON.
PETER VARGO AKA FANCY PANTS. PETER WESTAD. PETER YUEN.
PETTERI T. PHARM. G. PHIL ALLEN. PHIL BUTCHER. PHILIP HONG.
PHILIPPE DROLET. PHILLIP TAFFLEY. PHUONG NGUYEN. PRESTO39.
RACHEL M KITAGAWA. RAE MCKEE. REBECCA HABLE. REECE.
REESE MORIYAMA. REI TOWNSEND. RENÉ FABIAN.
RHEANNA STEHLEY. RICARDO GARCIA. RICH UNG.
RICHARD GACEK JR. RICHARD MILLIGAN. RICHARD ROOCROFT.
RICK ANDRES. RIK CROFTS. RISHI PATEL. RITA TSIONSKY. ROB LAY.
ROB MARTIN. ROBEN NEAL. ROBERT BEATTY. ROBERT WARREN.
ROBIN BERUMEN. ROLAND MACKINTOSH. RON WILHELM.
RONNY BUNARTO. RUBY LE. RUDY FLORES.
RUSHABH 'SHUBS' SHETH. RYAN EDGAR. RYAN EVANS.
RYAN GRIEGER. RYAN LEES. RYAN MCGUCKIN. RYAN RICE.
SABRINA GOMEZ. SABRINA SIMMONS. SAGAR SHAH. SALLY LAU.
SAM DIAZ. SAM FAUNT. SAM MCGRAW. SAM TROGOLO.
SARAH ZIEGLER. SCOTT BARNHILL. SCOTT FLICKINGER.
SCOTT GUENTHER. SCOTT HOGAN. SCOTT K. ZIMMERMAN.
SCOTT ONODA. SEAN KELLY. SEAN SHEERAN. SEBASTIAN MONSALVE.
SEBASTIAN WALLNER. SERGIO PABALINAS. SHAHAN CAWASJI.
SHANGELUS. SHANNON KILBERT. SHARIF KHALED (SH3RIFFO).
SHAUN HUGHES. SHAUN KENT. SHAUNA CRYSTAL MOYS.
SHINTARO ITAKURA. SHINTARO NAKANO. SIAN JONES. SIAN MARIE.
SIDDHANT KERHALKAR. SILVANA PALLISER. SIMO KOPONEN.
SIMON THIER. SOHAM ROY. SOKLIAN TEOW. SOMA STAHORSZKI.
SPACEMANNYC. STACEY DOUGHERTY. STÅLE H. BJØRDAL.
STAN SHYU. STEFAN SFOR. STEPH AUDREY TOLEDO. STEPH S.
STEPHANIE DAIGLE. STEPHEN MUDRA. STEPHEN RIPPON.
STEPHEN T FELKNER. STEVE KLEINBAUM. STEVEN RAMKUMAR.
STEVEN VANDENBURG. STEVEN WEAVER. STUART MITCHELL.
STUART RUGG. SUKÁLY RICHÁRD MÁRK. SUSAN RYOO.
SUSAN SCHNEIDER. TAMÁS SZABÓ. TAMI NGUYEN.

TANISHA MUQTADA. TANUJ J HARIA. TAYLOR OLSEN.
TERRY DONOVAN. TERRY WILLIAMSON. THANH LE.
THEODORE MELNICK. THERESA LUNA. THIEN DINH.
THIJS PERENBOOM. THIJS STOKER. THOMAS A.C. HILL.
THOMAS DOBBY. THONG LE. THUY-DUONG HA. TIANLIN CHANG.
TIFFANY & RICHARD LEE. TIFFANY CHAN. TIFFANY SMITH.
TIFFANY VO. TIM FREESE. TIM MONZURES. TIM PALAC.
TIM SHIELDS. TIM WAGONER. TIMMY . TINA TRAVIS.
TING WEI GUO. TODD FOX. TOM DENEHY. TOM VERHOEFF.
TOMMY TAM. TONI HUKKA. TORD STOKHOLM. TORSTEIN BERTEIG.
TRACEY CAPOBIANCO. TRACY VICKNAIR. TRAVIS RUIZ.
TREVIN CHARITY. TREVOR D KARASEK. TRISH LEUNG.
TRISH WIGGIN. TROY CIOCCHETTI. TRUEKAY. TUUKKA LEHTONEN.
TYLER BOWMAN. TYLER PETRIE. TYLER T. TRVN. VAN PATTHANA.
VICTOR APOSTOLOU. VICTOR HERNANDEZ. VINCENT ZUO.
VINNY TROIA. VITTORIO ROSATI. VLAD CHIRIACESCU. W8LESS.
WESLEY CHANG. WILL LEE. WILL MILLER. WILL NANCE.
WILLIAM FRAISEAU. WILLIAM SILVA. WITOLD OLEKSIAK.
XUE YING LO. YER LEE. YING CHYI GOOI. YUI POW REDFORD.
YUKA GARZENELLI. ZACH PHILLIPS. ZACHARY CHASE LOH.
ZACHARY GAMBLE. ZACHARY LOVLEY. СЕРГЕЙ ЖУЧКОВ.

Edited by Geraint Jones.
Design by Mike Jones @ X2 Design & Steven Cunniffe.
Gareth Emery Management: Kassy Ruimy.
Public Relations by JSloane Creative & Resonance PR.
Billboard quote by Katie Bain.
SPIN quote by Daniel Kohn.
Cover photo credit: Derek Bahn.
Back cover photo credit: Rukes.

While all of the stories in this book are true, some names and identifying details have been changed to protect confidentiality.

Gareth Emery Limited
7-7c Snuff Street, Devizes, Wiltshire, United Kingdom, SN10 1DU

garethemery.com

Printed in Great Britain
by Amazon

72528838R00163